Praise for Bill Harris
and his history of Kitty Hawk Village

Bill Harris was a friend, and a man for whom I had enormous admiration. His roots were in Kitty Hawk, and no one knew more about the history of that place than Bill. A generation of books on coastal North Carolina and the Wright brothers are richer for what he shared with the authors. His wise leadership of the First Flight Society, whether in office or out, kept that organization on a steady course. Many years ago, he took a then very young scholar under his wing and taught me to appreciate the past and present of that village on the edge of the continent where history was made. For that, and for his friendship, I am deeply grateful.

Tom D. Crouch, PhD, Curator Emeritus, Smithsonian Institution

My friend, Bill Harris was passionate about protecting and preserving the history of his beloved native community of Kitty Hawk. Bill happily shared the story of Kitty Hawk with countless researchers, authors, reporters, genealogists, political figures and many others. Bill understood that Kitty Hawk, though a small coastal community, occupies a gigantic spot in world history. He worked tirelessly to preserve the stories and the history of this place for future generations to enjoy.

Warren Wrenn, National Park Service Ranger - Retired

Bill, Rad and I spent a lot of time together when we were kids. Riding our bikes along the ocean was one of the things we did a lot. When we grew up, Bill moved away but his favorite thing to do on the weekends was to get back to Kitty Hawk. When he retired that is just what he did, he moved back to Kitty Hawk. There is one thing we can be sure of, Bill loved Kitty Hawk!

Margie and Rad Tillett, Kitty Hawk Friends

Bill was more like the "little brother" I never had. He was a good historian and loved his roots.

Lorna Staples Clark, Cousin

Bill loved history and brought it to life with his story telling. He was able to bring Kitty Hawk during the Wright Brothers era to life for me and many others. He told me the story of a young man and woman who lived up the creek & down the creek in Kitty Hawk. The 200 people that lived in Kitty Hawk were separated by a small creek. The young man & young woman grew up on each side of the creek less than a quarter mile apart and never met. They finally met when they were 16, fell in love & lived happily ever after. Once Bill told me the story it gave me a completely different view of Kitty Hawk at that time and brought it to life. I will forever be grateful.

John Harris, founder of Kitty Hawk Kites

Up-The-Road
Down-The-Road

Kitty Hawk Village From The Beginning

Bill Harris

Up-The-Road
Down-The-Road

Kitty Hawk Village From The Beginning

Bill Harris

Copyright © Judith Harris Fearing 2024
ISBN-979-8-9880171-5-8
Cover Image of Kitty Hawk General Store by Dawn Gray Morega
Cover Design by Barb Noel

First paperback edition 2024

Published by Gravity Well Books

Kitty Hawk, NC
Circa 1900

Note: House location numbers refer to 1900 Census data.

700   0   700   1400 Feet

Place names, families, and home locations were developed from a number of sources, including: 1900 Census, Atlantic Township, Dare County, North Carolina; historic maps; review of deeds from the early 1700's to the present involving Kitty Hawk lands; and oral history interviews by Bill Harris in 1960 with Kitty Hawk residents who were living in the community in 1900.

The base map is a current map of Kitty Hawk. Most of the waterways in 1900 were small channels that were enlarged in the 1950's and 60's for mosquito control. None of the subdivision channels existed in 1900.

Number	Name	Number	Name
18	Samuel B. Dowdy	47	Edward O'Neal
19	William Ivy Dowdy	48	Elijah Sibbern
20	Levi M. Perry	49	Avery B. L. Midgett
21	Decatur Beacham	50	William W. Midgett
22	William R. Perry	51	Charles C. Hayman
23	Frederick Perry	52	William W. Basnight
24	Thomas T. Baum	53	Oliver Twiford
25	Decatur Beacham, Jr.	54	James R. Hobbs
26	Theocarus Tillett	55	Thomas N. Sanderlin
27	Corrina B. Owens	57	Lewis E. Sawyer
28	John T. Beacham	58	Henry G. Smith
29	William C. Beals	59	Walter W. Best
30	Jordan D. Owens	60	William J. Tate
31	Caleb H. Toler	61	William A. Hines
32	Edward P. Rogers	62	John D. Cogswell
33	Benjamin D. Tillett	63	Franklin H. Midgett
34	Sylvanus Harris	64	Edward Baum
35	Samuel A. Perry	65	William R. Hines
36	Isaiah Perry	66	Lemuel T. Hines
37	James W. Beasley	67	George W. Baum
38	William T. Baum	68	George Wash. Twiford
39	William Grandy Beasley	69	Joseph E. Baum
40	Hezakiah D. Beasley	70	Daniel M. Tate
41	Penny Toler Harris	71	James Calhoun
42	Sarah Tillett Perry	72	William J. Baum
43	James C. Perry	73	Thomas E. Hines
44	Felix Beasley	74	Joseph J. Dosher
45	James W. Wicker	75	Dempsey B. Perry
46	Charlotte Gamsel Midgett	76	William T. Perry

Bull Ridge Marsh

Viney Swamp 69

Kitty Hawk Ridge

Dancing Ridge Pond

Dancing Ridge

47

Hickory Ridge

MAIN ROAD

Duck Pond

Sign Post

Chinquapin Ridge 35

Perry Baum Store

Ash Swamp

TURTLE ROAD

Blind Ridge

76

42

75

24

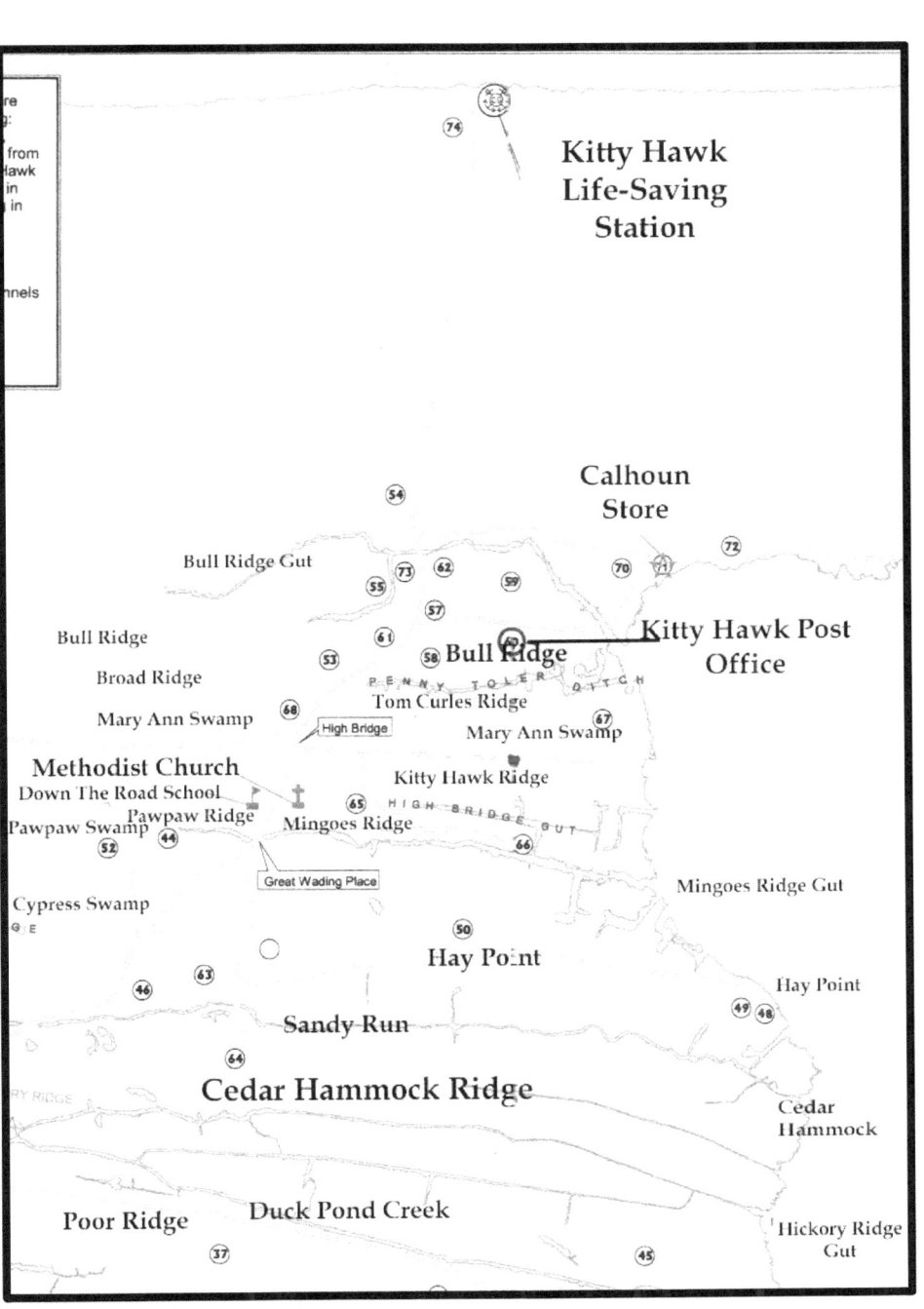

Kitty Hawk
Life-Saving
Station

Calhoun
Store

Bull Ridge Gut

Bull Ridge

Broad Ridge

Mary Ann Swamp

Kitty Hawk Post
Office

Bull Ridge

PENNY TOLER DITCH

Tom Curles Ridge

High Bridge

Mary Ann Swamp

Methodist Church

Down The Road School

Pawpaw Ridge

Pawpaw Swamp

Kitty Hawk Ridge

HIGH BRIDGE GUT

Mingoes Ridge

Great Wading Place

Mingoes Ridge Gut

Cypress Swamp

Hay Point

Hay Point

Sandy Run

Cedar Hammock Ridge

Cedar
Hammock

Poor Ridge

Duck Pond Creek

Hickory Ridge
Gut

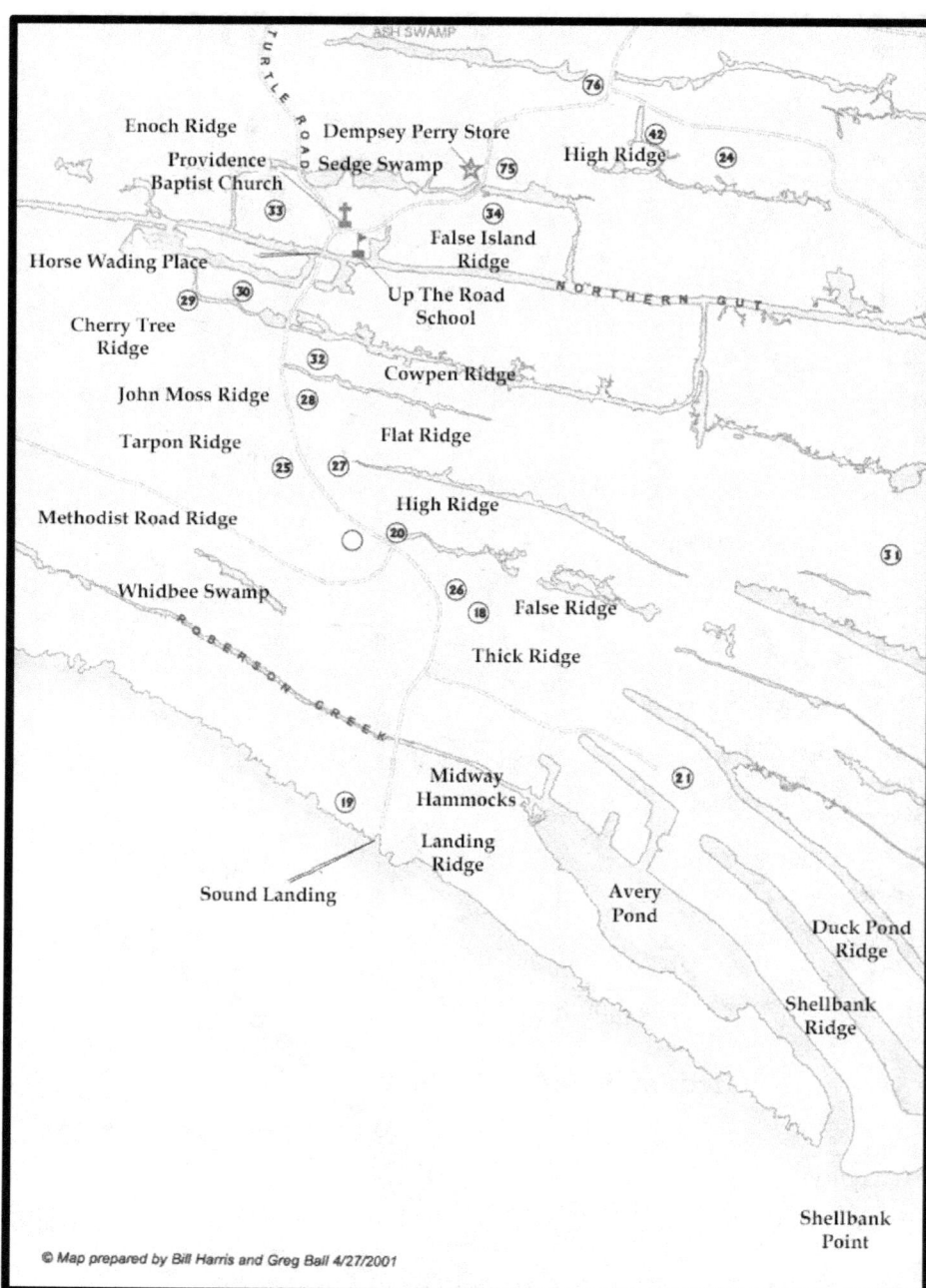

ASH SWAMP

TURTLE ROAD

Enoch Ridge

Dempsey Perry Store

Providence
Baptist Church

Sedge Swamp

High Ridge

Horse Wading Place

False Island
Ridge

NORTHERN GUT

Cherry Tree
Ridge

Up The Road
School

John Moss Ridge

Cowpen Ridge

Flat Ridge

Tarpon Ridge

Methodist Road Ridge

High Ridge

Whidbee Swamp

ROBERSON CREEK

False Ridge

Thick Ridge

Midway
Hammocks

Landing
Ridge

Sound Landing

Avery
Pond

Duck Pond
Ridge

Shellbank
Ridge

Shellbank
Point

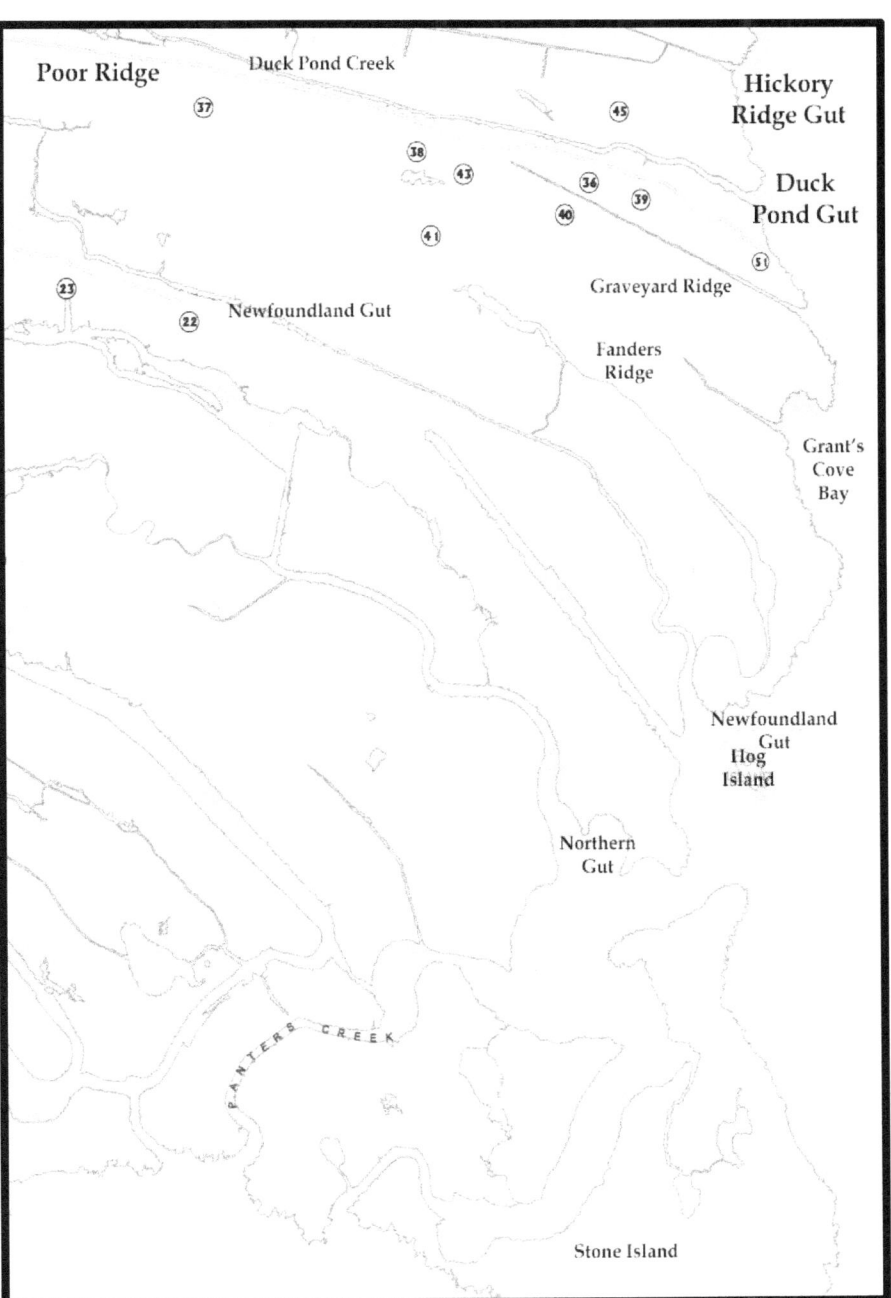

Poor Ridge

Duck Pond Creek

Hickory
Ridge Gut

Duck
Pond Gut

Graveyard Ridge

Newfoundland Gut

Fanders
Ridge

Grant's
Cove
Bay

Newfoundland
Gut
Hog
Island

Northern
Gut

CREEK

Stone Island

Number	Name	Number	Name
18	Samuel B. Dowdy	47	Edward O'Neal
19	William Ivy Dowdy	48	Elijah Sibbern
20	Levi M. Perry	49	Avery B. L. Midgett
21	Decatur Beacham	50	William W. Midgett
22	William R. Perry	51	Charles C. Hayman
23	Frederick Perry	52	William W. Basnight
24	Thomas T. Baum	53	Oliver Twiford
25	Decatur Beacham, Jr.	54	James R. Hobbs
26	Theocanus Tillett	55	Thomas N. Sanderlin
27	Corrina B. Owens	57	Lewis E. Sawyer
28	John T. Beacham	58	Henry G. Smith
29	William C. Beals	59	Walter W. Best
30	Jordan D. Owens	60	William J. Tate
31	Caleb H. Toler	61	William A. Hines
32	Edward P. Rogers	62	John D. Cogswell
33	Benjamin D. Tillett	63	Franklin H. Midgett
34	Sylvanus Harris	64	Edward Baum
35	Samuel A. Perry	65	William R. Hines
36	Isaiah Perry	66	Lemuel T. Hines
37	James W. Beasley	67	George W. Baum
38	William T. Baum	68	George Wash. Twiford
39	William Grandy Beasley	69	Joseph E. Baum
40	Hezakiah D. Beasley	70	Daniel M. Tate
41	Penny Toler Harris	71	James Calhoun
42	Sarah Tillett Perry	72	William J. Baum
43	James C. Perry	73	Thomas E. Hines
44	Felix Beasley	74	Joseph J. Dosher
45	James W. Wicker	75	Dempsey B. Perry
46	Charlotte Gamiel Midgett	76	William T. Perry

Table Of Contents

Introduction

My "Little Brother Bill" spent his childhood in various locations as we followed our US Coast Guard father's station assignments. Eventually duty stations brought us near enough that we had several youthful years living at home in Kitty Hawk, surrounded by loving parents, grandparents and a large family of relatives.

Bill grew up with our younger brother Roy doing all the young boy things like fishing, hunting, raising pets including a goat, pony and play toys like boats, tractors and things mechanical.They rode bicycles all over the village and knew everybody, young and old.

When young years reached the right age, he was off to serve in the US Coast Guard, attend college and follow his professional years in various National Park Service locations. But he was happiest when his journey brought him back to Kitty Hawk. Of course, Kitty Hawk was quite different from his young years, but he loved interaction with the older residents as well as the new ones. He never saw or met a stranger, he could make conversation with everyone, as he looked for the uniqueness of the area. He searched every nook and corner, checked every cemetery, and questioned everyone he met.

The "historian" used his professional experience to uncover the very beginning years of Kitty Hawk and its history. Public, local and state records, became his major reading materials. Recording his conversations with people he remembers from his early years was his most enjoyable pastime. Thus, the idea of writing a book became his passion, lest people forget the names of places and people who made the vast open, undisturbed area into a quaint little village and later a town.

It took all kinds of people, through the years, to build a village, have roads, bridges, churches, schools, education and employment for the people who lived here.

It was Bill's wish to preserve the history and names of families who grew the Town of Kitty Hawk. His research started with his college senior thesis and spanned 60 years. In fact, the last chapter was signed off just one week before his death, March 17, 2017.

We are delighted to share Bill's history of the town he loved, the people who lived, the stories and the roots from which we grew.

Geneva Perry-Ward
"Bill's Older Sister"

Lorna Staples, Geneva Perry Ward, with Bill and Roy Harris, In Kitty Hawk, 1945

Section One

The Origins Of Kitty Hawk

Chapter One

WHY KITTY HAWK

The Origins of the Name

Following a discussion of where the Wright brothers flew in Kitty Hawk or Kill Devil Hills in 1903, most people want to know how Kitty Hawk got its name. The quick and short answer is, "No one knows!" Though true, that response satisfies very few, if anyone. Every place name has a history of origin, or so most people think. For Kitty Hawk that origin is not clearly defined

Catherine Albertson in her undated booklet, *Wings Over Kill Devil; and, Legends of the dunes of Dare*, addressed the question of origin of the Kitty Hawk name. At least she borrowed the explanation from Captain William Tate, a native of Kitty Hawk, in a pamphlet he wrote and distributed at the 25th anniversary of powered flight, December 17, 1928. Tate's narrative is the first known written account of the origin of the name, Kitty Hawk.

This story, although legendary, has some very strong recorded facts to substantiate it. When the English first settled at Kitty Hawk and became sufficiently versed in Indian lingo, and the Indians had also become sufficiently versed in English so that a sort of mutual understanding could be had, the white man asked the Indian how he measured time, or how could the Indian tell when one year ended and another began. Now the word which in the Indian language meant goose (myriads of these fowls then frequented the coast and were eaten by the Indians and also by the whites) was Hauk, a sort of guttural sound made by the wild goose in its cry to its fellows. The Indian had learned enough English to say 'killy' when he meant kill, and he answered, "Fum a Killy Haunk to a Killy Haunk one white man's year," meaning that from the first time a wild goose was killed in its annual flight

5

in the fall of the year to the time the first wild goose was killed in the fall of the succeeding year was a white man's year.

Albertson also reported another story, which was popular when this writer was growing up in Kitty Hawk.

Several stories of the origin of the name of this little seacoast town are told. The one most common among the natives attributes it to the swarm of mosquito hawks that abound in that region at certain times of the year. Mosquito hawk in common parlance became skeeter hawk and in course of time evolved into Kitty Hawk, the name that finally fastened upon the little community.

It is a stretch of the imagination to understand how "skeeter" converts to "kitty," but that is one explanation of the origin of the name Kitty Hawk. Maybe it was just an easy story to remember and the logic of the explanation did not matter.

W. O. Saunders, one of the founders of The Kill Devil Hills Memorial Association, and publisher of the newspaper, *The Independent*, in Elizabeth City, N. C., in a little 1935 published booklet titled, *A Handbook of the Wright Memorial*, gave a similar Indian origin account to Tate's, but with a slightly different twist.

The popular accepted legend with respect of Kitty Hawk relates that its name is a corruption of "Killa Honk" or "Killy Honk." What is now Kitty Hawk was formerly a favorite winter-feeding ground and refuge for the Canada wild goose. Just across Currituck Sound from Kitty Hawk Bay is the tip of the Currituck peninsula where an Indian village was established, the remains of which are visible to this day. Legend says that in the late fall of any year when the wild geese came down from the north and began to congregate in Kitty Hawk Bay, the Indian, borrowing the white man's vernacular, said: "Killy Honk!"; which was his terse way of saying: "I think I'll paddle my canoe across the Sound and kill a honker," meaning a wild goose. And so, Kitty Hawk Bay came by its name. Old deeds and other records still in existence in Currituck show that the Kitty Hawk locality has been variously designated as Killa Honk, Killy Honk, Kitty Honk and Kitty Hawk, the latter having come to be accepted in late years.

Roger L. Payne in his 1985 book, *Place Names of the Outer Banks*, offers several other options for the origin of Kitty Hawk's name. The name bears a resemblance to kitty wake (kittiwake) which is the name of a gull-like bird of the Atlantic Coast. However, there is little evidence to support any relationship since the kitty wake is not generally known south of Chesapeake Bay. There is a Delaware Indian reference that translates Kitt to big and hakki to land which could be related to the name. The name is most likely an Anglicized corruption of an Algonquian Indian term Chickehauk which referred to an Indian settlement in the area. It is possible that the name is a corruption of Etacrewac, another Indian name for this general vicinity.

As referenced above, Chickahouk or Chickehauk have been suggested as the source of the place name Kitty Hawk. Isle Chickahouk appeared on a map by Jacques Nicholas Bellin printed in Paris in 1757. Twenty-one years later in 1778, Chickehauk I. appeared on a map published by Antonio Zatta in Venice. In both maps the names referenced the barrier island between Currituck Inlet in the north and Roanoke Inlet to the south, but not an Indian settlement. Neither name appears on any map after this period, there is no Indian settlement by either name in the area, and no documentation as to the source of the identification of this barrier island. Previously, the barrier island had simply been identified at "Sand Bank," and spoken of as "ye sand-banks." In later deeds, however, this island, and peninsula after Currituck Inlet closed in the 1820s, was referred to as the North Banks. The name Kitty Hawk was already in use before the publication of these maps so it seems highly unlikely that either Chickahouk or Chickehauk had any influence on naming the settlement. Kitty Hawk as a place name for the settlement appeared, maybe for the first time, on a very detailed 1886 map by Frank A. Gray. The community has continued to be identified on subsequent maps after that date.

There may be others theories on the naming of Kitty Hawk, but these are the only ones that have made it to print. Which one is the correct one is anyone's guess. The name Kitty Hawk appears to be unique in that there is no record of its use elsewhere; it was not brought over from the old country; it is not a replication of a name in the new world; and is not associated with any former resident of the area. However the name originated, it occurred very early in history.

The name Kittyhawk Bay appeared in a 1739 deed between Phillip Northern and Robert Paule, Jr. Northern's deed described "A piece of land beginning Currituck County near Kittyhawk Bay and joining on land called Rich. Smiths..." The land appeared to be in the area of present-day Poor Ridge.

Killehawk Bay was the name used in a 1763 deed from William and Jonathan Norton to Thomas Hill, Jr. Also in 1763, Tully Williams sold to Benjamin Paddrick 150 acres of land on the "...Banks land on Kitty Hawk Bay commonly called Blind Ridge and Smith Ridge, beginning at Ceder Hommack gut..." Blind and Smith Ridges appear to this writer to be what later became Hickory Ridge and Poor Ridge.

Citehawk, Cetehauk, Kittahawk, Kityhawk Bay, Kity Hawk Bay, Kityhauke Bay, Kitty Hawk Bay, and Kitty Hawk Banks appeared in various deeds throughout the 1700s. There is no clear explanation of why there were so many variations in the spelling except that deeds were separately prepared by those who could write and then copied by clerks at the Register of Deeds Office, sometime years later, in county deed book journals.

Kitty Hawk Bay and Kitty Hawk Ridge, with the name Kitty Hawk as is currently written, were common references in deeds in the 19th and 20th century. Kitty Hawk as the place name for the village did not become popular until the mid 19th century.

Settlers who lived on what we call today the Outer Banks were referred to as living on the "sand banks." Later, except for Nags Head which was frequently mentioned, the other villages and communities were simply lumped together as the "North Banks." The first mention of Kitty Hawk as a place name occurred in a 1795 deed from Thomas Best to William Etheridge, Sr. for "...North Banks land at Kitty Hawk at a swamp at a sweetgum, easterly to Kitty Hawk Ridge, along Zodock Gallop line to road...."

In April and May, 1852, and again in an 1853 entry, the Powells Point Regular Baptist mentioned services on North Banks, Kittahawk, in their church book. In August 1854 Brothers Hodges Gallop, Thomas McKimmey, Jasper Toler, Morris Beals, and

Sisters Alsey McKimey, Peggy Owens, Sally Toler and Betsy Beacham petitioned the Powells Point Regular Baptist church for a letter of dismissal "…for the purpose of constituting a church on the North Banks…" That church was formed as the Providence Baptist Church in Kitty Hawk. On September 7, 1854, the Powells Point Regular Baptist church book reported that "Letter of dismission to join Kitty Hawk church granted to Harriet Baum, Clarky Beasley and Iasiah Perry." Kitty Hawk was becoming a well-established place name for these residences of the North Banks.

Kitty Hawk as a place name received a degree of legitimacy in 1874 when the Federal Government established the Kitty Hawk Life-Saving Service Station on the beach east of the village. The village name became official on November 11, 1878, when Sophia D. Tate opened the first Kitty Hawk post office.

Regardless of its source of name origin, Kitty Hawk has been a viable community on the sand banks for well over 200 years. Through much of its history it has been the largest community on the banks, north of Cape Hatteras. The town may very well again be the largest community of the Outer Banks as it develops.

Chapter Two

KITTY HAWK

The Beginning and Growth of Kitty Hawk Village

For over 250 years, Kitty Hawk village, community, and more recently town, has been a quiet place where significant events occurred infrequently and the population grew slowly. Very little of Kitty Hawk's early past has been recorded, but events, sites, and landmarks define its history. The community was not in the mainstream of developments as experienced by other locations across the nation, and no one of great prominence originated from its people. Kitty Hawk was simply an isolated village moving slowly through time, not unlike many other coastal communities of its era, cut off from the rest of the world except by sailing vessels.

Kitty Hawk was not even the location of choice for early settlers to the "sand banks." Most newcomers settled either along the shores of La More Bay (a name no longer used), Colington Creek and Roanoke Sound in an area called Rousepock, near Kill Devil Hill, or around the shores of Jean Guite Creek and Currituck Sound in what is today Martins Point, Kitty Hawk, Southern Shores and Duck. The community around Jean Guite Creek was known by some as "the Perry Fields," probably because Josiah Perry, Sr. settled and lived here around 1800. And there were good reasons for settling in these locations - high land near the water's edge, adequate near shore water depths for boats, and protective anchorage from storms for vessels. By contrast, the high ridges in Kitty Hawk were separated from Kitty Hawk Bay by wide expanses of marshes in most locations, and the near shore water depths of the bay were relatively shallow.

By the second quarter of the 19th century people began settling in what became Kitty Hawk village. The change occurred because new people moving into the area and new adults in the Rousepock families wanted land of their own for their families. The land north of Kitty Hawk was being purchased by Willis Gallop and taken out of the real estate market as he added to his land holdings on the Outer Banks. The newcomers to Kitty Hawk established their homes along the village's main road and down the ridges towards the bay.

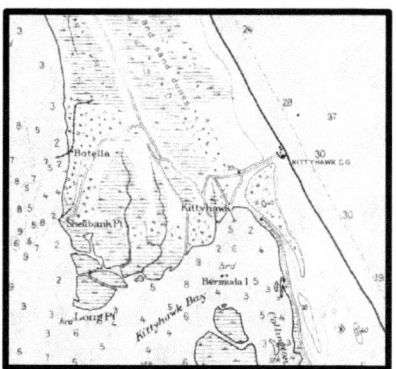

An 1860 map showing the name "kittyhawk" as one word

By 1850, Kitty Hawk was a well-established community. It recorded a population of 34 families and 192 people. Their occupations were usually given as a seaman, farmer, or fisherman. The 1900 Census reported 58 families and 282 people in Kitty Hawk, and their occupations had expanded to include service with the U. S. Life-Saving Service and Weather Bureau, grocers and merchants, carpenters, laborers, a schoolteacher, a preacher, and a physician, who was actually a pharmacist. As the community grew over the next decades, other occupations would be recorded.

Also, by 1850, most of the families normally associated with the history of Kitty Hawk, such as Beacham, Perry, Best, Twiford, Sibbern, Tillett, Baum, Hines, Owens and others, were living within the community and had started families. These names would reappear time and time again in the census over the next 80 years, and some of these same family names are recognized in Kitty Hawk today.

The isolation of Kitty Hawk, and its independence as a community, began to change in the last quarter of the 19th and first half of the 20th centuries. Developments that occurred along the Outer Banks during these years would forever change the course of history of the Kitty Hawkers and their neighbors.

Maritime commerce has always been a risky business and in the mid 19th century the United States was a major maritime nation. Maritime disasters with loss of ships, cargo, and particularly life were a significant concern to the citizens of nation, even to the point of pressuring the Federal Government to provide aid and comfort to those in peril.

Kitty Hawk Lifesaving Station and outbuildings, 1900

On April 20, 1871, Congress responded by authorizing $200,000 to establish a system of life-saving stations on the Great Lakes and along the Atlantic coast. The responsibility for the new service was assigned to the Revenue Marine Bureau within the Department of the Treasury. The Kitty Hawk Life-Saving Station was one of the original seven stations constructed along the North Carolina coast in 1874 as a result of this authorization. Its sister station to the north was Caffey's Inlet Life-Saving Station and Nags Head Life-Saving Station to the south. Eleven additional stations were added along the coast in 1878, including the Paul Gamiels Hill Life-Saving Station and Kill Devil Hills Life-Saving Station, immediately north and south of the Kitty Hawk station. The significance of the establishment of these stations to Kitty Hawkers was that, in addition to the assistance it provided for mariners, the Life-Saving Service offered employment opportunities for able-bodied men in the community. At some point in their history nearly every family had a relative serving with either the Life-Saving Service, or later the U. S. Coast Guard.

Shortly after life-saving stations were established, the U. S. Army Signal Corps assigned weather observers at key locations along the coastline to report on weather conditions. A telegraph line was also established from Dam Neck Mills, Virginia, south to a weather station building near the Kitty Hawk Life-Saving Station. Later the line was extended further south along the coast to Morehead City, North Carolina. The telegraph line was installed for the purpose of transmitting weather reports to a central office in Norfolk, Virginia. The U. S. Army Signal Corps, and later Weather Bureau, did allow other official uses of the line such as the LSS (Life-Saving Service) reports on wrecks, calls for assistance from other station and salvage information. Even later, they allowed some private transmissions including the Wright brothers telegraph of their first powered flight success to their family in Dayton, Ohio. The Signal Service telegraph system did not have a significant impact on the local population, but it did serve to connect the Outer Banks to the outside world and was the basis for telephone service that came to the area after the area was opened for developments.

Another window to the outside world opened for Kitty Hawkers with the opening of a post office in November 1878. Mrs. Sophia D. Tate was the first postmaster and operated the post office out of her home at the head of Kitty Hawk Bay. For the next seventy-five years either a Tate or a Baum were postmasters. The Kitty Hawk post office not only served the local community, but its neighbors to the north in what became Duck, and to the south the Kill Devil Hills Life-Saving Station and residents of Colington Island. Even today the Kitty Hawk post office serves the towns of Southern Shores and Duck.

Although Kitty Hawk was some distance from Elizabeth City, it was not impossible to travel there. With a fair wind, a sailor could sail from Kitty Hawk to Elizabeth City in about 5 hours, a distance by water of about 40 miles. While it was possible to sail to Elizabeth City when desired, there is scant evidence that Kitty Hawkers made the trip with any degree of frequency.

The trip to Elizabeth City was made somewhat easier in 1890s when Willis G. Banks of Currituck County established a water freight and passenger line connecting Kitty Hawk communities bordering Currituck Sound and North River with the regional trade center. The freight line business for Kitty Hawk was probably as much to support his small general store at the end of Poor Ridge as it was to transport general freight to and from the community. His freight boat, the *Filena*, named for his wife, was one of the early gasoline powered boats in northeastern North Carolina and probably the first powered boat to enter Kitty Hawk Bay. Apparently, the store and freight business in Kitty Hawk was not as lucrative as Banks had hoped and by 1900 the store was closed and the freight boat no longer called on Kitty Hawk. Banks continued to serve the other communities in the region for the next decade from his base at Newbern's Landing in Powells Point.

After the Banks line ceased to operate locally, William Robert "Bob" Perry opened a water freight line in Kitty Hawk and a small general store with Thomas T. Baum, another Kitty Hawk resident, on the main road in about the center of the village. That freight line no doubt was started to serve their store and any freight needs the locals may have had. It was short lived, however, as Bob Perry sold the freight line and equipment to Franklin Harris Midgett in 1902 and closed his store.

It was an opportune time for the new freight service. A number of new homes were constructed in Kitty Hawk after the turn of the century for which the Midgett line transported the lumber and building supplies. Tunis Lumber Company began a 10-year program of timber harvest in the Kitty Hawk woods and the Midgett freight line transported supplies and materials for the company and their large work crew. New stores in the village opened and had much of their supplies delivered by the local freight line. Captain Harris Midgett also became a fish buyer and transported the fish to market.

The freight line operated successfully for well over two decades, connecting not only Kitty Hawk village, but also over time all other coastal communities bordering Currituck Sound and North River. Although Captain Franklin Harris Midgett owned and operated the freight line himself he quickly involved his sons,

Truxton, Frank, and Spence Midgett in the business when they became old enough to handle the business and vessels. His brother William Wellington Midgett was associated with the operation through most of its history. Freight hauling was the principal purpose of the operation, but passengers were transported on space available bases.

The Midgett freight line service's place in history was secured almost from the beginning, though no one realized it at the time. The Wright brothers in their correspondence and diary entries during 1902 and 1903 mentioned Captain Midgett, his sons, and their freight boat, the *Lou Willis*, frequently. The Wright brothers and their camp guests were regular passengers on the freight boat and the Midgetts procured supplies for the brothers in Elizabeth City and transported them to Kitty Hawk and the Wright camp at Kill Devil Hills. After the successful flight on December 17, 1903, the Kill Devil Hills Life Saving Station crew crated the Flyer and had the Midgetts transport it to Elizabeth City for shipment by rail to Dayton, Ohio. Truxton Midgett remembered the incident vividly in an interview later in life as he and his brothers had to strap the Flyer crate to the top of the Lou Willis cabin for the trip from Kitty Hawk. It was an awkward arrangement for their small vessel, but they made the trip without mishap.

Within a few years the Midgetts added a second vessel to their fleet, the B. M. VanDuesen, and were able to provide expanded freight and passenger service to the community and the Wrights when they returned to Kitty Hawk for further experiments in 1908 and 1911.

Like the rest of America, Kitty Hawkers fell in love with the automobile, and it in turn forever changed the life of these people who for centuries have been semi-isolated on the"sand banks" coast of North Carolina. The automobile did not change the isolation, but improved roads, ferry connection and eventually bridges opened the area to travel and visitors, and offered the residents an opportunity to travel to distant places.

The identity of the first person to bring an automobile to Kitty Hawk has been lost to history and several families make that claim. Charlie and George Perry, sons of William Robert Perry, were among the first to own a vehicle in Kitty Hawk. Charlie reported in a 1960 interview that he bought a car in Norfolk around 1920 and brought it to Kitty Hawk down the beach from Sand Bridge, VA. It was not an easy task as he told in his story because with small tires fully inflated the vehicle had to be pushed through the soft sand as much as it could be driven. It would be several years before the roads could be worked to accommodate this new mode of travel. Without bridges or ferries most early vehicles arrived in Kitty Hawk by being brought down the beach from Virginia.

The vehicles were extremely popular in spite of their limited range of operation, but within a few years a number of families and individuals owned them. Silas Guard, Truxton Midgett, Elijah Baum and Robert Wescott were early local car owners. Sometime in the early 1920s, Silas Guard, a Coast Guardsman at one of the nearby stations, asked Captain Bill Perry if he would transport his vehicle from Kitty Hawk to Point Harbor. Captain Perry agreed and loaded the car on a small barge and pushed it across Currituck Sound with his powered shad boat. Others made similar requests and Captain Perry responded by getting a barge that would carry two cars. Business expanded, and he replaced this barge with one that carried six cars. Without planning it, Captain Bill Perry became the first person to offer ferry service between Point Harbor and Kitty Hawk. An undated handbill in the possession of Mrs. Carl Perry reported on the Point Harbor Ferry schedule. It stated that "The Perry and Dowdy Ferry will leave Point Harbor Thursday, Saturday and Sunday at 8 o'clock A. M. of each week, and after June 15th will leave Point Harbor at 8 o'clock Saturday P. M. in addition to the other dates." The handbill also referenced the Roanoke Ferry Co., Inc., service between Point Harbor and the north end of Roanoke Island operated by Captain Thomas A. Baum. Old timers remember that at least one of his ferries was named *Rebecca*, but whether or not it was the one serving Kitty Hawk is unknown at this distance in time. The "Dowdy" in the Perry and Dowdy Ferry operation was no doubt William Ivey Dowdy of Kitty Hawk, a waterman and Captain Bill Perry's neighbor.

Captain Baum bought out the Dowdy-Perry ferry operation in 1926 and continued to offer ferry crossing of Currituck Sound until the Wright Memorial Bridge opened to toll vehicle traffic September 17, 1930. The bridge toll of $1.25 per car and driver and 25 cents for each additional passenger help defray the cost of maintain the bridge and to recover the company's investment. The tolls were removed in 1935 when the State of North Carolina bought the bridge from the Wright Memorial Bridge Co.

The 1930 Wright Memorial Bridge was the first of three bridges constructed between Point Harbor and Kitty Hawk. The first two wooden bridges were subject to occasional ice flow damage and interruption of traffic. The third bridge, opened in 1966, and its 1982 duel parallel companion, were of concrete construction and continue to serve the Outer Banks today.

Connecting the Outer Banks to the mainland Currituck County was the last major obstacle of isolation for Kitty Hawk and its neighbors. The privately funded bridge was not constructed for transportation of the inhabitants of the Outer Banks, though it served that purpose, but rather for access to the Wright Memorial Bridge Company's seven miles of beachfront land holdings. The development company had plans to develop their beach property. Some lots were sold in the Kitty Hawk beach area and a number of beach cottages were built during this early period. A few of those early cottages survive, but are disappearing quickly. Unfortunately, before the Wright Memorial Bridge Company's plans fully materialized the country experienced the Great Depression of the 1930s and World War II, which delayed and slowed their project.

For Kitty Hawkers, the bridge and the 1931 state highway constructed along the beach connecting Point Harbor and the 1926 Roanoke Sound Bridge were major improvements to their transportation needs. They could now drive south over a modern highway and bridge to Manteo, the county seat, or go north to Elizabeth City, Norfolk, and beyond. Isolation was no longer a problem for the residents of Kitty Hawk, or their neighbors.

Development of the Kitty Hawk beaches began in earnest following World War II, and with it came improved electrical and telephone services, new cottages and cottage courts, service stations and retail outlets, and fishing piers. In time motels and hotels, condos, fast food establishments, recreational playgrounds, national business chains, and health facilities made their appearance on the Outer Banks. Today, Kitty Hawk and its neighboring towns are much like most other beach resorts with amenities to meet everyone's needs.

It is hard to visualize the Kitty Hawk that Edmond Beacham, a shoemaker, saw when he purchased 150 acres of land at the head of Kitty Hawk Bay from Mathias Toler in February 1781; or the 43 acres John Lewark secured in 1785 for his home site on the west side of Bull Ridge Marsh in the deep woods north of the village; or Joshua Guard's 50 acres on Cowpen and Flat Ridges at the Horsewading Place near Northerns Gut, which he purchased in 1785; or the land Thomas Best purchased for his residence in 1791 of Daniel Hayman at Mingers Gut, on the northeast side of Kitty Hawk Bay, Mill Point and Seder Hammock Ridge, where William Dunston Ridge formerly lived. While the topography of the land has changed and place names are all but lost to history, what has not changed and is reminiscent of the original Kitty Hawk are the beautiful fall sunsets over Kitty Hawk Bay. It symbolizes why Kitty Hawk is a special place for those who have lived here, or wish to.

Chapter Three

WHAT'S IN A NAME?

The History of the Place Names of Kitty Hawk Village

Any kid growing up in Kitty Hawk in the 1940s or 1950s could easily direct a stranger to Moore Shore, the Signpost, Sound Landing, Army Camp Hill, Hay Point, Shellbank Point, Poor Ridge, Duck Pond Bridge or the Devil Oak. These were locations within the village that everyone knew and referenced. Earlier generations would have known about High Bridge Creek, Ash Swamp, Cowpen Ridge, Grant Cove Bay, and Newfoundland Gut. And even earlier residents could talk about Viney Swamp, Bull Ridge Marsh, Mary Ann Swamp, Mill Point, Mingoes Ridge Gut, the Horse Wading Place, Pawpaw Ridge, and Northern Gut. These were place names in the community that served as addresses before the days of numbered lots on Herbert Perry Road, West Kitty Hawk Road, Bob Perry Road, Ivy Lane, Seascape Drive, and the multitude of other streets and roads names that have come because of postal requirements, fire and police department's needs, and subdivision developments. The early names included large areas and are no longer relevant in a town that is becoming more populated and developed with minimum lot sizes for homes.

The naming of ridges, swamps, guts, creeks, and other landmarks however did serve a very useful purpose for the early inhabitants and landowners. It helped everyone to identify land ownership and boundaries on the ground. Describing a piece of property as: "…beginning at a stake in a ditch, westerly along main road over two ridges to the center of a gut, south down the gut to the bay, easterly along the bay to the ditch, north up the ditch to the first station, the same containing 75 acres…" would be hard, if not impossible, to locate within the village as several parcels of land might meet the description.

This same property described as: "beginning at a cedar post in Penny Toler Ditch at the main road, westerly along the course of the road across Tom Curles and Kitty Hawk Ridges to a cedar post in the center of High Bridge Gut at Elijah Sibbern's line, southerly with Elijah Sibbern line down High Bridge Gut to Kitty Hawk Bay, easterly along the bay shore line to the mouth of Penny Toler Ditch, northerly up Penny Toler Ditch to the beginning, the same containing 75 acres," would easily identify the property location.

When the first settlers arrived in the Kitty Hawk area in the mid-18th century, they found the land behind the sand dunes as a series of sand ridges separated from each other by low lying swales, which generally supported water most of the year in swamps and marsh areas. Both the high land and swamps were forested. A fringe of marsh occurred at the head of Kitty Hawk Bay, but west of Mill, or Hay, Point the marshes were extensive and, in some locations, extended a half-mile or more within the village.

Army Camp Hill - "Army Camp Hill" was the common local name, but not an official or deeded name, for the sand hills on the road east of the village. In the spring of 1942, the US Army established a radar station there that included a steel radar tower and an operations center at its base on land now occupied by the Holy Redeemer Catholic Church. A little further east, six barracks, an office building, mess hall, and several ancillary buildings, including an underground magazine, were located at the crest of the sand hills on the south side of the road between Kitty Hawk village and the beach. The camp was removed before the end of World War II.

Austin Cemetery - The cemetery was named for Avery Joseph Austin, owner of the property from the late 1870s until his death in 1902. Austin was from Wanchese before moving to Kitty Hawk to serve as the Keeper of the Poyners Hill LSS Station and later the Keeper of the Paul Gamiels Hill LSS Station. Even as a

Life-Saving Service Keeper he also served as the Elder (preacher) of the Providence (primitive) Baptist Church in Kitty Hawk. Married to Martha Perry of Kitty Hawk he purchased land in the village from Moses D. Lane so he could be near his LSS Station assignments. The Kitty Hawk land included a cemetery which had already been established and in use and he allowed it to continue to be used and even expanded. In time it became the unofficial community cemetery for Kitty Hawk. Avery J. Austin, his wife and several of their children are buried in the cemetery.

Avery Pond - The pond was most likely named for an Avery Tillett, who moved from Tyrell County to Kitty Hawk before 1800, or one of his descendants who also carried the Avery name. The pond and land surrounding it was purchased from John Dough and passed on to decedents of Avery Tillett after he died around 1810. Although a popular hunting pond through the years its name was never documented in any land records, but was known locally as "Avery Pond" by the residents.

Blind Ridge - From an early deed description it appears that Blind Ridge may have been what was later called Hickory Ridge and located as the next ridge east of Poor Ridge. The ridge fits the description of Blind Ridge that appears in a deed between Daniel Savils and Robert Paule in 1737/38. "4 Apr 1738 Daniel Savils of Currituck, wheelwright to Robert Paule of Currituck, planter, cons. The patent which Richard Sanderson, Jr. received on 24 Oct 1717, 264 acres on Sand Banks, adj. Bay. ... which land Parker, by a power of attorney from Sanderson, made over to Daniel Savils: land called Blind Ridge in westernmost end of tract adj. Ceder hammock Gutt…"

Bull Ridge and Bull Ridge Marsh - Bull Ridge is the first ridge in the Kitty Hawk maritime forest west of the active sand dunes. Being flat it is not an impressive ridge as one enters Kitty Hawk village by the main road but its flatness was ideal for home sites. There have been homes scattered along the ridge from the earliest days of settlement in the village. The flat and openness of the area also permitted cultivation for farming although the farm land was not extensive, 5 acres or less. Bull Ridge or Bull Ridge Marsh is mentioned several times in deeds of the late 1700s and early 1800s. "Mathias Toler to John Lewark - 43 acres - west side swamp Kitty Hawk Ridge, west side Bull Ridge Marsh" "Thomas Best to Shadrick Gallop - 50 acres - Citehawk -begin at road, John Luark line, Bull Ridge, Thomas Beacham's line, Edmon Beacham's line." "Mathias Toler to John Walker & O'Neal Walker - North Banks at Bull Ridge and Bull Ridge Marsh, Neal Walker line, bordered both Asa Walker and John Walker lines." "Matthias Tolar, Senr. to John Walker State of NC and County of Currituck, 'I Matthias Toller Senr. do gibe and bequeth to my cousin John Walker the son of Spencer Walker a sertain peace or parcel of land containing by estamation fifty acres lying and situate on the North Banks in the county afsd. Beginning at a place caled the Viney Swamp and running along James Lewark eastwardly to the Bull Ridge thence along the Bull Ridge northardly as far as to contain the fifty acres and from thence to the VINEY SWAMP and thence along said swamp to the first station. May1802'"

Cedar Hammock Ridge – Located between Sandy Run and Hay Point Ridge to the east, and Hickory Ridge and Duck Ponds Creek on the west, Cedar Hammock Ridge was the location of one of the early home sites in Kitty Hawk. The ridge site appears to be where William Dunston resided during his lifetime. This is also land later owned by Edward and Letitia Baum, Jesse and Letitia Partridge and more recently by Edward "Nettie" and Emeline Baum and their heirs. Today, the property has been subdivided into smaller home site lots.

Chinquapin Ridge – Although there are only a few references to Chinquapin Ridge in deeds it appears to have been located between Kitty Hawk Ridge on the east and Dancing Ridge to its west. The associated swamp is sometimes identified as Chinquapin Swamp but also as Cypress Swamp. In the early history of the community a ridge name may change from one location to the next, particularly a ridge that extended on both sides of the main road. Chinquapin Ridge may have been an extension of Pawpaw Ridge which was an extension of Mingoes Ridge on the south side of the main road where the Kitty Hawk Methodist Church was built. Chinquapin Ridge appears to be at the south end of Viney Swamp in an area that has never been cultivated or developed and thus has no memorable distinguishing landmarks. The name chinquapin was well known to the local people as the trees were native to the area. Chinquapin trees, which seem to enjoy a long life, were sometime identified in property line boundary descriptions. The location of the ridge and associated swamp was north of the main road as reported below, "Elijah Sibbern to B. F. Perry - 'adjoining the lands of Oliver O'Neal, F. H. Midgett and others, bounded as follows, viz: Beginning at log wood post in Chinquapin Swamp running southeasterly along the H.M. Lyons line to a maple tree, then westerly along F. H. Midgett line to a gum tree, thence Northeasterly along Oliver O'Neal line… marked ash tree, thence easterly along the line of Edward O'Neal to first station. The said tract of land contains ten (10) acres more or less.'"

Cowpen Ridge – Cowpen Ridge, Flat Ridge, and High Ridge, were south of the main road and side by side west of Northern Gut. They were three of the very early ridges cited in original deeds and grants. In the alignment, Cowpen was the eastern most ridge, Flat Ridge next and High Ridge the western most of the three ridges. Their names appear in a 1778 land grant to James Gamuvell (Gamewell, later Gamiel) for 100 acres in the Up-the-Road section of Kitty Hawk: "Oct. 29, 1778, James Gamuvell, of Currituck Co., enters 100ac in Currituck Co., near Kitty Hawk Bay on the banks; border: a large lying down tree in the footway that crosses the bay that makes out of head of Northerns Gut at W side of Moses Capps field, runs S down said glade to Haman's entry, W. across Cowpen Ridge and Flat Ridge to E. side of High Ridge, N along said ridge to a corner, E along Flat Ridge and Cowpen Ridge to a corner in the valley, to the beginning." The origins of the names are not known but Flat Ridge and High Ridge suggest a name descriptive of the physical appearance of the ridges. In the early history of the village, the land was treated as open range for livestock grazing, but some owners would fence across a ridge to keep the livestock in place. While the fence helped keep the livestock from moving north while swamps and marshes kept the livestock on the ridge and from straying east, west and south of the ridge.

Cypress Swamp – Appears to be the same property as also identified as Chinquapin Swamp, above.

Dancing Ridge – There are two major ridges in Kitty Hawk that can be traced from Kitty Hawk Bay to Southern Shores; KittyHawk Ridge and Dancing Ridge. These two names have gotten lost to history because other names have been applied or the use of the ridges has changed over time. At one time a cart path was open on Kitty Hawk Ridge from Kitty Hawk Bay to what is today the shopping center at Southern Shores. Without public use the cart path became over grown and was abandoned.

Dancing Ridge, the second major ridge through Kitty Hawk, extended from Hay Point on Kitty Hawk Bay to the Kitty Hawk School area on Dogwood Trail in Southern Shores and beyond. Historically, the road along Dancing Ridge was known locally as the "Main Road," but that name was changed to "the Woods Road" by an early Kitty Hawk Town Council Board. Although the ridge is essentially one unit but not always in one straight alignment, it has different names at different places in the community: i.e.: Hay Point, Herbert Perry Road, Midgett Road, and the Woods Road north of its intersection with Twiford Road. A series of open ponds north of Kitty Hawk village and east Dancing Ridge are known as Dancing Ridge Ponds. In the past the ponds had been a favorite hunting site for water fowl, pond and wood ducks, and similar species, particularly during periods of inclement weather. The Dancing Ridge Ponds are sometimes referred to as Cypress Ponds because they are within the Cypress Swamp east of Dancing Ridge.

Duck Pond, Duck Pond Creek, Duck Pond Bridge - Duck Pond Creek parallels Poor Ridge along its east side and extends to Kitty Hawk Bay. Although there is not a bridge there today, historically there was a bridge on the main road over Duck Pond

Creek near the old Kitty Hawk School building. The Duck Pond itself probably was an open water pond historically and was located a few yards east of the Kitty Hawk School building and north of the main road. The pond is mentioned in many deeds like the deed here: "93 Aug 1764, April 1765, 15 Oct 1765: Richard Sanderson, of Perquimans county, to Mathias Toler of Currituck, planter, cons. '7 pounds cm NC. – 100A on Kityhawk Bay' on n. Branch, beginning at Middle Ridge called "Hickory Ridge," n. to Duck Pond, s. to Bay, as by a patent will appear…" A number of property lines appear to meet and merge at a point within the Duck Pond.

Emeline Lane – The lane is a short spur road that extends west off the present-day Herbert Perry Road and crosses Sandy Run branch to the former Baum property on Cedar Hammock Ridge. The road was named for Emeline Guard Etheridge Baum, but not during her lifetime (1845-1932). Emeline Guard grew up in a section of north Nags Head Woods known as Rowseypock. She went to school on Roanoke Island, met and married Truxton Sykes Etheridge and returned to Rowseypock to start their family which became 2 boys and 6 girls. The boys died young. Father Truxton Etheridge also died and Emeline moved with her girls to Kitty Hawk village where she met widower Edward "Ned or Neddie" Baum. He promised to build her and her girls a nice home on his Cedar Hammock Ridge property if she would marry him. She agreed and they married in 1881. They had two sons together, Edward Nelson Baum and Ellsworth Jackson Baum. Edward "Neddie" Baum lost his position with the Life-Saving Service and never built the house he promised Emeline; and she never forgave him. In fact, when he was stricken by probably a stroke and fell out in the front yard of their home, he begged Emeline for help. She stood on the porch looking down on him and said, "Dry up Neddie Baum!"

The Cedar Hammock Ridge property was divided between sons Edward and Ellsworth Baum when they became adults and they built their homes on the property.

Flat Ridge – see Cowpen Ridge above.

Hay Point – see Mill Point.

Hickory Ridge (also referred to as Middle Ridge) - Hickory Ridge was one of the early ridges identified in early Kitty Hawk land grants and deeds. The ridge was located between what we know today as Poor Ridge on the west, and though not often cited, Cedar Hammock Ridge on the east. The origin of the name is unknown but hickory trees were common in the Kitty Hawk woodland and most likely the origin of the ridge name. It was not a very prominent ridge, had a low profile, flooded often and did not support many buildings. James W. Wicker and his wife Nancy had a home on the south end of the ridge near Kitty Hawk Bay, and Samuel Joseph "Joe" Harris lived with his wife Mary Sibbern Harris in a home at the north end of the ridge near the main road. Joe Harris died in 1878 and Mary remarried. The home became the community school house for a number of years until the village constructed two school buildings; one Up-The-Road and a second Down-The-Road. Dempsey Perry and William Robert "Bob" Perry operated a general store in the building for a short time but Dempsey Perry left the partnership in a few years to form his own store business. Bob Perry continued to operate the store before he starting a freight boat business operating between Elizabeth City and Kitty Hawk.

High Bridge Creek – see Northerns Gut.

High Bridge, High Bridge Gut, High Ridge – see Cowpen Ridge above.

Kitty Hawk Ridge – Kitty Hawk Ridge was one of the early named ridges in deeds describing lands in Kitty Hawk. The name first appeared in a 1783 deed for land from Thomas Jones to Edmond Beacham, but it also appeared many times in deeds thereafter down to the 1940s. Kitty Hawk Ridge is the second major ridge in the village from behind the sand hills east of the village. There are a few other minor ridges in the same general area but they only extend for a short distance and then terminate or combine with another or other ridges. Kitty Hawk Ridge starts at Kitty Hawk Bay and goes north to US 158 at Seaside Shopping Center and originally may have extended even further north. Elijah Baum Road is located along the west slope of Kitty Hawk Ridge at the south or village end of the ridge.

Lillian Street – Named for Lillian Koerner of Interlaken, New Jersey, a family friend of Frank Stick and owner of the land on which the street and subdivision was developed. She also purchased West Hill at the Kill Devil Hills for inclusion in the lands to be transferred to the Federal Government for the Kill Devil Hills National Memorial, renamed the Wright Brothers National Memorial. Mrs. Koerner's husband, William H. "Bill" Koerner, was a business partner with Frank Stick in several real estate ventures on the Outer Banks.

Long Point – It is not a very prominent point of land along Currituck Sound but in 1870 it represented the southernmost boundary line as it extended eastward to the Atlantic Ocean for Currituck County along the seashore banks. When a portion of the banks land from here to Caffey's Inlet was transferred to Dare County in 1919 it became the boundary line for Atlantic Township and later the boundary between the Towns of Kitty Hawk and Kill Devil Hills.

Main Road – As a rule the community public roads, those roads maintained by the men of the village under the "road days" work program, were not named. In most cases "main road" was written in lower case which did not designate a place name. The public roads were however acknowledged in deeds as they often formed property boundaries. They were listed in deeds as "main road" and all the public roads in the community from Moore Shore to Sound Landing or from the Signpost north to Caffey's Inlet were known as "the main road." While there were no street numbers, locals would qualify the location by references such as: "main road by Devil Oak Hill," "at High Bridge on main road," "main road near school house," and similar descriptions. Locals knew what "main road" meant even if newcomers were lost.

Marsh Road – (New Road) Maintaining a passable road into the village from the south became a problem for the road day work crews in the late 1800s because of migrating blowing sand from the nearby sand hills. The community work crews solved that problem by building a sand causeway across the marsh from Bull Ridge to Moore Shore, approximately 300 yards. It included a bridge across Bull Ridge Gut to allow for drainage of the interior swamps and wetlands north of the Bay. When completed around 1895, locals referred to the causeway as the "New Road" or simply, "Marsh Road."

Mary Ann Swamp – Mary Ann Swamp is located between Tom Curles Ridge and Kitty Hawk Ridge, or more specifically the low area at the 730-731 address of West Kitty Hawk Road. This land appears to be within the 40 acres purchased by Edmond Beacham from Thomas Jones in 1783. The deed description was from a gut (Penny Toler Ditch) at the head of Kitty Hawk Bay northwardly to a corner tree between said Jones and Beacham line, southwestwardly to Kitty Hawk Ridge, down the eastwardly side of ridge to the bayside and then to the first station. The deed would include Tom Curles Ridge and the swamp on its west side, which fits the Mary Ann Swamp location. Edmon Beacham left these 40 acres to his daughter, Mary Ann Beacham, in his 1792 probated will. Mary Ann sold the land to William Best, Jr., in 1795. The name Mary Ann Swamp does not appear in any deeds until 1898 when Elijah Sibbern and wife sold 20 acres of land to James R. Best, which would become the location of his home place in Kitty Hawk Village. In this deed, the swamp on the north side of the main road would also be called "Mary Ann Swamp". Mary Ann Swamp on the south side of the main road has been filled in over the years and does not appear as a swamp, but it was a true swamp up until the 1950s.

Methodist Road - William Best to Thomas Allen - 50 acres - the sound, Methodist Road, and James Best line (Probably north of Sound Landing.) Thomas Allen to James Wall - "begin sweet gum tree soundside William Best line, thence east with Best line to hickory, thence to Methodist Road, thence northerly course of said road to James Best's line, thence west with said Best line to sound side…"

Mill Point, Hay Point – Mill Point and Mill Point Gut are names that appeared in a Land Entrie Grants in 1778 and repeated in other deeds of the period. The last deed reference to Mill Point, or Mill Point Gut, was in 1831. In a deed dated 1851 the Mill Point at the end of what we today call Herbert Perry Ridge was identified as Hay Point and that name has come down to the present. No one knows the origin of the name Mill Point, but it would have been an ideal location for a windmill. At the end of the ridge there is a high hill overlooking Kitty Hawk Bay on the east and south faces of the ridge, while marshes occupy the area to the west of the point of land. The nearest trees of any size were 500 or more yards away, so there would have been very little disruption of wind currents to run a center post windmill that could be rotated to face the wind. This writer has not found any documentation that there was ever a windmill at the site, but there could have been. The name Hay Point is another name whose origin is unknown. Again, the name may suggest a use of the land at the south end of the ridge, a field used to grow hay, and it would be ideal for that purpose. There is probably 10 to 15 acres of flat land around the hill at the end of the ridge. Herbert Perry farmed the flatland during his lifetime so it stands to reason that a hay field could have been here at one time.

Mingoes Gut – (also: Minga's, Mingues, Mingers, etc.) The name "Minga's Gut" appeared in a 1787 deed and with various spellings other deeds down through the years. The name Mingoes, or its derivation, is thought to be for the Mingo Indians who were an Iroquoian language group, a part of the Algonquian group of Native Americans. The Mingos were not however native to this area; nor were there any Native Americans living permanently on the Outer Banks. Native Americans, probably Tuscarora Indians, did seasonally visit the banks on food gathering expeditions, but did not establish any permanent villages. How this name Mingoes became attached to this waterway which runs from the interior swamps and ponds of Kitty Hawk down to Kitty Hawk Bay is unknown, but the name has been in use for well over 200 years. Mingoes Gut crosses under West Kitty Hawk Road about 300 yards west of the Kitty Hawk United Methodist Church.

Mingoes Ridge – The name explanation is the same for Mingoes Ridge as for Mingoes Gut. The Kitty Hawk United Methodist Church is located on the north end of the crest of Mingoes Ridge at West Kitty Hawk Road. The ridge runs south toward Kitty Hawk Bay, ending where the marsh replaces fast lands. O'Neal Lane road traverses most of Mingoes Ridge.

Moore Shore and Moore Shore Road –

The area appears to have been named for a Moore family who lived on the east side of Kitty Hawk Bay, probably in the 1880s. In a 1914 deed W. J. Tate referred to "the Moore lands." Tract number seven: "Beginning at the water's edge on Kitty Hawk Bay at the south line of the John Baum lands, running N. Easterly course along the dividing line of the John Baum heirs and the lands known as the Moore lands to the ocean, thence southerly along the ocean to a post, thence westerly to Kitty Hawk Bay, thence along said bay to the first station, containing one hundred acres more or less, being land purchased by W. J. Tate from R. L.

Griggs Sheriff of Currituck County at Sheriffs sale of lands for taxes on the first Monday in May 1912 at the Court House door..." Capt. William J. Tate also mentioned the "Moore place" in an article he wrote in opposition to one by Frank Stick who had said that the drifting of the sand dunes was a great hoax. The Tate article appeared in the May 22, 1931, issue of the Elizabeth City, NC, *Independant*.

I will cite to you what is locally known as the Moore place at Kitty Hawk and I cite to you J. R, Best, Jackson S. Twiford, Mrs. Mary Midgett and Mrs. Matilda Baum, all of Kitty Hawk. These parties will remember and will bear me out in the following. They, as well as myself, remember when at the Moore Place there was a nice little plot of cultivated land and a nice home with woods to the east and northeast of it. Now the site is back under the hill, buried under many fathoms of drifting sand. No vestige of the place appears to the casual passerby. This old colonial home was built in 1800 and had soldiers quartered in it in 1812, and among the generation of my age, was known as one of the oldest homes on that part of the coast. Captain Tate cited several other places up and down the coast where the drifting or migrating sand dunes had buried other building and cemeteries. The home he was born in at the head of Kitty Hawk Bay and north of the Moore place had to be removed to salvage the lumber before it too had been buried by the drifting sand dunes.

Northard Neighborhood – "Northard Neighborhood" appeared in the Providence Baptist Church Book for July 1870 as a reference to the community north of Kitty Hawk, now known as Duck, but not called that in 1870. Duck was the name assigned to the 1909 established post office in the community and became the common name for the community. Lillie Jacob Baum, who lived at the Pine Island Club north of Caffey's Inlet in the early 1900s, recorded in her diary trips to "Bank Woods"; apparently another name for the North Banks community that would become Duck.

Northern Gut – (also: Northerns Gut, Northers Gut, Northan Gut, other similar spelling) John Northern of Charles

Parish in the county York and Colony of Virginia was involved in real estate purchased on the Sandy Banks in North Carolina from at least 1710. His purchases included land and marsh in the up-the-road section of Kitty Hawk. Northerns Gut was undoubtedly named for him or his son, Peter Northern, a resident of Currituck Co. at the time, who also purchased and owned lands in Kitty Hawk. Although the name Northern Gut appeared in deeds for at least a century and a half, the gut today is known as High Bridge Creek, a name that appeared maybe for the first time in a 1922 deed between B. D. Tillett and wife Almira B. Tillett to H. O. Tillett.

Panters Creek - Panters Creek was mentioned in deeds as early as 1710 and continued to be identified as a landform and boundary until the 1850s. It was one of the small creeks south of Shellbank Point and connected Currituck Sound with Northern Gut creek and by extension Kitty Hawk Bay.

Pawpaw Ridge - This is a very old ridge and swamp name associated with Kitty Hawk village, but it does not appear often in deeds because it was a small tract of land that did not exchange hands often, thus few documented references."John Luark to Willis Gallop - 10 acres - by William Etheridge line on Cypress Swamp to beech, old line, Poppaw Ridge" "Elijah Sibbern wife Fanny Sibbern to W. W. Basnight- beginning at a sweet gum in the middle of Pawpaw Swamp, running Northward along said Swamp to a Bay tree at the Lyons line, thence along said Lyons line westward to the Middle of Viney Swamp to an Elm Tree, thence Southward down said Swamp to a Cypress Tree at W. Beasley line, thence along W. Beasley line to the first station, containing ten (10) acres more or less..."

Some people have thought that Pawpaw Ridge was a substitute name for Poor Ridge, but they are in fact two separate ridges. Poor Ridge is in the Up-the-Road community with Duck Pond Creek forming its east boundaries. Pawpaw Ridge is in the Down-the-Road community on the north side of the main road across from Mingoes Ridge where the Methodist Church is located. The pawpaw trees and bushes for which this ridge is named are believed to grow in Kitty Hawk woods, but not in any great numbers.

Pawls Creek – Although it is not documented as such, the series of creeks in the southwest marshes of Kitty Hawk were sometimes referred to as the "Pawls Creek." The reason for this is that from a bird's eye view, the creeks flow southerly and seem to turn further southward the closer they approach Kitty Hawk Bay or Currituck Sound. With that curvy style, they look like the paw of a wild animal, maybe a bobcat which are known to live in this area.

Poor Ridge – (i.e., Smith Ridge) The name Poor Ridge appeared for the first time in an 1873 deed from Jasper Toler to Isiah Cain of New York for the lease of 30 acres of land for 4 years, 9 months at Poor Ridge Landing, for the purpose of keeping a store and fish house. The earlier identification of Poor Ridge as Smith Ridge is from a description of the property as outlined in a 1763 deed from Tully Williams of Perquimans Co. to Benjamin Paddrick of Pasquotank Co. That deed references two ridges, Blind Ridge and Smith Ridge, and Ceder Hommack gut. Comparing this description to other deed description, it appears that Blind Ridge is present day Hickory Ridge, and Smith Ridge is present day Poor Ridge. "Tully Williams of Perquimans Co., to Benjm Paddrick of Pasquotank Co. – 150A - being or supposed 1/2 of a large quantity of land holden by and between the afsd Tully Williams & Richard Sanderson, called Banks land on Kittyhawk bay commonly called Blind Ridge and Smith Ridge, beginning at Ceder Hommack gut, thence the said gut the various courses of it to the head, then of thence a westerdly course to southerdly and so to the ____, such a manner as shall include one half a quantity of said and thence to the 1st station..." The origin of the name, Poor Ridge, is unknown. No one by that name ever lived or owned property on the ridge. Nor is it a corruption of the name, Paw Paw Ridge, which is located in a different section of Kitty Hawk. Poor Ridge may have been a descriptive term, not a legal one, and could have been inserted in a deed by anyone at any time. The simple explanation of the name may be that that was the name local people called the ridge, such as, "I live down on Poor Ridge!" The name stuck and became the name of the ridge and the road that extend its length.

Robersons Creek – This is a very old place name and appears in a 1787 deed as: "Walter Sykes to Thomas Garrett- 50 acres - head of Robinson's Creek at Sam Woodley line, the named '...the manor plantation where Thomas Hill formerly lived.'" (Comment: This land was probably part of the 400 acres granted to John Norton in 1725. It appears that Thomas Garrett deeded this land to John Dough in 1788.) Its location is between Sound Landing Ridge and Methodist Ridge and is drainage for Whidby Swamp into Avery Pond, and in turn to Currituck Sound. The origin of the name "Robersons Creek" is unknown. There appears not to be any records of anyone by the name "Roberson" or "Robersons" having lived in Kitty Hawk or owned property in the community before 1787, or for that matter any early period of time.

Sandy Run Bridge, **Sandy Run Dream** (drain), **Sedge Swamp** (also Sage) – References to Sedge Swamp appear in deeds several times during the period of 1857 to 1901 and describing swamp property in the vicinity of where the Providence Baptist Church was constructed. In some deeds the name "Sedge" has been miss-written as "Sage," however, an examination of the grounds around and near the church will display an abundance of "White-topped Sedge" grasses during the blooming season. Sedge Swamp itself appears to be north of the church property itself and extend south to at least the West Kitty Hawk Road and north beyond Twiford Road. Deed references for Sedge Swamp appear as: "William Wicker to Ivey Dowdy - 5 acres - at Nothand's Gut, adjoining heirs of Elijah Wicker - Sedge Swamp next branch, heirs of William Keys..." "Ivy Dowdy to Jasper Toler - 5 acres - N. Banks, Northerns Gut adjoining heirs of Elijah Walker, Sedge Swamp next Branch" (Appears to be land Ivy Dowdy purchased from Wm. Wicker. "James Wicker and wife to Sylvanus Harris (Sr.) - 'adjoining the lands of the Avery Tillett heirs others, bounded as follows, viz: Beginning at a pine stump at the corner of the Tillett Wicker lands running easterly to the middle of Sedge Swamp, thence a northerly course along the middle of said Swamp to the A. B. L. Tillett line, thence a westerly course to the middle of Northern Gut, thence a South course along said gut to the first station, containing 2 acres or there about..."

Shell Bank - *Signpost, or Headquarters* - Before the State of North Carolina took over the maintenance of the public roads in the 1920s each community of any size had a Signpost, or Headquarters. It was the point in the community where the "road day work crews" worked toward or from. In Kitty Hawk the Signpost, or Headquarters, was at what is now the intersection of The Woods and Twiford Roads. The Down-the-Road road crew worked the road from Moore Shore to the Signpost, the Up-the-Road road crew worked the road from the Signpost to Sound Landing, and the people in the community that became Duck worked the road from their community to the Signpost. The road from the Signpost to Duck was a very long distance when compared with the other assigned roads, but the Duck Road was mostly over high ground without swamps, ditches, creeks, or marshes to cross and was much easier to maintain than most other unimproved roads. Truxton Midgett in a 1976 interview reported that at one time there was a sign at the Signpost giving the mileage to Caffey's Inlet and Nags Head. The sign was not replaced when it was no longer readable. Although they did not know its meaning or purpose, every kid growing up in Kitty Hawk in the 1940s and 1950s knew of the Signpost and its location. The Signpost is a lost term today.

Sound Landing –

Western most point of land reached by the public road through Kitty Hawk on Currituck Sound. In 1838 and maybe before, Ivey Dowdy lived next to Currituck Sound and the area was called Doudey (Dowdy) Landing. Sound Landing was also the site of the Thomas Baum ferry landing during the period of 1926-30.

The Neck – Several people who were interviewed in 1960 on the history of Kitty Hark referred to the Up-the-Road community as"The Neck." There was no real explanation for the term, unless you have a great imagination. If one were to look at the Up-the-Road community from a bird's eye view, the road system west of Duck Pond Creek appearing like the outline of a body and neck of a heron stalking for food at a marshes edge. The Neck never appeared in any known historic documents.

Tom Curles Ridge – This ridge name does not appear in any known land deed or area map, but it was known by several old members of the community during research work in the 1960s. The ridge was located between Mary Ann Swamp (adjoining Kitty Hawk Ridge) on the west and Penny Toler Ditch on the east.

It was a relatively short ridge extending about ½ mile from Kitty Hawk Bay on the south end and just beyond the main road to the north. The ridge name is attributed to Tom Curles who lived in the area in the 1850s and may have had a house or home place on the property. His daughter, Affe Frances Curles Lewark and husband, John H. Lewark, are buried on the property in a small family cemetery plot near the head of Kitty Hawk Bay.

Turtle Road – A place name that appears not to have a long shelf life was Turtle Road. The two descriptions deeds below seem to give two separate locations for Turtle Road. In the 1857 deed Turtle Road appears to be west of Northern Gut, probably near the east end of what became Austin Cemetery. In the 1861 deed, Turtle Road appears to be east of Northern Gut on land which the Walker family is known to have owned at one time. Based on these two deeds one could surmise that at one point in time the road between the "Signpost" (Twiford Road) and what became Austin cemetery was referred to as the Turtle Road. That section of road is low and would have been an ideal spot to observe turtles sunning themselves, and to pick up a snapper for turtle stew. "William Tillett to Ivey Dowdy 5 acres - begin at bridge in the marsh that crosses Turtle Road running easterly and various courses of the road to pine still easterly to another pine to another pine to Joseph B. Owens line, thence a southerly course to said Ivey Dowdy line, then westerly along Ivey Dowdy line to 1 station, being in shape of a jib, 5 acres…" "Affie Walker Guard to Nichodemus Best - 33 1/3 acres - 1/3 share (inherited from father Norris Walker) lying … on Turtle Road adj. land of Hodges Gallop on North & East, land of Elijah Sibern (Wicker?) and Wicker heirs on South and Northern Gut on West." (This is probably the land that Nick Best sold to Robert O'Neal in 1867.)

Viney Swamp - (sometimes appearing as Piney Swamp) – Viney Swamp is a name very few Kitty Hawkers have ever heard of and fewer still have ever seen on the ground, including this writer. It is reportedly a very swampy, densely vegetated area in the interior of Kitty Hawk woods west of Bull Ridge, the first major ridge in the woods west of the Kitty Hawk sand hills and behind Sea Scape Golf Course. Although it has not been plotted, it is believed that the swamp and its environs drain out to Kitty Hawk Bay through Penny Toler Ditch and Bull Ridge Marsh. The name Viney Swamp appeared in an 1802 deed from Matthias Toler to his cousin John Walker. A couple of 1840 deeds referred to the area as "Piney" Swamp. Apparently when the deeds were being transcribed to the County Deed Book, the letter P was substituted for the letter V and the deed read Piney Swamp instead of Viney Swamp. An 1897 deed from Elijah Sibbern and wife to W. W. Basnight again referred to the swamp as Viney Swamp. The area today is part of the Kitty Hawk Woods Coastal Reserve which should assure its preservation in its natural setting for the future.

Wading Place – The terms "Wading Place, Horse Wading Place, and Great Wading Place" occur in many deeds of the 1775-1825 periods and describing land boundaries. The terms apparently reference location where it was necessary for a horse to carry its rider or pull a wagon over a short body of water hazard such as a creek or swamp. Also, for those walking it would require them to remove their shoes or boots and wade the hazard. The road crossing of Mingoes Gut, west of the current Kitty Hawk Methodist Church, was referenced in deeds as "the Great Wading Place," probably because of its width rather than its water depth. It apparently was a major hazard as a corduroy road was built from each bank. The "Wading Place" or "Horse Wading Place" described the crossing of Northern Gut, which was located opposite the inactive Kitty Hawk Providence Baptist Church. The crossing today is known as High Bridge Creek. After the village increased in population the men in the community performed "road days" work and bridged the water hazards.

Whidby Swamp – Whidby Swamp was not a well-known landmark but was reported as a place name by an interviewer in discussion of Kitty Hawk locations in the 1960s. The name "Whidby Swamp" does appear in an 1803 deed as follows: "Samuel Dough to Avery Tillett - 55 acres, plus 8 acres on Northern Gut - North Banks land joining land of William Best, Jr., begin at Whidby Swamp, running easterly course to head of John Dough patent, thence southerly course by line of marked trees, Jack Dough's line, thence north to said swamp, thence northerly to 1st station..." The deed does not precisely pinpoint the location of Whidby Swamp, but by comparing this deed with others it appears that the swamp was north of the Sound Landing Road and between (Sound) Landing Ridge and the Methodist Road Ridge. Robinson Creek appears to drain Whidby Swamp and empties it into Avery Pond.

Section Two

Kitty Hawk In Businesses And Schools

Chapter Four

MAY I HELP YOU MA'AM...

How the Villagers Brought General Stores to Kitty Hawk

A bird's eye view of Kitty Hawk would suggest it would be an ideal location for a town or area trading center. The heavily forested land is at the widest spot approximately 3 miles across, east and west, and about 2 to 3 miles long, north to south. The village set well back from the ocean, but had a beautiful bay connecting to both Currituck and Albemarle Sounds. By water, it was about 45 miles from Elizabeth City, the city that emerged as the principal economic center in northeastern North Carolina. Norfolk, Va., a much larger trading center was less than 100 miles by water to the north. Seemingly ideally located, Kitty Hawk should be a great place to set up an area trading center, or so it would appear. The topography under the tree canopy reveals a land that does not have a very large development base because the soil was laid in ridges, separated by dense swamps in the interior and marshland along the southern fringes. In spite of its size there is very little contiguous property on which to site buildings, stores and businesses. Because of the extensive inland swamps and marshes, connecting the land together would require an elaborate system of bridges and causeways. But the biggest deterrent to business development in the village was the shallowness of Kitty Hawk Bay. While a beautiful body of water to view, Kitty Hawk Bay was and is very shallow and does not have the natural depths to allow vessels with drafts above 3 to 5 feet to navigate, and those depths occur only in a few short channels in the bay. The limited water access correspondingly limits development of the land. While Kitty Hawk did not develop as a trading center it did manage to support a few small stores and other business ventures through the years. The earliest listing for businesses for Kitty Hawk and northeastern North Carolina appeared in "Branson's North Carolina Directory 1884." The listing was reprinted in *The Daily Advance* newspaper for June 18, 1962, and included the identification of three boarding houses in the community, a wheelwrighting and blacksmith business operated by Baum Sadler, two fish dealers, a livestock operator and three general store merchants. William J. Baum, Daniel M. Tate, and James R. Hobbs were the operators of the three boarding houses in Kitty Hawk at the time and each was "licensed to operate an ordinary" by the county government. "An ordinary" was the term used by the county to identify a boardinghouse. Daniel J. Baum and James M. Baum were identified as two local Kitty Hawk fish dealers. More than likely they were fish buyers for Elizabeth City and Tidewater Virginia fish dealers working the Kitty Hawk Bay - Currituck Sound areas.

The Beasley-Daniels Stores - Hezakiah Wateman Beasley and Theoflus L. Daniels were each identified as operating general stores in the community in 1884. Those stores would have been located at the end of Poor Ridge. Theoflus Daniels is also known to have had a freight boat which he uses to transport fish to market. The vessel was operated for Mr. Daniels by Franklin Harris Midgett.

The Dan Tate Store - Daniel M. Tate was the proprietor of another small store in the village on the east side of Kitty Hawk on Moore Shore Road. Daniel M. Tate, was reported to have shipwrecked with his brother William Douglas Tate along the Kitty Hawk coast around 1849-1850. Brother William Douglas stayed in the area although according to census records he may have continued to be a mariner working out of the port of Norfolk. He married locally, invested well in local property and became a community leader. Daniel Tate returned to Maine, married a lady there and lived in Maine until after she died around 1865. He returned to Kitty Hawk and continued he maritime sailing life for a few years and then settled in Kitty Hawk village. When Daniel opened his store is unknown, but a receipt to Elijah Sibbern for

$40.00 dated July 18, 1883, and issued by D. M. Tate as agent for

DAN TATE

Singer Sewing Machines, suggests he was in business at least by that date. Without question that sewing machine was probably one of the first, if not the first machine of its kind in Kitty Hawk, and with seven girls in the Sibbern family the sewing machine would undoubtedly have been a welcomed addition for wife, Fannie Twiford Sibbern. The Tate store appeared to have been located along Kitty Hawk Bay where Moore Shore Road turns from a west-to-east direction to a southern orientation. No pictures or descriptions survive of its existence so one can only guess at its appearance. Apparently, Daniel M. Tate lived within the building so the salesroom was probably very small. William J. "Capt. Bill" Tate lived with and helped his Uncle Dan Tate with the store when Bill was not attending school at Oxford Orphanage or enrolled in tutoring courses with Samuel Lloyd Sheep in Elizabeth City. Bill Tate was appointed Kitty Hawk Postmaster in January 1892 and as was customary at the times the post office was moved to a site selected by the postmaster, in this case most likely the Tate store. The post office was again moved around 1896 to the William J. Tate home after the house was constructed.

The Calhoun Store - The old Tate store building burned of unknown causes sometime after Bill Tate moved the post office to his new home. A Mr. James Calhoun built a replacement building there before 1900 but the store did not last very long as Calhoun sold it in November 1900. Before doing so, Orville Wright gave a humorous description of shopping in a Kitty Hawk store to his sister Katherine Wright in an October 14, 1900, letter: "I suspect you sometimes wonder what we eat, and how we get it. After I got down we decided to camp. There is no store in Kitty Hawk; that is, not anything that you would call a store. Our pantry in its most depleted state would be a mammoth affair compared with our Kitty Hawk stores. Our camp alone exhausts the out-put of all the henneries within a mile. What little canned goods, such as corn, etc., [there is,] is of such a nature that only a Kitty Hawker could down it. Mr. Calhoun, the grocery man, is striving to raise the tastes of the community to better goods, but all in vain. They never had anything good in their lives, and consequently are satisfied with what they have. In all, other things they are the same way, satisfied in keeping soul and body together. Mr. Tate is probably the one exception. He gets interested in anything we have, wants to put acetylene gas in his house because he saw my bicycle gas lamp, has decided to buy our gasoline stove when we leave. Gasoline stoves are a curiosity in this neighborhood, and more feared by the natives than those "bars" up North River where Israel Perry wouldn't land "for a thousand dollars." Mr. Tate would also like to spend his remaining days-which might be few-in experimenting with flying machines, He is already post-master, farmer, fisherman, and political boss of Kitty Hawk. Doc Cogswell, a man from N.Y. City, who married a sister of Tate's wife and who has settled down here, says Tate will be dead before Christmas - from excitement if we don't get out. Tate can't afford to shirk his work to fool around with us, so he attempts to do a day's work in two or three hours so that he can spend the balance with us and the machine. We need no introduction in Kitty Hawk. Every place we go we are called Mr. Wright. Our fame has spread far and wide up and down the beach. Will has even rescued the name of Israel Perry, a former Kitty Hawker, from oblivion, and it now is one of the most frequently spoken names about the place. Will admits that Israel meant well. I believed I started in to tell what we eat. Well, part of the time we eat hot biscuits and eggs and tomatoes; part of the time eggs, and part tomatoes. Just now we are out of gasoline and coffee. Therefore, no hot drink or bread or crackers. The order sent off Tuesday has been delayed by the winds. Will is most starved. But he kept crying that when we were rolling in luxuries, such as butter, bacon corn bread and coffee. I think he will survive. It is now suppertime. I must scratch around and see what I can get together. We still have half a can of condensed milk, which amounts to six or eight tea spoonfuls."

When the brothers could not find items they wanted in the local store they often prepared a list of their needs and gave it to the freight boat operator to purchase for them on his next trip to Elizabeth City. The freight boat usually traveled to Elizabeth City weekly, but weather conditions dictated the schedule so they may not get what they wanted for days, or a week or so later. In spite of the inconvenience, the system worked for them for the most part.

The Beasley Store - There were several store operations in Kitty Hawk before those reported in 1884 Branson directory. Hezekiah Beasley was listed as a merchant in the 1870 census with his location somewhere on Poor Ridge. The business was probably not a very financially successful operation as he only reported $30 of real estate value and $15 personal estate value in the 1870 Census. By 1880 Hezakiah is reported to be a widower and a sailor, but in the 1884 Branson directory he is once again listed as a general store operator. Hezakiah W. Beasley was an interesting person and had a varied life. He married three times, had a number of children, and listed his occupation at various times as a fisherman, a merchant, or a sailor. He served as clerk to the Providence Primitive Baptist Church of Kitty Hawk, but resigned that appointment to become the church Elder. He was expelled from the Church for failing to attend some services but was later restored to full membership. Several times he was appointed as Register and Inspector of Elections by the County government and was even appointed commissioner of Atlantic Township on the Currituck Board of Commissioners, but refused to qualify, could not serve and was replaced. The Providence Baptist Church Book reported his death as April 1891. His burial site is unknown.

The Morse Store - William J. Morse was listed in the 1880 census as a retail grocer in Kitty Hawk. The location of his store is unclear but it may have been in the Up-The-Road section of the village between Northern Gut and the Austin Cemetery. Morse was an active member in the community serving on the Atlantic Township School Committee and as a poll taker for several elections. He was also a register inspector on other occasions. He served as a standing clerk with the Providence Primitive Baptist Church while living in the community. In 1881 he closed his Kitty Hawk store and moved to Elizabeth City where he opened a new store and became a grocery merchant again. His daughter, Essie V. Morse, became a teacher and returned to Kitty Hawk in 1908 to teach in the Up-the-Road school. She met and married Cal Veston Harris in 1912, built a house across the road from the school and lived there until 1917 when they moved to Elizabeth City for the remainder of their lives. Their Kitty Hawk home building is still standing at 1090 West Kitty Hawk Road. The house has been well maintained and recently been risen to get it above the flood plain.

The Perry-Perry Store - Dempsey Perry, formed a partnership with William Robert "Bob" Perry in 1890, opened a small store on land across from his home on the main road through Kitty Hawk. The store would have been located around 1078 West Kitty Hawk Road on a map of today and would have principally served the Up-the-Road community in it day.

The Dempsey Perry Store, with Dempsey Perry, in hat, left

The Perry-Baum Store - The Dempsey Perry-Bob Perry partnership did not last and Bob Perry moved out, formed a new partnership with Thomas T. Baum and opened a new store business in a former residence near the Duck Pond Bridge. The residential building had belonged to Samuel J. Harris who died in 1878. Before being the Tom Baum - Bob Perry store, the building had also served as a school house for the Up-the-Road students. Around 1900 while still in the store business, Bob Perry bought out the Kitty Hawk service line of the Willis Gallop Banks freight business. Bob Perry operated the freight line for a time and then closed his store and sold the freight line to Franklin Harris Midgett in 1902. Thereafter he mostly fished for a living.

The Banks Store - Although he did not appear in the 1900 Census, residents of the time reported that Willis Gallop Banks owned a store on Poor Ridge. Banks is believed to have been living in the Powell's Point community of Currituck County when the census was taken and most likely his Poor Ridge store was being "run" by someone else. Willis Bank's principal line of work was operating a freight line from Elizabeth City serving communities around Currituck Sound and adjoining waters. He owned his own freight boat which he named *Filena*, after his wife. It was gasoline powered and may have been the first motorized vessel to ply the waters of Kitty Hawk Bay.

The Dempsey-Zene Perry Stores - The Perry store, first operated by Dempsey Perry and then by his son, Zene, was the longest operating business in Kitty Hawk in the 19th and 20th centuries. Dempsey Perry built his first small store in 1890 but then enlarged it to about 20 X 30 feet in 1900. The Zene Perry store, even larger than the second Dempsey Perry store building, opened in May 1926.

The Dempsey-Zene Perry Store with a visible gas pump to serve the newly acquired automobiles of Kitty Hawk

Zene Perry reported in a 1960 interview that he left Kitty Hawk in 1907 to work in the Charles Robinson wholesale dry goods store on Water Street in Elizabeth City. He got along well in Elizabeth City and became acquainted with many of the wholesale merchants in the town. Some of the merchants, including Charles Robinson, encouraged Zene to return to Kitty Hawk and help his father run his store. Zene thought his father was too generous a person and "trusted out" too much from his store which resulted in heavy debt for the business. While Dempsey Perry had over $5,000 on his books owed to him, he in turn owed $700 to Elizabeth City merchants but had only $300 worth of stock in the store. Zene made a deal with his father to operate the store and provide for both families, but he, Zene, would be the boss and would determine who to "trust" with credit. Zene took over his father's store in the summer of 1910 and went about cleaning up old debts and establishing good credit with suppliers. By 1924 Zene Perry had purchased the store from his father and cleared all debts on the store and merchandise. The Perry family operated a store in the community for the better part of 80 years. Even as he approached old age, Mr. Zene continued to go to the store daily when his health permitted. The store finally closed with Mr. Zene's death in 1972. In the 1980s the store building was sold and moved to Nags Head to be a new business with an old store appeal. It did not attract the public attention necessary to grow the business and it closed after a few years. The building was razed to make way for a chain auto parts store.

The Perry store did hold a special place in the communities, at least during the 1960s. At that time, Russell Perry, Zene's son, was Voting Register for the Kitty Hawk precinct. This writer had just moved back to Kitty Hawk and needed to register to be eligible to vote in an upcoming election. As I drove toward the Perry store I met Russell traveling east so I flagged him down to ask about getting registered. He told me to meet him at the Shannon - Beacham store Down-the-Road, which I did. When I got to the store, Russell had his voter register journal open on the tailgate of his truck and we proceeded to get me registered.

Later that year a general election was held to fill local and state government offices. Also on the ballot was a school improvements referendum tax, which was not popular with some of the older members of the community. When I arrived at the local polling location, the Zene Perry store, there was a small congregation of older men on the porch greeting the voters as they entered the building. One called out to me, "Billy, you know how to vote on the school bond issue, don't you?" I replied, "I sure do Mr. Pennel, I understand the issue!" and proceeded to the ballot table. Using the Zene Perry Store as an election polling place was an interesting experience. There were no individual booths so you had to find your own private spot to mark your ballot. I found a stack of paint cans under a 40-watt bulb, filled out my ballot and placed it in a locked box at the registers table. Later I learned that I voted with the majority who wanted to improve the local school system. While it was a very casual and informal affair, I never heard anyone saying anything about voter fraud back in those days.

The Holland Perry Store - Around 1900/01, William Avery "Captain Bill" Perry purchased the Samuel B. Dowdy home place at Sound Landing and about 12 acres of adjoining land. He tore down the old home place and built a new house for his family. Shortly thereafter he built a small store building next to the Landing road. His wife ran the store, which became known as the "Frances Holland Perry Store", or simply the "Holland Perry

Store". He also applied for a post office outlet which was granted and the Otila post office was established on Sept. 20, 1905, in the store building with Mrs. Frances Holland Perry as Postmaster. The store operation was very small but it, along with the post office, helped to serve the basic need of the Up-the-Road community. Both operations were timely since a major logging operation of Kitty Hawk Woods which would last for over ten years was just beginning. Mrs. Perry's husband, William A. Perry, was appointed Otila Postmaster on Aug 29, 1913. He was replaced as postmaster by William J. Tate on April 6, 1914, but then was reappointed postmaster on 20 July 1914. The post office was discontinued on May 15, 1918. Mrs. Frances Holland Perry died January 25, 1922.

The Elijah W. Baum Stores - Elijah W. Baum opened a new general merchandise store for Kitty Hawk on September 9, 1906. It was approximately 24 feet by 30 feet in size and located on Kitty Hawk Bay at the south end of Kitty Hawk Ridge in what was then known as the Down-The-Road community. Ordinarily one would simply note the opening of the store and move on but in this case the circumstance of the opening was special. Elijah Baum was a young merchant at 21 years of age, single, who did not inherit an established store but built a new one for himself without any retail experience or training. He apparently saw a need and an opportunity and took the chance of going into business for himself. The one advantage he did have was that there were no other stores like his in the Down-The-Road community so he had limited competition.

Elijah Baum's first store, 1916

On June 10, 1914, Elijah W. Baum was appointed Postmaster for Kitty Hawk and the postal operation was incorporated within his store building. Having the post office with the general store was a convenience for the postal users and a valuable service for the store patrons – and the postal-store operation was a good fit. In the early days stock and merchandise for the store was delivered to Kitty Hawk by the freight boat *Lou Willis* operated by the Franklin Harris Midgett family. The *Lou Willis* had originally been a sailing vessel when purchased around 1902 from Bob Perry. Harris Midgett converted the vessel to power by installing an engine built by Andrew Sanders of Elizabeth City.

Materials delivered to the store were off-loaded to a flat barge and brought to shore by poling the barge. It was a cumbersome operation so Elijah Baum built a wharf and dock system that connected the front porch of the store to a loading dock approximately 400 feet into Kitty Hawk Bay. To move the stock and merchandise down the dock to the store he adapted a two-axle push cart with railroad type wheels which matched a track on the wharf. Items that were ready to be sold in the store were delivered directly to the building, but bulk items such as barrels of fuel, hay or other large items were stored until needed in one of the freight storage buildings next to the wharf near the shoreline.

Elijah Baum's wharf, with the rail cart system he installed to move stock

An ice storage building was located at the south end of the wharf where the freight boats docked. It was about 20 feet by 20 feet in size and was insulated with sawdust to keep the ice insulated. The building had a 4-inch concrete floor with a 3-foot square trap door and opening to allow ice to be shoveled on to the fish cargo when the boats were positioned under the floor opening. The ice would have been purchased in Elizabeth City and brought to Kitty Hawk principally to ice downmarket fish, but the ice was also sold for household use. Sometimes when Kitty Hawk Bay froze over, Elijah Baum and helpers would saw out blocks of bay ice and store it in the ice house for later use.

Throughout his career as a merchant businessman Elijah Baum tried to keep pace with the evolution of changes in the industry and provide the materials desired by the needs and convenient of his customers. Early on he installed a DELCO electric power system to make shopping and using the postal service easier for his patrons in his store. He even extended the electric power to his wharf and dock operations to facilitate late or early arrivals and departures. As a personal spin off he extended the electric power to his home, which adjoined the store.

With Truxton Midgett joining the USCG in 1917 and his brother Spencer following a year later, the Midgett freight line had to make adjustments in its services. Elijah Baum, realizing for him to continue his store operation he too would have to make adjustments to his services. He had a small boat that he could use to haul some of his freight, but it was not adequate to meet his overall needs. His real

The *Hettie E* docked at Elizabeth City

needs would be to secure the services of a regular size freight boat and he made arrangements with John P. Pugh, a carpenter and master wood craftsman of Colington, NC, to build a vessel for him. With the launching of his 40 foot *Hettie Mae*, Elijah Baum had the freight boat he needed to support his general merchandise store. The vessel was originally built to allow him to service his own business operation, but as the Midgett freight boat operation closed he began to pick up freight for other communities around Currituck Sound. Even a fish dealer in Virginia contracted with him to purchase North Carolina fish and deliver the catch to their Virginia docks. Charles William Perry was the freight boat operator for Elijah Baum when necessary and Jim Beacham or Herbert Gard served as the engineers when the *Hettie Mae* was underway. Joe Ed Baum, Elijah Baum's father-in-law and a longtime cook at the Kitty Hawk Life Saving Station, served as the cook aboard the *Hettie Mae*. While the vessel was primarily built to haul freight, passengers were allowed on a space available basis. The passenger fare was $1.00 for travel one way, Kitty Hawk to Elizabeth City, or Elizabeth City to Kitty Hawk.

When automobiles began to arrive in Kitty Hawk in the mid-1920s, the store operation was expanded to provide gasoline and repairs service. Texaco products were brought to Kitty Hawk in barrels and cases and kept in the wharf side storage buildings until needed. Gasoline was stored in an underground tank which had an above ground hand operated pump. Gasoline would be hand pumped to the visible glass storage cylinder at the top of the pump and gravity dispensed to the vehicle through a flexible hose and hand operate nozzle. In addition to gasoline and oil, tires and tubes and general repair service was offered the customers. William Thomas Beacham was one of the early mechanics hired for the Baum garage. Orville Baum and Aubrey Alonzo Harris also worked in the garage.

In 1920, Jessie Baum and his cousin Edward Baum opened a general mercantile store on the main road through Kitty Hawk near the Methodist Church. Initially it did not present much competition for the E. W. Baum Store which was located about ½ mile away on a side road. However, with the introduction of ferry service in 1926 and the opening of the bridge across Currituck Sound in September 1930, traffic patterns through Kitty Hawk changed and the E. W. Baum store began to become isolated. A paved road from the beach highway to a point near the Methodist Church would isolate the store even more. Rather than to be sidelined by development, Elijah Baum devised a plan to continue his business. He secured the vacant Down-the-Road school building located on the main road through the village just east of the Methodist Church and remodeled it to serve as his store and to accommodate the post office operation. The gasoline pump from the store at the bay was moved to the new store operation. Later, Elijah Baum built a service station and garage on land on the west side of the dirt road leading to the bay landing from lumber salvaged from the bay side store. Apparently, there was not a need for the service station in the community and it closed. During the period of operating the new store, Elijah realized the building was on his sister's land so around 1938 he had the store building moved west about 200 feet to his land. It was on this new location when the store and post office accidentally burned to the ground on Dec. 12, 1944. Only a building for the post office was built back.

The 1935 Elijah Baum store and post office

The Baum & Baum Store - opened for business in the spring of 1920 under a written partnership agreement between cousins Jessie E. Baum and Edward N. Baum. The store, built mostly by Edward Baum, was located on the north side of the main road through Kitty Hawk diagonally across from the Kitty Hawk Methodist Church on land leased for $1.00 a year for 99 years from James Raleigh Best. Although it was not written into the agreement, there was a mutual understanding that gasoline would not be dispensed from the leased property, and none was. Later Jessie Baum did install pumps on his property across from the store and sold gasoline as part of the store operation. And later still Jessie Baum permitted the construction on his property of a small building to serve as an auto repair shop. Ernest Pugh was the auto mechanic who ran the shop for Jessie Baum. At the time of the new store opening, the main village road was unpaved and the bridge across Currituck Sound had not been constructed so there was limited traffic through the community. That would change with the new bridge and increase in auto ownership. After only a couple of years of business, Edward Baum opted to sell his interest in the partnership and for the next 20 years Jessie Baum was the sole owner and operator of the Baum & Baum store.

After Jessie Baum's wife died in 1943 and with failing health, Jessie Baum decided to get out of the retail grocery store business. Early in 1944 he sold his interest in the merchandise business to neighbors, Guy Hayman and Roy Beacham. Later, Lionel J. Shannon replace Guy Hayman as co-owner in the store operation. Other later store owner-operators were Sidney and Leola Toler (1967-1973), Wayne and Mary Helen Parker (1973-1978) and Rocky and Judy Kemper (1978-1980). The store closed in November 1980.

Jessie and Fanny Baum in front of the Baum & Baum Store, later named the Kitty Hawk Country Store

The Foreman Grocery - In 1947 Bill and Mildred Perry Foreman opened a small grocery store in Kitty Hawk. Mildred Perry had grown up in Kitty Hawk and had met and married Bill Foreman while he was in the US Navy in Norfolk, Va., during World War II. The store was located about 600 yards west of the Baum & Baum store on the main road. They lived with their infant son, Coby, in accommodations in the rear of the building.

Their merchandise display and sales area was located at the front end of the building facing the road.

Mildred and Bill were popular among the villagers and especially so with the youth of the community. They supported the school kids in their sports and school activities and the students adopted "Foreman's" as their community meeting place. Foreman's Grocery also became a popular shopping store for summer residents who had cottages on Kitty Hawk Beach and spent most of the summer in them.

In 1953 the Foremans sold their store to Ezekiel Mathias "Little Zeke" Midgett and became involved in beach real estate ventures, an emerging business on the Outer Banks. Little Zeke continued to operate the store for a few years but a declining business finally forced him to close the store. He utilized the old store space as his home. Some years later an accidental fire destroyed the building and there is no trace of it on the site today, ending an era of over 100 years that "mom and pop" store operations had served the local community. The Baum & Baum store building was razed in December 1999

Chapter Five

EDUCATION FIRST SCHOOLS

The Strength and Positive Growth of Education in the Area

Public education in Kitty Hawk developed slowly over the years, but probably no more so than other isolated rural communities across the state or the nation. Education of the masses had not been a priority of either the colonial government, or the new state. Government funds allocated for education were usually quickly diverted to other more pressing government needs and it was up to the individual to find opportunities to learn to read and write. Self education was the rule of the day, except when religious orders attempted to fill this need in colonial times and through the early years of the new state. Their purpose, however, may have been as much to promote their form of religion as it was to educate the citizenry.

During the Colonial period the Church of England sent missionaries to the colony to administer to the spiritual needs of their people; some missionaries also served as teachers. The Society for the Propagation of the Gospel in Foreign Parts sent at least three collections of books to the colony for public libraries, but only one collection is known to have reached its destination in Bath in 1709. Also, that year, Charles Griffin, a lay reader in an Anglican church, opened in Pasquotank County the first known school in North Carolina. In a few years, he moved on to Edenton, but the Pasquotank County school continued for some time. No doubt other communities experienced similar educational initiatives, but by and large education opportunities were limited throughout the colony.

As Presbyterian, Quaker and Moravian settlers moved into the interior of North Carolina they built homesteads, cleared land for farming and the raising of livestock, formed communities, and constructed churches, court houses and jails, but there was still no organized movement for educating the populous within the colonial government.

Educational opportunities did not materially improve with the end of the Revolutionary War and the formation of the new state government. The state constitution did encourage the establishment of schools, but without state financial support. The constitutional provision, however, resulted in over a hundred private academies being chartered across the state over the next half century, including one in Currituck County near Indiantown. While the academies were a step forward in the educational training process, they primarily served their immediate communities, and did not address the state's overall educational needs. Finally, in 1825 the Legislature passed a bill establishing the Literary Fund to support common schools with proceeds from the sale of state-owned swampland and tax receipts on liquor and bank stock. The Fund never accumulated much reserve since it was often raided to pay other state expenses, but it established a mechanism for funding public education in the future.

After state constitution reforms in 1835, a period of more progressive government emerged with education receiving a higher priority. In January 1839, the General Assembly passed the first common school law, or free school as it was called, designed to establish a statewide school system for the teaching of reading, writing and arithmetic, and the county governments were authorized to tax the public for the program. By the end of that year Currituck County had appointed a Superintendent of Common Schools for each of five school districts in the county. Lewis Mann of Nags Head was appointed the Superintendent for the North Banks district. The following year the county initiated a $.10 poll tax in support of the schools. This tax was later increased to $.20, and a land tax added.

Over the next several decades, the organizational structure of the county school system evolved from having a superintendent in each district, to a countywide board of education with a school committee in each school district, and later a school committee for each school. The school committees were caretakers for the school facility, helped with selecting teachers for their school, securing private funds to extend the school term by paying for additional teachers or extending their employment period beyond that provided by the county. The portion of the school year paid for by the county was known as the "Free School," but when the community paid for teachers through their private contributions, the school was known as "Pay School."

The first common school in Kitty Hawk was probably located at the "Signpost" on the main wood's road between Kitty Hawk and the "Northern neighborhood." At least, that is where a schoolhouse was shown on the 1848-49 U. S. Coast Survey map. No further documentation has been found for this school. The location of the schoolhouse was the same as that of the new Providence Baptist Church, which was established in Kitty Hawk on August 26, 1854. It is not inconceivable that the structure was built by Hodges Gallop to serve both purposes; he owned the land, was a person of considerable wealth, had a large family of school age children, and was an active member of the Primitive Baptist religion, which had grown popular with North Banks residents. Hodges Gallop was the first resident Elder of the Kitty Hawk Providence Baptist Church.

The next school, and one remembered by the older residents of the community when interviewed in 1960, was located east of Duck Pond Creek on the main Kitty Hawk village road where the road turns off to Duck. The location today would be on the south side of the 900 block of West Kitty Hawk Road. The schoolhouse was most probably the former home of Samuel Joseph Harris, who is reported to have lived on this site and died in April 1878. After his death, his widow returned to live with her parents so the house may have been available for school purposes.

Hildegard Etheridge, who started attending school at this location in 1882, reported that it was an old house converted to a school building; adding that "it weren't bigger than nothing." Her sister, Mary Holland Etheridge described the school as one room with a wood stove, a single desk in the back, hand made benches for seats, and no wall maps. Students used slate board and slate pencils. In spite of its primitive nature, the schoolhouse continued in use until almost the turn of the century. After this old-school building was no longer used for school purposes it was converted to a store by Tom Baum and Robert Perry.

UP-THE-ROAD/DOWN-THE-ROAD

In December 1889, the county School Board divided the Kitty Hawk school into two districts, West Kitty Hawk and East Kitty Hawk; locally referred to as the Up-The-Road(west) school and the Down-The-Road (east) school.

The Up-The-Road school continued in the same location as before the division of the schools until December 1897 when A. B. Love Tillett and wife donated for school purposes a ¾ acre parcel of land near the new Providence Baptist Church site for a new Up-The-Road school. Today, that site would be along Northern Gut at 1089 & 1091 West Kitty Hawk Road where there is a small boat basin and docks. A one-room school was built on the site, but later enlarged to a two-room structure.

The Up-The-Road School, with teachers and students, 1914

No one is quite sure what happened to the 1897 Up-The-Road school building after the schools were consolidated. Some have said that Zene Perry salvaged its lumber for his store, but he reported that he opened his new store in 1924, while the Up-The-Road school building was still in use. It would be a fair guess to say, however, that the lumber from this building was indeed salvaged and used in another building somewhere in Kitty Hawk, even if the building cannot be identified.

The first Down-The-Road one-room schoolhouse was constructed around 1890. In a 1960 taped interview, Elijah Baum remembered the building as being about 16 feet by 24 feet in size. He reported that it was located on James Riley Best property across from the Methodist church. The county furnished the lumber, but local people built the building. A curtain drawn across the center of the open room divided the classes.

Down-The-Road School, with students gathered outside, 1916

Around 1896, this building was moved about 400 yards east to George Washington Baum's property, which today would be at the southeast corner of West Kitty Hawk and Elijah Baum Road. No reason is known today as to why the school was moved, but it could have been that the original structure had been built in a flood prone area. Over the years, the school building in its new location was remodeled, made wider and longer, and ceilings heightened. Much of that work was done by Thomas N. Sanderlin and Edward N. Baum, both of whom had a special interest in education for community children. No doubt other neighbors helped as well. Thomas N. Sanderlin, as a carpenter, was especially noted for his skills as a custom casket maker who kept seasoned lumber on hand for just such a purpose. Edward N. Baum served on many school committees through the years and two terms as Chairman of the Dare County Board of Education. Two of Thomas Sanderlin's daughters and all four of Edward Baum's daughters became teachers.

After the consolidated school opened in 1926, Elijah Baum bought the Down-The-Road schoolhouse building and converted it into apartments. In 1931 he again remodeled it for his general merchandise store, which included the Kitty Hawk post office. Later he moved the building west across the dirt road leading to Kitty Hawk Bay to place it on his land. The building burned in December 1944.

CLASSROOM STUDIES

In spite of encouragement from the State and support from the County, educational programs for Kitty Hawk students were slow in developing. In the 1850 census, approximately 30% of the adult Kitty Hawk population could read and write, but less than 20% of the 70 odd community children attended school that year. In the next census, attendance had doubled but was still way short of the percentage of students attending school in other Currituck County school districts. With a lifetime of subsistence living on and near the water and no real prospects for the future, apathy no doubt affected the local public interest in education, but that would change over time.

Initially there seems to have been very little consistency in the level of education available to students. There were few teachers to serve the needs of communities. Typically, during the year teachers moved around from school to school much in the same way that circuit preachers moved from church to church. School terms were short, measured in weeks, rather than months, and school sessions were staggered to accommodate teachers' schedules.

School facilities were of the most basic style and some lacked heating during cold periods. School books were not standardized and were limited in number, as were most other teaching aids. Despite these many limitations, improvements were evolving slowly in the field of education for children.

By the 1890s many of the earlier problems in school administration had been worked out. A new Down-The-Road school house had been built and a new Up-The-Road school house would be finished before the end of the century. The school population in the district, which included the community that later became Duck, was over 110 students. At least one county paid teacher was assigned to each school, and that position was often supplemented by a teacher privately paid by the community.

By 1920, when Kitty Hawk became part of Dare County, two or three paid teachers were assigned to each school. Each school had a "school committee" appointed by the County Board of Education to look after the school facilities, assist with the selection of teachers, and advise the Board of school needs. Membership on the "school committee" rotated frequently enough to keep the school program progressive.

The school term sometimes fluctuated, probably due to funding, but the Board of Education tried to provide 16 weeks of school each year. While the school term in early years had been from April through June, by 1900 the Kitty Hawk schools were scheduled to start in October or November. Spence Midgett, in a 1960 interview, remembered one year, probably around 1910, when he went to school five months; three months of "free school" and two months of "pay school." There must have been some flexibility within the school term schedule because some teachers, who taught in Kitty Hawk during that period, also taught in other schools in Currituck County the same year.

By the turn of the 20th century, the school curriculum had improved to include arithmetic, geography, grammar, physiology, hygiene, reading, and North Carolina and United States histories. Approved books for school use included Harrington Speller, Webster Dictionary, Harvey's Grammar, Holmes's Readers 1, 2, 3, 4, and 5, Sanford Arithmetic, Mitchell's Geography, and Stephen's United States History. A few schools still used Webster's Blue Back Speller and McGuffey's Readers 1, 2, 3 & 4, in their program, but those books would soon be replaced. Although the classes were ungraded, a level of educational achievement could be determined by the level of reader the student was studying. Once they had mastered McGuffey's Reader Number 4, or Holmes Reader Number 5, and finished the other subjects offered, their education was essentially complete. Shortly after the turn of the century, the State school system developed a class grade structure. Before the advent of the high school program, grades 1 through 7 was the norm across the state, particularly for rural school systems.

There seemed to be a new awareness and concern by parents and guardians for children's education in Kitty Hawk beginning in the 1880s. William James Tate had been orphaned in 1880 and was being cared for by his uncle, Daniel M. Tate. His uncle arranged for him to attend the Oxford Orphanage as a teenager where he studied printing among other general education subjects. Later, Bill Tate attended The Atlantic Collegiate Institute in Elizabeth City, NC, operated by Samuel Lloyd Sheep, and then received further tutoring from Matt Ransom in Hertford, North Carolina. When he returned to Kitty Hawk around 1891, he was probably the best educated person in the village, and maybe anywhere along the banks. He was soon appointed Postmaster and later served as a Justice of the Peace. Neighbors frequently called on him to draft wills and deeds, and attend to their other legal document needs.

Elijah William Baum boarded in Norfolk, Va., with his Uncle William "Bill" Partridge's family and attended Norfolk Business School. After earning a business degree, he returned to Kitty Hawk in 1906 and taught in the Down-The-Road school. He left the teaching field after a couple of years, opening his own general merchandise store at the head of Kitty Hawk Bay. On January 10, 1914, he replaced Mrs. Addie Tate, wife of Bill Tate, as Postmaster after the Tate family moved to Martins Point. Elijah Baum continued his education in adult life through correspondence courses.

Franklin Harris Midgett, who operated a freight boat service between Elizabeth City and Kitty Hawk, with occasional stops at other communities along Currituck Sound, was a strong advocate for education. When his daughter, Bertha Mae Midgett, had finished the educational program in Kitty Hawk around 1909, he sent her to Elizabeth City for advanced training in the school system there. After marrying Jessie Etheridge Baum in 1913, she returned to Kitty Hawk and helped him establish and run the Baum and Baum store in the village.

Spencer Midgett, another of Harris Midgett's children, was sent to Elizabeth City around 1911 to study under Richard Benbury Creecy, Jr., who operated a private school, which was popular with students who wanted advanced training in basic educational courses, or tutoring in specific subjects. Creecy also offered correspondence courses for men who needed to pass civil service tests to join the Life-Saving Service. After two years, Spencer Midgett returned home to serve as an engineer on his family freight boats. He joined the U. S. Coast Guard in May 1917 and remained in the Service until retiring as a full Lieutenant with 30 years of service. His education from the Kitty Hawk schools and studies under Richard B. Creecy served him well in his professional life.

Others from Kitty Hawk attended the Creecy School, including Carlos Dowdy, and Shelton and Eldridge Beacham. Their parents, William Ivy Dowdy and Decatur Beacham, were active on Kitty Hawk school committees and worked hard to see improvements in school facilities and the educational program within the community.

Lloyd B. Owens attended Trinity College, later named Duke University, sometime around 1915 to 1920. It is not known if he finished college, but it is significant to note that a native from rural Kitty Hawk found his way to a college in the central part of North Carolina.

Several students followed a different path to completing their education. Franklin Linwood Tillett and Dexter Beacham both attended and graduated from Poplar Branch High School in Currituck County, N. C., Tillett in 1924 and Beacham two years later in 1926. Oscar Sanderlin also left Kitty Hawk to attend high school in Manteo, where he graduated in 1927.

CONSOLIDATED SCHOOL

There were several proposals to consolidate the two schools in Kitty Hawk while they were still a part of Currituck County, but nothing came of them. In 1920, in a redrawing of county boundaries, Kitty Hawk, Duck and Caffeys Inlet became part of Dare County, and their local school systems came under the Dare County Board of Education.

On April 8, 1924, a Kitty Hawk School Committee composed of John Wescott, Ellsworth Baum and Elijah W. Baum appeared before the Dare County Board of Education with a petition for school consolidation and a request for a special tax election to erect a consolidated school in Kitty Hawk. The vote on the referendum was held July 8, 1924, and with a 91 percent turnout of Atlantic Township voters, the consolidation and tax proposal passed 72 to 15. Kitty Hawk and its neighbors wanted a better school system for their children and were willing to tax themselves to achieve it.

The School Committee, Board of Education and Board of County Commissions moved quickly to secure suitable property for the school. The Washington Perry tract of slightly over 5 acres in the middle of the village seemed to meet their needs and with the support of Washington Perry they entered a friendly condemnation to clear title to the property. It was purchased for $200.00.

Spencer Midgett, in an interview with Donald and Carol McAdoo for their 1976 book, *Reflections Of The Outer Banks*, reported that voters of Atlantic Township bonded themselves for $20,000 for the construction cost of the new consolidated school. He also reported that local timber was sawed from a virgin cypress stand for the building framing. Construction of the school appeared to have been by local carpenters under the direction of the Kitty Hawk School Building Committee: Edward N. Baum, James R. Best, Elijah W. Baum, Decatur Beacham, and Banister J. Hines.

Between the time of the 1924 referendum vote and the opening of the new school in 1926, the Kitty Hawk schools were authorized to extend their school year to 8 months and to offer classes through the 10th grade. In a 1976 interview, Tom Beacham reported that when he realized Kitty Hawk was going to have a high school, he returned to school to finish the 7th grade so he would be eligible for high school. He had quit school after the 6th grade and had worked several years as an automobile mechanic and freight boat engineer for E. W. Baum, who operated a garage and a freight boat connected with his general merchandise store at the head of Kitty Hawk Bay. Tom Beacham graduated as valedictorian of his class in May 1928, one month short of his 22nd birthday.

Edward N. Baum, a Kitty Hawk resident and member of the Dare County Board of Education, reported to his fellow Board members in October 1926 that "the work on the building at Kitty Hawk was not complete, but it was in use." Thus, the fall of 1926 appears to be the opening date for the new consolidated high school. That date also corresponds with the availability of the first Principal, Alton E. Baum.

The new Kitty Hawk School soon after opening.

The new school must have been something of a culture shock for Kitty Hawk students. For the first time in over 40 years all Kitty Hawk village students would be in one facility instead of separated by communities, and they would be joined by students from Duck, Caffeys Inlet, and Paul Gamiel Hill. Instead of attending a one or two room school with all age students together, the new school had 6 classrooms, generally with two grades per room under one teacher, although initially first grade students were in a single classroom with a teacher. Nags Head and Colington students would be assigned to the Kitty Hawk school over the coming years as roads, bridges and transportation improved.

The new school was built in the general shape of the letter H, with an east and west wing of class rooms running north and south. The wings ran parallel approximately 60 feet apart and were connected by a porch and auditorium near the south end of the wings. The exterior of the building was finished in green stain on the cedar shingles with white trim on corner and fascia boards, windows, doors, and columns. The classrooms were spacious with high ceilings and windows on the outer wall. Both the ceiling and walls were of tongue-and-grove beaded pine paneling and varnished in a natural wood finish. One room, however, was shown in an early photograph as being painted white. In 1940 all rooms were painted white. Tall nine-over-nine pane windows along the outside wall provided the principal lighting for the classroom, and shades at each window blocked direct sunlight. Later a Delco plant located at the north end of the west wing supplied lights for the building. Commercial power was extended to the school around 1939. Blackboards were located on three of the walls in the classrooms. Heat was provided by a potbellied coal stove in each classroom. Initially, the school did not have a cafeteria so students had to bring their own lunch. In 1935, the Board of Education authorized cafeterias in schools that had space to accommodate the service. Kitty Hawk had an extra room in its east wing and by 1937 the school's PTA was operating a cafeteria for the students. Not all students used the services of the cafeteria and some continued to bring their lunch to school. At least one objection to the cafeteria was that one of the cafeteria workers had a habit of licking off the spread spatula when making sandwiches, a practice they deemed unhealthy.

During the late 1930s the county sought permission to use WPA funds to build restrooms in the schools, which was granted, and new restroom facilities replaced the outdoor privies at Kitty Hawk. A water pump installed in the Delco plant shed room provided water for the cafeteria, restrooms and an outdoor drinking fountain.

As was customary at the time, most of the students in the village walked to school, but since it was in the approximate center of the community no student had to walk more than a mile and a half. The school district did acquire a "school truck," or "school bus" as it was called later, to transport students from Caffeys Inlet, Duck and Paul Gamiels Hill to the new school. A 1922 Model T Ford truck, fitted with a passenger body and roll-down side curtains without see-through panels to keep out the weather, was originally acquired by the East Lake School District for transportation of their students. After a trying year of muddy and impassable roads the East Lake district asked that the truck be replaced with a boat. The Dare County Board of Education directed that the truck be sent to Manteo and assigned to Kitty Hawk for their consolidated school needs. That one year in East Lake must have been a hard one on the Model T, because the engine had to be replaced before it could be used at Kitty Hawk.

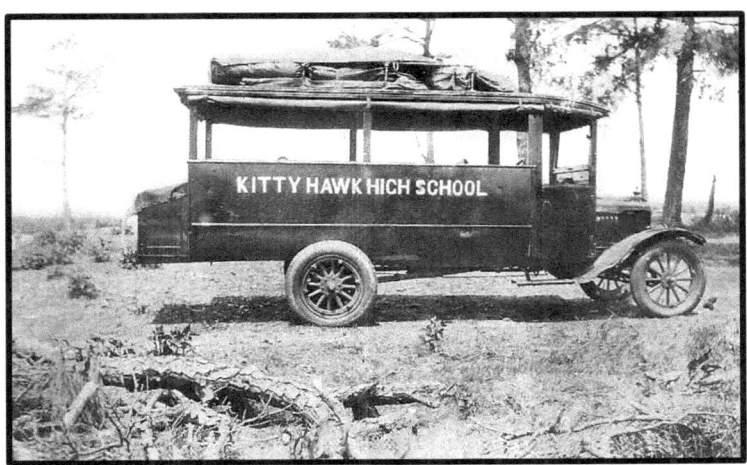

Kitty Hawk school bus that was acquired from East Lake.

Tom Beacham, who was living with the Walter Beacham family in Caffeys Inlet, was the first school truck driver at a salary of $30.00 per month. Each morning he picked up the Caffeys Inlet kids, then the ones in Duck, and finally the children in the houses around the Paul Gamiels Hill Coast Guard Station for transportation to Kitty Hawk. The trip could be routine and an easy ride, but in the dry seasons when the sand was exceptionally soft, or when the sound tides were running high and forcing the truck to travel in the dunes, the trip could be as difficult as the East Lake mud. Like the kids in East Lake, the North Banks students would have to get off the truck and help push it through tough spots.

Alma Rogers from Duck, who was a first grader at Kitty Hawk in 1927, remembered one disturbing trip that made her cry. When Tom Beacham heard her crying, he stopped the truck and went back to find out why she was upset. She told him that she had forgotten her lunch! He told her, "Don't worry about it, Honey, I have plenty to eat in my lunch pail and will be happy to share with you." True to his word, when lunch time came, he went to her and opened his lunch pail. It was full of "sea chickens" and "sweet potatoes!" She made a full meal of sweet potatoes, but passed on the sea chickens, which were small shore birds usually found along the ocean beach. She never liked "sea chickens" and did not eat them at home, so she was not about to eat them at school, but she never told Tom of her dislike for them.

Nags Head and Colington were not initially within the Kitty Hawk School District as they were in a different township. Both communities had elementary schools through the 7th grade, but no high school. Levin Worth Stetson and his wife, Sadie, of Colington, wanted their daughter, Mary Frances Stetson, to attend the new Kitty Hawk High School and decided to board her in the village. Since there were no bridges connecting Colington to the banks, Levin Worth Stetson would transport his daughter by boat to Kitty Hawk each Sunday afternoon and then pick her up to return home each Friday afternoon. The first school year, 1926-27, Mary lived with the Zene Perry family in the village. The second school year, 1927-28, she boarded with the Edward Baum family. By the third-year bridges connecting Colington Island with the banks had been completed and her father had bought a new car which she drove to school. She also carried Harry Meekins, Irene Meekins and Del Haywood to school. The county paid Mr. Stetson $6.00 per month for providing a car and driver for student transportation. Mary Frances Stetson graduated in May 1930.

SCHOOL ACTIVITIES

Although the School Committee and the Superintendent of Dare County Schools probably did not realize it at the time, Alton E. Baum was an ideal selection as the first principal of the new consolidated Kitty Hawk School. He was born and raised near Fairfield in Hyde County, N.C., and finished school there, so he was familiar with rural school needs. He graduated from the University of North Carolina in 1924 and worked at Camp Butner north of Durham, N.C., before becoming the Kitty Hawk principal in 1926.

Alton Baum in front of the new consolidated Kitty Hawk School

At 23, he was probably one of the youngest principals ever in a North Carolina school system. His youth and progressive outlook for education in a totally new school environment were probably his strengths for this position. As a first-time principal, he was committed to providing the best education possible for the students, but was not encumbered with set patterns and strong opinions about how the school should operate, or how the students should respond. His flexibility related well with the students and he built a strong commitment from them for the school and education and opened new avenues of challenge and opportunities for the students. He also built a strong support base within the community for the school. Years later when his former students spoke of him there was an obvious expression of pride and respect for him and his administration of the Kitty Hawk School.

Beyond the normal classroom program there is little information about student activities in the early years at the new school. It is known that within the first school year the high school boys organized themselves into a group called The Lucky Thirteen. Its origin and purpose have been lost to history, but apparently 13 may have been the number of male students in high school at the time. The boys adopted a dress code which included white pants, a long sleeve white shirt, black belt, and a dark blue tie with the initials LTS down the front. The society had a banner with the words, Lucky Thirteen, displayed diagonally across the flag and the numbers 19 in one corner and 27 in the other, for the year 1927. There was also a pennant with The Lucky Thirteen across its face. The obvious goal of the Society was to build a bond of unity within the student body and pride in the school. Principal Alton Baum and teacher R. L. Parlier apparently served as faculty advisors to the society and they too adopted the society's dress code for special occasions. At least one member of the society, Orville Baum, was so taken by the organization that he had the numerals "13" in gold color attached to the radiator of his 1927 Ford roadster.

The Lucky Thirteen Society

In 1928, not to be outdone by the boys, the high school girls formed the Ideal Literary Society. Its origin and purpose are also obscure, but like the boys it served to build support and pride in their school. Their dress code was a simple short sleeve white dress, white stockings, black shoes, and a leather belt worn low on the hips. A diamond shaped patch with the initials ILS was displayed on the left front of their dress. They too had a banner with Ideal Literary Society across the center and 1928 under the name. In a 1993 interview, Edna Baum Harris reported that the Ideal Literary Society met informally at various members' homes after school to socialize and plan parties and group activities.

Both societies were in attendance and participation in the May 2, 1928, unveiling ceremonies of the Wright monument on the grounds of the Kitty Hawk Methodist Parsonage. In their official dress, The Lucky Thirteen boys stood as honor guards at the speaker's platform, while the Ideal Literary Society girls performed a similar function next to the granite marker to be unveiled. Neither group had a formal part in the program, but their very presence added formality and dignity to the event. The unveiling of this monument at the site where Wilbur Wright began assembling the first glider was undoubtedly the most important celebration in Kitty Hawk's history; and was a nationally significant event in that it was the first monument in the

United States erected to the Wright brothers. Additionally, the monument was totally funded by the citizens of Kitty Hawk.

Ideal Literacy Society

The students were proud of their new school and exhibited that pride in the adoption of a school song, which they wrote "In Kitty Hawk, there is a high school noble friends so true. We will ever sing its praises dear old white and blue. Hail to the school that ever grows pure in its work and play. Let us all make it the best school in the U. S. A." It was still the school song when the last graduate of the consolidated Kitty Hawk High School left in 1956, though a few words had been altered to reflect the change in school colors, from white and blue to gold and blue, and to improve the rhythm of the song.

The Lucky Thirteen and the Ideal Literary Society apparently did not survive and may have disbanded by 1930; but other school clubs and organizations were formed to serve the students and the school. At various times through the years the students had both a Senior and Junior Dramatic Club, a Music Club, an Art Club, a French Club which was also called The Les Contents, an English Club sometimes known as The Emerson Society, a Science Club, and at least by 1939 a 4-H Club which split into a Senior 4-H Club and Junior 4-H Club. The 1939 4-H Club had as a project the promote of good health in their community and even elected that year a King and Queen of Health - Billy Toler and Shirley Dowdy. The students organized to print several mimeographed school newspapers over the years including *The Hawk Eye* in 1940-41, *The Kitty Hawk Beacon* in 1949-50, and *Sea Breeze* in 1953. Although there was not one every year, several yearbooks were published by the students. The mimeographed 1945 yearbook was named *The Falcon*, while the printed yearbook for 1953, 1954 and 1955, was called *Ocean Echo*.

Historically the school student body population was always small in numbers and their opportunities limited compared with larger schools, but those who attended the Kitty Hawk School were satisfied that they had had a very active and challenging school life. They would not have traded it with any other school system.

CENTER OF THE COMMUNITY

Former students and long-term residents of Kitty Hawk remember the Kitty Hawk School as the social center of the community. The school was used for a host of activities, both during the school day and after school hours.

School plays were always a big occasion for the school, students and community. Several times a year, the student body, a school club, or an individual class, and on occasions even teachers, presented plays, many of them three acts, for the enjoyment and benefit of the students. Most of the plays were also presented to the public at night, usually for a modest fee of 15 cents for students and 25 cents for adults. A history of plays offered through the years has not survived, but a few were announced in local newspapers or through the limited school newspapers issued by the school. In 1930 the Kitty Hawk High School launched a little theatre movement under the direction of English teacher, L. W. Anderson. The students were totally involved in the play including making scenery and costumes. One of the plays they produced was *Who Wouldn't Be Crazy*, which was presented to a full house.

In 1932 the students recruited a couple of their teachers for parts in the play, *Old Fashion Mother*. Charlie Caldwell played the part of Jonah Quackubush, while first grade teacher, Miss Nora Baum, was Miss Lowry Loving Custard. With their teachers playing characters with cast names like these, the students did not need to be entertained by good acting.

In May 1933, at the invitation of the Kitty Hawk School administration, the Poplar Branch High School seniors presented their highly-acclaimed play, *More Power to You*, in the Kitty Hawk School auditorium. Their twenty-piece band played before the performance and during intermission. The presentation was well received by the school and community.

The 1940-41 school newspapers reported that the Senior Dramatic Club presented *Cats Whiskers*, while the Senior Class presented *The Path Across the Hills* and *Murdered Alive* for the students and the public. The Junior Class play for that year was *M'LISS*.

The 1944-45 Kitty Hawk year book also reported that the high school boys staged a womanless wedding for the entertainment of the school and public, while *Little Nell* was presented by the sophomores and *Indian Village* by the seventh and eight graders.

School plays continued into the 1950s with *Peck's Bad Boy* in 1951 and *Happy Daze* and *Boarding House Reach* in 1953. One of the last plays given by the high school students in the 1950s, before the students were reassigned to the Manteo High School, was *Hillbilly Weddin'*.

In addition to programs put on by students, occasionally there were outside entertainers, such as a play and musical by the Johnston County Ramblers, the string music, singing, dancing, and comedy of "Julian Hill's Dude Ranch Cowhands" and "Sunshine Sue and Her Rangers," and a "Rip-Roaring Comedy" with the Gleason family.

The Kitty Hawk Parent-Teacher Association (PTA) formed shortly after the new school opened in 1926 and continued to support the school during its 30 plus years of operation. One of the PTA's first objectives was to get lights for the school which they did by securing a Delco plant in the early 1930s. The PTA was very active in developing entertainment programs for the school and public including sponsoring a talent night and musical show featuring Dare and Currituck County amateurs. The PTA also were known to have organized square dances on the new concrete basketball court featuring the Charlie Shannon band, with Mrs. Rosaline Swain or Jep Harris calling squares, the annual Halloween Carnival with games and refreshments, and Christmas programs where every student received a present of fruit and candy. Homemade ice cream at a modest price was a special treat at those sponsored functions. The tradition of holding square dances continued and in the 1950s David Stick called squares for a new generation of dancers. Usually there was a small admission fee for these special programs which the PTA used to support the school cafeteria, or to buy educational materials, school furnishings, basketball uniforms, recreational equipment and related services for the school. They even sponsored a Boy Scout troop in the 1950s.

One of the most popular PTA program with the students and public in the early 1940s was full length feature movies presented in the auditorium. Diane Baum Johnson, daughter of Thomas A. Baum and native of the area, arranged through a film distributor to have Hollywood movies delivered to the school, sometimes as frequently as weekly. Usually, the films were shown free to the students in the afternoon and for a fee of 10 cents per student and 25 cents for adults to the public at night. The movies were shown on a 16 mm RCA Victor projector. Each reel had to be rewound after shown, so there was a built-in intermission during the presentation. Additional intermissions could occur spontaneously when the film broke and had to be repaired, or sections skipped when repairs were not possible. Many of the movies were B-Westerns such as Roy Rogers and Gabby Hayes in the 1939 film, *Days of Jessie James*, Gene Autry and Frog Millhouse, as Smiley Burnette, in the 1939 film, *South of the Border*, and the 1937 film, *Western Gold*, with Smith Ballew.

Not all movies were westerns; sometimes a classic, such as the 1939 film *Adventures of Huckleberry Finn*, with Mickey Rooney, was shown; and a few students from that period still remember seeing it when it was shown. Another non-western was the 1942 film, *Winning Your Wings*, with James Stewart as himself, Lieutenant James Stewart. The 18-minute film, directed by John Huston, was used for Army Air Corps recruitment, and was nominated for an Oscar for Best Documentary in 1943. Occasionally there were cartoons, news reels, and the serial, *Flash Gordon* with Buster Crabbe. While the school auditorium did not have all the comforts or amenities of a theater, and there were interruptions in the film presentation, having local access to the movies was a good source of entertainment for the students and community, particularly with gas rationing and travel restrictions in effect at the time.

These 1940 period film presentations were not the first exposure to motion pictures for the local people. Earlier, in the late 1920s, the Liniger family of Currituck County would visit Kitty Hawk each summer with a traveling show which featured movies, or "picture shows" as they were called. They set up a large tent with seats on the school playground southwest of the school near the road. The Linigers also had a Delco plant for lights which was placed some distance from the tent to keep down the noise of the motor. The main feature of their entertainment, in addition to vaudeville acts, was the showing of silent motion pictures, complete with accompanying piano music by Mrs. Elizabeth Liniger synchronized with the action on the screen. The shows were well attended by the community, and long remembered by the people because for most of them this was the first time they had ever seen a motion picture. Usually, the Liniger shows would be offered nightly for about a week, then they would pack up their equipment and move to another community. The showing of a flickering silent black and white movie in an open tent in this rural community was just a prelude to the many changes that would impact the people in the years ahead and a lifestyle that had evolved ever so slowly over two hundred years of living in Kitty Hawk.

The PTA's monthly meeting was a special occasion for the school and community as the attendance by parents determined which class would be allowed to display the "Attendance Banner" for the coming month, or until the next PTA meeting. As could be predicted, the elementary school classes usually won the banner, but on at least one occasion in 1924, Principal Talmage Page's room was awarded the banner. This was most unusual since his home room class was the eleventh grade.

Not all uses of the school auditorium were school related. On September 23, 1927, a special meeting of the community was called to discussing the possibility of erecting a monument to the Wright brothers within the village. After much discussion, the public agreed to the proposal and 70 citizens of the community, plus the Ladies Aid Society of the Kitty Hawk Methodist Church, contributed over $200 to the cost of the granite monument. To assure that it was a totally local effort, no donations were sought or accepted from anyone who was not a native of the village. The monument was placed in front of the Methodist Parsonage and officially unveiled on May 2, 1928.

Though not recorded in newspapers of the day, other meetings, such as the State's plans for paving the roads in the village, and Virginia Electric and Power Company's plans for extending electric power throughout the village, were discussed at public meetings in the school auditorium.

The Kitty Hawk Men's Club regularly met at the school after World War II. The meetings were so well attended by the wives that the name of the organization was soon changed to the Kitty Hawk Civic Club. The Club provided a forum to discuss issues of importance in the community, such as the problem of a large school of porpoises that had entered Currituck Sound and stayed for an extended period. Local fishermen were concerned that the porpoises posed a threat to the fishing stock and sought help from the Club to have them removed. In turn, the Club contacted the North Carolina Wildlife Resources Commission to have the porpoises removed from the sound, and they were. Another successful program, and one that helped the public become better acquainted with their county government, was having elected officials attend Club meetings to discuss the work of their offices. The program gave the residents an opportunity to learn about local government and to discuss local issues with their elected officials in a setting other than an election campaign. These sessions were much appreciated by the public.

The Civic Club also participated with the school's PTA in sponsoring an annual Thanksgiving turkey shoot in November. The three shots for a dollar was an excellent fund raiser for the school improvement fund. For a number of years, a bulletin board erected by the Club near the post office was used to announce the time and place for the turkey shoots, square dances, school plays, basketball games and similar programs in the community.

Two projects that can be directly attributed to the work of the Civic Club were the placement of mile markers along the beach road, and later the bypass, and the relighting of the Wright Memorial with flood lights. Both projects survived the passing of time.

By the mid 1950s, however, several new civic organizations had formed on the Outer Banks and interest in a local civic club began to wane. The Club became more and more inactive and soon passed into history.

When newlyweds David and Phyllis Stick moved to Kill Devil Hills in 1948, they recognized that teenagers had very little recreational opportunities after school hours. They proposed the formation of a Kitty Hawk Youth Club, which was well received by the young people of the community. With approval of the School Committee, the club met on Friday evenings in the Kitty Hawk School auditorium. It was a great success and drew teenagers from not only Kitty Hawk village, but Duck, Colington and friends from Currituck county as well. Even grandchildren from Elizabeth City, Norfolk and elsewhere who visited their grandparents on weekends wanted to be there early enough for Friday evening Youth Club meeting. The club offered games, dancing and refreshments, and a highlight of most meetings was square dancing with David Stick calling the squares. The kids were also introduced to the Virginia Reel dance, and some couples would sneak in a slow dance now and them. When weather permitted and there was enough daylight, club members and guests played softball, volleyball, basketball, and other games on the school playgrounds and basketball court.

The young people of Kitty Hawk were so pleased with their youth club that they proposed that the community establish a youth center for their use. Youth Club President Kenneth Clay

Tillett appeared before the Kitty Hawk Civic Club in February 1951 to solicit their help and support for a center. The Civic Club gave a unanimous pledge of assistance whenever called upon, but without a facility to work from, or funding, the project died. And with it the Youth Club began to die as well. By the mid 1950s many of the earlier youth center participators had graduated, entered the military, gone to work, gotten married, or simply gotten their drivers license and enjoyed "riding around" more that "hanging around."

In 1956 the last graduating class finished school at Kitty Hawk and thereafter all high school students were bused to Manteo High School. An exciting period in Kitty Hawk's history had run its course and the old consolidated school would no longer be the center of the community. The Kitty Hawk Youth Club suffered a similar fate.

BASKETBALL

Students in the new consolidated Kitty Hawk School were quick to take up basketball, both as a playground activity and school team sport; well, initially anyway. Even before the playground had been cleared of brush and trees, or the stumps removed and ground leveled, the school had installed a backboard and goal on a lone pine sapling left for that purpose. A second backboard and goal was attached to a pine post at the opposite end to form the court. The court was crowded during recess despite a stump sawed off at ground level in the middle of the playing area. A second court was added later for use of scheduled basketball games at Kitty Hawk. On game day, a rope stretched along the ground marked the playing boundaries. Many schools used powdered lime to mark their court boundaries, but Kitty Hawk used rope.

Kitty Hawk High School did not field a basketball team the first year the school opened, but used the time to prepare for the future. Constructing a playing court, securing equipment, practicing and assigning positions, and designing and selecting uniforms occupied the students' time initially.

The Kitty Hawk girls basketball squad uniforms looked rather funky by today's standards, but was the style of the period. In fact, the Kitty Hawk girls' uniforms appear to have been copied from the uniforms worn by the Elizabeth City High School girls team, even to the colors of blue and white, which also were Kitty Hawk school colors in 1926. Their uniform consisted of dark blue knee length bloomer shorts, white pull over jersey with a banded bottom and sailor collar, dark blue scarf worn under the collar, tied in front and tucked in a loop on the jersey, knee high socks and athletic shoes, but no numbers on the jersey.

Sanford Corbell, Lyle Midgett, Unk Beacham, Norman Perry, and Russell Dowdy, with the Falcon mascot on the jersey

The boys' uniform, which did not appear to be in school colors, included medium dark boxer shorts, a light-colored tee shirt with a broad band around the chest that matched the color of the shorts, a number on the back, ankle length socks and athletic shoes. The boxer shorts and tee shirt style uniform stayed consistent through the years.

School colors changed in the 1930s from blue and white to blue and gold and the uniforms changed to reflect the new school colors. Like other schools which were adopting nicknames and logos, Kitty Hawk High School adopted (in 1938) the nickname, Falcons, and a falcon in flight as their logo. The new girls uniform was shiny gold satin with the letters KITTY HAWK across the front of the buttoned blouse, a number on the back and boxer shorts as replacement for the bloomer shorts. The boys wore blue boxer shorts and a sleeveless gold color tee shirt with a Falcon in flight on the front, and a number on the back. In the following years, both sets of uniform style changed several times, but the basic school colors of blue and gold continued in use as long as Kitty Hawk School fielded basketball teams.

In the 1920s, and until gyms were built in the late 1930s and early 1940s, all rural schools played afternoon basketball games outdoors on dirt, clay, or sand courts. The dirt or clay courts were by far the best since they could be compacted and offered a smooth and firm playing surface. Kitty Hawk's sand courts were something else, as it was almost impossible to dribble a basketball on the sand. At best the ball might return to the dribbler, but more likely than not the ball would ricochet away from the player. Knowing this the Kitty Hawk teams developed a playing style that included many passes and limited dribbling. The girls developed a technique they called "jiggling." Girls by rules were not allowed to take more than two dribbles before passing. In "jiggling," when a Kitty Hawk girl had the ball and was closely guarded, she would throw the ball in the air, run under and catch it, and then pass off to a teammate. It was a playing style that confused the opposition, and led to scoring opportunities for Kitty Hawk.

Most schools hated to play Kitty Hawk on its home court. An elderly Currituck County resident who played against Kitty Hawk in the early days in a recent interview accused Kitty Hawk of playing unfairly because of their sand court. And the Manteo boys must have complained that the Kitty Hawk sand court caused them to lose to Kitty Hawk in January 1936 since an article by sports writer Woodrow Price appeared in *The Daily Advance* which spoke to this subject: "Kitty Hawk is just as much out of place away from home as the other teams are at Kitty Hawk. Forced to rely on a passing attack and trained to compete against that, they are helpless on dribbling and defending their goal against a team with a well-developed attack. With players like Reber, Dowdy and Wise, it is quite possible that were the Kitty Hawk team adequately trained to compete with teams on their own grounds they would have a conference championship team. So, if a team loses at Kitty Hawk and comes out with the sand alibi, just remember that the Kitty Hawk boys face a similar handicap when playing on the courts at Central, Shiloh, South Mills, Poplar Branch, Moyock, Newland and Manteo."

Probably the real complaint was that the sand court helped to equalize the play of a small school against a larger one. In November 1936, the Kitty Hawk School administration submitted an application to the Works Progress Administration for construction of a gymnasium on the school campus styled after the one in Weeksville. Apparently, the school felt comfortable that they would get the gymnasium because in January 1937 they withdrew from further Albemarle Rural Conference competition until the gym was constructed. Nothing happened, Kitty Hawk did not get a gym, but Manteo's gym was under construction by December 1938. In 1940 WPA completed construction of outdoor concrete courts at Kitty Hawk, thus giving the school a hard-playing surface in place of the sand courts, but play would still be outdoors in the weather. After 1948 and until the Kitty Hawk school closed, most of Kitty Hawk's home games were played in the Manteo gym by agreement with the Manteo administration and scheduling by the conference.

There is no evidence that Kitty Hawk fielded basketball teams during their first school year of 1926-27, but they did field both girls and boys basketball teams in 1928. Orville Rodgers, a third grader in 1928, remembered the first Kitty Hawk boys team as being very good, and there is some support for his assessment. The starting squad for the first Kitty Hawk boy's team included forwards Hallett Perry and Billy Betts, center Tom Beacham, and guards Grady Beacham and Jennings Beasley. Ernest Midgett was one of probably several substitutes. Several of the team's starters were six feet or taller so it was a tall team for a small rural school. While they had height, they were inexperienced in competitive basketball.

Rural northeastern North Carolina schools played a limited basketball schedule in the late 1920s, probably because of travel difficulties. Also, the schools were not initially organized in a conference that would have facilitated multiple game schedules. Weeksville, one of the larger rural high schools in the region, played only six games in 1928, and Central High School, just outside of Elizabeth City, played their first ever basketball game in February of that year, although like Kitty Hawk they had opened as a new school in 1926. From newspaper accounts and old photographs, it appears that Kitty Hawk High School probably played six basketball games in 1928.

One of the first games, and maybe the first ever played by Kitty Hawk was against Poplar Branch at Kitty Hawk in January 1928. It was a hard-fought defensive game and the outstanding star of the contest was forward Hallett Perry, who scored three field goals for Kitty Hawk; in fact, he scored all of Kitty Hawk's points as they won by a score of 6 to 4.

In February, Kitty Hawk traveled to Moyock for a double header. Unfortunately, both Kitty Hawk teams lost; the girls by the score of 35 to 9, and the boys, 13 to 8. The reporter who filed the news story of the game stated that Kitty Hawk made Moyock boys "hustle," so maybe there was a ray of hope for the team even in defeat. Later that month Kitty Hawk had a return match with Poplar Branch at Poplar Branch and won again, this time by a score of 18 to 12. Hallett Perry once more was the top scorer with 12 of his team's 18 points. His teammates, Billy Betts and Tom Beacham, scored 2 points each and Grady Beacham added one foul shot. The girls' team against Poplar Branch was not as lucky, losing by a score of 30 to 7. Forward Virgie Perry led the Kitty Hawk team with 5 points. Her teammates included forwards Mae Dowe and Irene Lewark, and guards Minnie Parker, Mary Stetson and Aurelia Tillett.

1928 Kitty Hawk Girls basketball game

In addition to the few newspaper reports, historic photographs show Kitty Hawk boys playing Manteo at Manteo, and then at Kitty Hawk. Two different visiting girls teams were shown in the photographs of games played on the Kitty Hawk home court. The visiting teams were most likely Poplar Branch and Manteo. Of interest in the photographs view of the games was the large crowd of spectators. High school basketball had become a favorite sport of the community, as well as the school.

Records for the 1928-29 basketball season are limited; in fact, only two games are reported in the Elizabeth City Daily Advance. The Kitty Hawk High School boys' team won at Poplar Branch 11 to 10, but the local girls lost to Manteo 2 to 0. After the 1929 season, no competitive Kitty Hawk basketball team played until the fall of 1934; at least they did not join the four-county basketball conference formed in 1931, nor have any box scores recorded in local papers during that period.

Basketball returned to Kitty Hawk in 1934 and the teams played nine games. In their first conference game with Manteo, Manteo played their three strings against both the Kitty Hawk boys and girls' teams – in reverse order; so much for courteous respect for a new upstart school team, and no doubt the beginning of the intense rivalry between the two schools. 1934 was not a good year for the Kitty Hawk boys team as they lost all their games; their worst loss was 52 to 0 to Central. The girls team ended the season with 3 wins, 1 tie and 5 losses. In some respects, it is not surprising that Kitty Hawk had problems winning in their first year. Most of their players on both the girls' and boys' teams were 6th, 7th, and 8th graders and Foster Spruill and Guy Hayman as 8th graders were the senior players on the boys' team. Most of their opposition had been playing competitively for years and were seasoned by experience so it is not surprising that Kitty Hawk lost so often and by such lopsided scores. It is probably more surprising that the girls' team could win three of it nine games.

In 1935 the Albemarle Rural Conference was reformed and provided for home and away games for each of the 9 teams in the conference. Kitty Hawk teams did not fare much better in the new conference alignment than they had previously, but the boys beat Manteo at Kitty Hawk 13 to 12 that year, somewhat avenging the snub they received at Manteo the previous season.

Over the next several years Kitty Hawk teams, particularly the girls, improved their play and their win-loss records and in the process becoming competitive within the conference, particularly when games were played at home. Neither team won the conference title or the tournament championship, but their games were respectable and they surprised some of their opponents. The girls' team won their first ever tournament game in 1940, but lost in the semifinals after one of their star players, Nettie Fulcher, was injured. Had that not occurred, maybe they would have played for the championship - but that did not happen.

1939 Boys basketball team

One of Kitty Hawk's all time outstanding basketball teams was its 1941 girls' team - and they were good! The Falconettes, as they were called, were led by forwards Jean Midgett, Minnie Tillett, and Shirley Dowdy, and guards Lessie Perry, Alma Beacham Hayman and Bernice Stetson. Because of a dislocated shoulder injury, Ellen Dowdy replaced Bernice Stetson as the starting guard after the third game. Nettie Fulcher at forward contributed quality time to many games as a substitute.

Lessie Perry, who had been an outstanding guard for three years, was expected to receive All-Tournament recognition in her final year. Alma Beacham Hayman, an under five-foot guard, who had great timing skills in disrupting shots and recovering rebounds and was quick with the ball, was nicknamed, "mighty mite," by the sportswriter in *The Daily Advance* for her tournament play the previous year. She was another potential All-Tournament candidate. The forwards were seasoned players and developing into high-scoring threats. Minnie Lee Smith, who graduated in 1940 and was an outstanding player the previous year, volunteered to work with the team members to improve their play.

The girls opened the season with two wins over a makeup team of Manteo Independents and a cherished win over Manteo High School with a score of 20 to 18. They breezed through the season schedule and before going into the last regular scheduled game against Manteo, their chief rival, Kitty Hawk enjoyed an 11 – 1 win-loss record. The conference championship was not, however, to be for Kitty Hawk this year; losing the last conference game to Manteo 11-10. Kitty Hawk people expected to redeem themselves in the conference tournament, maybe at the expense of their old rival Manteo. Unfortunately, however, Kitty Hawk lost 17 – 15 in the first round to Perquimans County High School and was eliminated from tournament play. The girls' basketball record of 11 wins and only 3 losses was undoubtedly the best of any Kitty Hawk basketball team, and a record that the players and school could be justly proud, but it did not bring the individual recognition to Lessie Perry and Alma Beacham Hayman they deserved. Alma did receive from the school a gold

94

basketball medal as the Best Girl Player of the Year, but she felt that the medal really should have gone to Lessie Perry.

For the boys, 1939 was another disappointing year; they only won one game despite good performances throughout the year by Tom Dowdy, Claude Parker, Carlton Smith, Jim Scarborough, and others. The 1939 graduation hit the boys basketball team hard with many of their first team regulars finishing school. The graduation caused Kitty Hawk to start building a new competitive boys' team for the 1939-40 basketball season. But building a quality team was not easy. With losses of 59 to 0 to Poplar Branch and 73 to 5 to Central most teams would have folded. Alvis "Sam" Beacham, Grady Tate, Clyde Twiford, Billy Toler, Fred Haywood, Dick Mann, and others took their licks in stride and would see better days ahead.

Kitty Hawk had new basketball facilities in 1940, thanks to the WPA. They consisted of outdoor concrete courts, but not a gym. Instead of playing on sand where passing was the principal way of moving the basketball, on the new courts the teams learned to dribble and pass like other teams they played. The concrete courts were good for practice and game day, but tough on athletic shoes, basketballs, elbows and knees. The school committee, students and faculty built new backboards for the courts and A-style bleachers between the two courts so that spectators could watch the teams play.

The 1941-42 girls' team also played well, including winning two games from the Elizabeth City High School

An outdoor boys basketball contest at Kitty Hawk School

Lady Jackets on the Jackets' home court. Elizabeth City was probably the largest school Kitty Hawk ever played. The girls also won their opening game in the Albemarle Rural Conference Tournament, but lost in the semi-finals. That was the last tournament game a Kitty Hawk girls' team would win in the school's history, but they did not know that at the time. To this point, the boys had yet to win a tournament game.

The Albemarle Rural Conference suspended play for the 1942-43 school year because of travel restriction and gas rationing. Several schools played games with nearby schools, but distant games were not scheduled. There are no records of a Kitty Hawk basketball program for that period but they may have played Manteo and Poplar Branch, or possibly service teams from the Poyners Hill Naval Radio Station, Coast Guardsmen from the Kitty Hawk station, or maybe even a team from the Army installation on the sand hill east of the village.

The Albemarle Rural Conference reformed for the 1943-44 season, but Kitty Hawk did not join until the 1944-45 season. Kitty Hawk again dropped out of the 1948-49 conference schedules, but rejoined in the fall of 1949 and remained a conference team until the high school was permanently closed in 1956.

According to the January 1950 school newspaper, *The Kitty Hawk Beacon*, Shelby Hines, known as "Speedy Ace," hated to lose and would decide to "quit" after each loss; but was the first one on the court the next day for practice. His patience and practice paid off in the 1951 Albemarle Rural Conference Tournaments when both he and G. C. Curles were selected to the All-Tournament Team, after the boys had won their team's first ever tournament game. They lost their semifinal tournament game to Manteo that year but they had already established their team's reputation. The reporter for THE COASTLAND TIMES, who gave an account of the 1951 tournament, summed up the frustrations probably many Kitty Hawk teams faced over the years: Manteo met the tough team the night before the finals. Kitty Hawk had beyond doubt the smoothest working first five men to show in the tournament, but a basketball game is full of lots of minutes for just five men to cover the court at top speed. After holding Manteo's high scoring five to just seven points in the first half, while acquiring 14 points for themselves, the Kitty Hawk iron men ran out of gas midway in the last half. The champions-to-be caught them up and were going away at the finish. The 1950-51 Kitty Hawk Falcons, which included Marvin Midgett, Jr., Wayne Parker, Kenneth Clay Tillett, Roy Dale Sowers, Hope Beacham, Barney Midgett, Pernell Perry, Jack Tinnin, in addition to Hines and Curles, may have been the school's best boys team ever. They played well in the conference, won their first ever tournament game, played Manteo in the tournament on even terms most of the game, and had two of their members selected to the All Tournament Team. Not bad for a high school with a population of just over 30 students, of which less than half were boys, and not all of them played basketball.

Kitty Hawk's basketball fortunes began to wane after the 1951 tournament. They had good performances from Roy Dale Sowers, Bryan Meekins, and later D. A. Perry and Larry Parker, but won few games between 1952 and 1956. Bobby Duvall and Major Curles led the Kitty Hawk boys during the 1955-56 season, the last year Kitty Hawk High School played basketball which ended with a 4 and 8 record.

In spite of losing all their games, both the boys and girls were awarded the sportsmanship trophies for their conference play in the 1954-55 season; but they would have preferred to have won some games.

Except for the 1954-55 season when the Falconettes failed to win a single game, the girls managed to stay out of the cellar most of the time. Clara Faye Haywood was considered by many to be the outstanding basketball player for the Kitty Hawk girls team during the early 1950s. She was frequently the high scorer for the team, but Kathleen Rogers, Zelda Gamiel, Phyllis Scarborough, Charlotte Meekins and Melba Haywood also contributed to the team's effort. As the seniors graduated and moved on other students stepped forward to be on the team. Norma Spruill, Genes Faye Partridge, Kaye Whitfield, Barbara Wise, among others, answered the call and played on the 1953 to 1956 teams. Guards rarely got recognition for their contributions to the team, but occasionally a reporter would mention a player for outstanding defense. Dawn Tillett, Susan Sanderlin, Jenelle Haywood and Angis Toler were among those guards who caught the attention of the media. Angis Toler was especially good and received the school's outstanding female athlete award in 1954.

Some victories are more satisfying than others and that is the case with the Kitty Hawk girls' victory over Manteo, at Manteo, in February 1956. At the time, Manteo was among the conference leaders and Kitty Hawk was winless. At the end of regulation play, the two teams were tied and the game went into overtime. Kitty Hawk came out of overtime ahead, 51 to 49, for its first and only victory that year. In the game, freshman Elsie Hines scored 34 points and only missed four shots from the floor all night. Her 34 points was the second most points scored by a Kitty Hawk player in the school's history. (Pearl Lewark, mother of Barbara Wise who was a teammate with Elsie Hines in this win, had scored 38 points in a game with South Mills in 1937 to establish the individual record of most points scored by a Kitty Hawk player.) The boys lost their game to Manteo by thirty points, but no doubt savored the girls' win as if it were their own.

Both girls and boys teams played in the 1956 Albemarle Rural Conference Tournament without success and brought to an end a basketball legacy for the Kitty Hawk High School that started in 1927. Graduates moved on to the next phase of their life and basketball players, if they played did so under a different school banner in 1957.

BASEBALL

Basketball was the Kitty Hawk consolidated school sport through the years, but in 1951, 1952, and 1953, the school also fielded baseball teams. The school did not join the regular Albemarle Rural Conference for baseball, but did play several teams from the conference. Their most impressive baseball wins were probably in 1951 when they beat both Central and Griggs. The Central game was impressive in that G. C. Curles and Cecil King divided time on the mound and collectively pitched a no-hitter. Their season record that year was 2 wins in 9 games.

In 1954 Kitty Hawk citizens sponsored an independent community baseball team called the "Tomcats." It was not affiliated with the high school, though it played games on the school playground. The team was chiefly sponsored by W. C. "Bill" Foreman, owner and operator of Foreman's Grocery in the village. He provided uniforms and some baseball equipment, and served as the team's coach. In appreciation, the team named the baseball field at the school "Foreman's Field."

The Kitty Hawk Tomcats lost two games to the Griggs Tater Diggers during the summer of 1954 and were ready for them in the return match at Kitty Hawk in September. The Tomcats won the doubleheader from the Tater Diggers at Kitty Hawk behind Major Curles, who pitched both games. The next contest for the Tomcats was with a Harbinger team, but since local contests were not always posted, no record of the game is available. It appears that the Tomcats did not survive after the 1954 season.

With consolidation of Kitty Hawk High School into the Manteo High School after the 1956 school year the final chapter of Kitty Hawk High School sports closed. The next chapter would be written by the Kitty Hawk Elementary School.

SCHOOL TRIPS

Principal Alton Baum was a firm believer in high school graduates going to college if possible and he encouraged them at every opportunity. At one time when he was principal of Lake Landing High School in Hyde County near Lake Mattamuskeet, after leaving Kitty Hawk, he had the highest percentage of high school graduates enrolled in collages of any school in North Carolina.

At Kitty Hawk, he had encouraged students to go to college and as a way of introducing some of the students to college opportunities he organized an educational sightseeing trip to western North Carolina. The students would need transportation for the tour and in April 1927 a delegation of boys from the Kitty Hawk School appeared before the Dare County Board of

Education with a petition requesting the use of the school truck (bus) for the trip. They had already secured permission from the Kitty Hawk School Committee and had agreed to put the truck in good working order for the trip, and return it in the same condition. The Board of Education granted the request.

Kitty Hawk School seniors prepare the school truck for their trip

After school graduation exercises May 12, 1927, Principal Alton Baum, Teacher R. L. Parlier and the students prepared for their trip. The truck was loaded with camping gear including a big wall tent, cots, cooking pots and pans, camp stools, a portable table, provisions and personal clothing. Items were stored in a rack on the roof of the truck, in an extended rack attached to the back of the truck, and in whatever space was available inside the vehicle. Extra tires and water bags hung from the side of the truck. The party probably looked like a group of traveling hippies moving to the promised land.

A trip log or diary for the trip has not been located, but photographs taken by the boys give an indication of the tour. The party camped across the state in open fields and on school property. They traveled south of Charlotte to the North Carolina/South Carolina line and then turned north and crossed the North Carolina/Tennessee border on US 19E, and continued on to at least the community of Shell Creek, near Roan Mountain, Tennessee. The trip lasted three weeks, but one week was spent in Cranberry, N. C., a small community southeast of Elk Park, N. C., while several boys recovered from measles.

Tom Beacham and Orville Baum served as drivers. In an interview for *The Coastland Times* in 1977 Tom Beacham told of at least one harrowing experience on the trip. As the party was returning down the mountain from a visit to Blowing Rock, the truck brakes gave out about halfway down a steep grade. Downshifts helped to slow the vehicle, but Tom had to run the truck into the side of the mountain

The camping trip for Kitty Hawk seniors travels up to the twisting mountain roads

to get the vehicle stopped. When Tom and Orville removed the gear box cover, the gear bands were chewed up and smoking. The bands were replaced and they could have proceeded, but the boys were so shaken up that they camped there for the night. Replacing bands became such a common occurrence that Tom and Orville could replace them within 45 minutes. They acquired additional sets of bands for the remainder of their trip.

For students who had probably been no further from home than Elizabeth City or Norfolk, the trip to western North Carolina must have been an exciting and memorable experience, a highlight of their school experience. If the purpose of the trip was to encourage the boys to attend college, there were some successes. Ernest Midgett and Grady Beacham attended the University of North Carolina where Ernest Midgett graduated, and Orville Baum attended North Carolina State College for three years before the effects of the depression caused him to withdraw.

In 1946 many Kitty Hawk School students went on another field trip, this time to Raleigh and in a full-size bus. In all, 38 students from grades 8 through 12 were on the trip with Principal

Talmage Page and his wife, Olga Page, a teacher, as chaperones. Mose Basnight of the Virginia Dare Transportation Company in Manteo, N. C., was the bus driver. The students paid a modest fee for the bus rental and took a picnic lunch to keep the cost of the trip within their means. According to those who made the trip it was a fun occasion and they visited several public buildings in Raleigh, including the old State Capital Building where the Legislature met.

Another noteworthy trip occurred in October 1948 when the Kitty Hawk students chartered a bus for a trip to the State Fair and to hear President Harry S. Truman speak. Principal W. V. Wilkerson and Miss Hall, the French and English teacher, were chaperones on the trip.

For Kitty Hawk students, field trips away from the school were rare occasions and the trip to the capital of North Carolina or the State Fair would be special treats and long remembered by those who were fortunate enough to make them.

GRADUATION

Few events are as important to students and their parents as graduation. The citizens of Kitty Hawk had worked long and hard to improve education opportunities in the community, and finally in 1926 Kitty Hawk had its own high school which gave the young people the tools to improve their lives through the coming years. But not all students who attended Kitty Hawk High School graduated. Typical of the times, the dropout rate among students was high. They left school for a variety of reasons; some because of poor grades or a lack of interest, others got married, some left to pursue a working career, others joined the military and a few moved to other school systems. In spite of the drop out rate, nearly 250 students graduated from Kitty Hawk High School during its 30 years' of life between 1926 and 1956.

The 1927 graduation class of Kitty Hawk High School was especially important and meaningful for the community, because it was a first. A capacity crowd of parents and friends attended the Baccalaureate services held in the school auditorium on Sunday,

May 8, 1927. Reverend W. A. Betts, Minister of the Kitty Hawk Methodist Church, delivered a sermon on "The Secret of a Long and Happy Life." A quartet sang the program anthem, "Building, Daily Building," and Miss Minnie Parker sang a solo, "Whispering Hope." Graduation exercises occurred four nights later May 12, with Etta Gurganus Baum being the first graduate from Kitty Hawk High School, and the only graduate in the 1927 class. Etta Baum's father was Edward N. Baum, a member of the Dare County Board of Education, who later served as its chairman. Etta Baum went onto college, earned her teaching certificate and taught for many years in the Dare County school system.

Graduation exercises were greatly expanded for the 1928 class. Unlike 1927, when only one student graduated, the 1928 class had nine seniors. The graduation services that year extended over seven days. Baccalaureate services were held Sunday, May 6, in the school auditorium with Reverend William A. Betts once again delivering the sermon, this time titled, "The Primary of Obedience". On Thursday evening, May 10, an operetta, "The Golden Whistle," was presented in the school auditorium for the graduates and the public. Graduation day, May 11, started at 10:30 a.m. with a Commencement Address by Dr. Boone "Bone" D. Tillett of Norfolk, Virginia, an educator who was born and raised in Nags Head. His sister, Ester Tillett, was a member of the graduating class. Medals for winners of the school's Declamation and Recitation contest were presented by Kitty Hawk School Committee members, Captain Will Lewark and Ellsworth J. Baum. The formal graduation exercise was held Friday evening, May 11, in the school auditorium with Grady V. Beacham delivering Salutatory remarks; William T. Beacham presenting Valedictory remarks; Ernest E. Midgett giving the class history; Mae P. Dowe presenting the class poem; the class prophecy was read by Ester B. Tillett; and Orville Baum offered the last will and testament; William A. Betts made the class presentation to the school; and Minnie Parker offered a presentation on seniors as juniors see them. The senior class sang both the class and school songs for the last time as students. Dare County Superintendent of Schools, E. W. Pearson, presented diplomas to the graduates. The final graduation week presentation was a play, "Go Slow Mary," given by the school's junior and sophomore classes on Saturday night to officially close the 1927-28 school year. The programs and activities of the 1928 graduation set a pattern for subsequent graduating seniors in the years to come, depending on the interest and size of the graduating class.

The 1939 graduating class

The 1939 graduating class was special; it was the first class to wear caps and gowns for graduation and with sixteen seniors, the largest class ever to graduate from Kitty Hawk High School. Several other classes were close in graduating totals including 15 in 1941, 14 in 1954, 13 in 1942, and several years with 12 graduates.

Usually there were few graduates. In 1943 Elmo Whitson was the only graduate and no one graduated in 1948. The "no graduate in 1948" was caused in part by the State extending the school year after 1946 to twelve years instead of eleven, which had been the standard since the school opened. The students who could have graduated in 1948 started dropping out earlier to get married, go to work, or simply quit, so there was no one in the pipeline to graduate that year. While there was no high school graduation, ten eighth graders received certification to advance to high school at graduation exercises held at the school the first week of June of that year. Superior Court Judge Chester R. Morris was the commencement speaker for the eight-grade graduating class.

The 1940 graduating class added a new dimension to their graduating exercises by including mascots. Marlene Scarborough of Duck and Shelby Hines of Kitty Hawk were the first mascots for a Kitty Hawk High School graduating class. Most of the later graduating classes followed this lead.

Having a Junior-Senior Banquet idea originated with the 1943 class of juniors and the lone senior, Elmo Whitson. The program was held at the school and included singing, toasts with responses from students and faculty, and a skit by Norman Perry and Russell Dowdy. Probably the local PTA catered food for the banquet. The Junior-Senior Banquet program continued through most of the remaining years of the school's history. There was even a Junior-Senior in 1948 when there were no senior graduates. The juniors held their dinner banquet at the Carolinian Hotel and moved to the Casino for dancing. In 1952, the students held their Junior-Senior Banquet at the Point Harbor Grill. The roast turkey with dressing dinner was topped off with a generous helping of apple pie a la mode. It was a grand affair for the five seniors, three juniors and their guests.

The last commencement exercise for Kitty Hawk High School graduates occurred May 30, 1956. The five graduates included Gary Scarborough, valedictorian, Susan Sanderlin, salutatorian, Phillip Sawyer, Conley Beacham and Janice Pugh. With Gary Scarborough's name being listed last in the alphabet listing of students, he had the honor of being the last graduate of Kitty Hawk High School. The following year, Kitty Hawk, Duck, Colington, Nags Head, and Southern Shores high school students attended Manteo High School.

The old-school building continued to serve as an elementary school for three additional years while a new school building was under construction. In January 1959, all students in Kitty Hawk School moved into the new Kitty Hawk Elementary School at the corner of US 158 and the old main road between Kitty Hawk and Duck. This move brought an end to an era of over 100 years of schools in Kitty Hawk village and closed the old-school house as the social center for the community.

TEACHERS

Seventy-five or more persons served as teachers in the Kitty Hawk school system from 1848 until the school closed in 1956. Many teachers only taught for a year or two and then moved on, though several gave long periods of service to the community.

Noah T. Hurdle, a native of Gates County, moved his family to Kitty Hawk around 1900 and served as a teacher in both the Down-The-Road and Up-The-Road school through 1913. He died in 1917, but his family stayed on in the community. His daughter, Beulah Hurdle, married Zene Perry and at least one of their granddaughters still lives in the area

Nora Baum, a native of Kitty Hawk, taught from 1906 until 1948, both as a "free school" county teacher and as a "pay school" teacher. Without question, with over 40 years of teaching in the community, Nora Baum taught more Kitty Hawk children than any other individual, before or since.

Charles and Nellie Baum Caldwell each spent nearly twenty-five years as teachers in Kitty Hawk after the consolidated school was opened in 1926.

Nellie and Charles Caldwell

The history of early teachers is not well documented, but a few persons are recorded as receiving pay for teaching and could have taught in Kitty Hawk. Sarah Mathias and Alfred Jones are listed in the 1870 census for Kitty Hawk as "school teacher." Sarah Mathias was shown as a member of the Hodges Gallop household at Martins Point and could have been a tutor for the Gallop children, but she could have also been a common school teacher in the neighborhood. On the east side of the village, Alfred Jones was with the James R. Hobbs family, who had no children, so he most likely was a community teacher.

Both Hezekiah W. Beasley, in 1874, and John D. Wicker, in 1876, were paid as teachers by the county. There is no record as to where they taught, but they both lived in Kitty Hawk at the time; John D. Wicker was an Elder of the Providence Baptist Church, and Hezekiah Beasley was a general store merchant. In 1876 also, Lucetta Gallop, daughter of Hodges Gallop, was paid for teaching in the county, but the school or schools, in which she taught were not identified.

Hildegard Etheridge Perry, in a 1960 taped interview, remembered one of her teachers as "old man Brice," who she describes as "a mean old thing." Of course, when she made that comment there was a twinkle in her eye and a slight smile on her face. She never said why he was "a mean old thing," so maybe the years had mellowed her views of him.

George Percival Delencles Brice apparently left a family in Baltimore, Maryland, before serving as an officer in the Virginia 15th Regiment of Cavalry during the Civil War. He appeared in the Currituck County area around 1870 and married a local woman from Colington. In 1872 he was examined and approved for teaching in Currituck County by V. L. Pitts, County Examiner, and appointed Free Public-School teacher at Reedy Branch School. Reedy Branch School's location today has been lost to history, but like many other small neighborhood schools of its time it was undoubtedly combined with other schools and took on a new identity.

Although no official records have survived, George Brice must have also been approved in Dare County because he was known to have taught on Roanoke Island during this period. Incomplete Currituck County school records report his being paid as a teacher in 1872, 1873, 1874, and 1877; but he undoubtedly taught in other years and into the early 1880s as well. He was also involved in civic affairs and served as a Superior Court Judge and later a County Commissioner for Currituck County. He died in 1885.

William Ivy Dowdy remembered Charles Stetson as a peg leg schoolteacher who taught in Kitty Hawk. Charles Stetson served with the North Carolina Confederate troops and lost part of a leg in the Battle of Roanoke Island in 1862. His occupation is listed in both the 1870 and 1880 census as "school teacher." Ivy Dowdy fondly remembered a song Charles Stetson wrote about a "bear" incident in Kitty Hawk. Here's how he told the story, and recited the song.

Robert F. Sanderlin, before he married in 1879 and moved to Wanchese, NC, lived with his widowed mother in Kitty Hawk. He had many hogs in the woods near his home, which he fed several times a week to keep them tame and close at home. At one feeding he sighted something in the woods that apparently frightened him. Charles Stetson's song memorialized the incident in "Killing of the Bear."

It was in Atlantic Township one morning in the spring Rob Sanderlin got frightened at a dreadful big thing. He waddled and he toddled as hard as he could to tell Nettie Baum what he saw in the woods Oh...

Nettie said to William (Baum), this beast we must kill. They went and got John Tillett, Jessie Partridge and Oliver O'Neal.

John Tillett, he was never known to tell a lie. He swore upon his honor he could see the animal's eye. Bobbie O'Neal, he was a man of the law. He swore he could see the animal's paw.

They all came to the conclusion that #4 shot would do to shoot in the hump.

They sent one man out to get shot, but found that the animal was a stump.

Chorus: We need a bear hunter from Tyrrell. We need a bear hunter from Tyrrell We need a bear hunter from Tyrrell, To kill that wonderful beast.

William Ivy Dowdy was too young to have known about the incident when it occurred, but apparently, the story was retold through the years to the point that he memorized it and could recite it 80 years later.

Zene Perry reported that Dr. W. T. Griggs was one of his teachers, but it is doubtful that Griggs had received his medical degree before he taught in Kitty Hawk. Records show that William Thomas Griggs taught in the Up-The-Road School in the spring of 1893. He also taught in several other schools in the county during the period of 1893 and 1894. While teaching in Kitty Hawk he probably lived with the Elijah Sibbern family.

Griggs attended the University of Virginia and finished medical school in 1896. He returned to Currituck County and started a medical practice and became interested in improving the public education program in his county. He served seven years as the Currituck County Superintendent of Schools and was instrumental in the construction of one of the first North Carolina rural high schools at Poplar Branch. The Poplar Branch High School was named for him when it was rebuilt in 1947.

Another of Zene Perry's teachers was Bertha Muse from Pamlico County, N. C. School records indicate she taught in the Up-The-Road School in 1900. Perry spoke fondly of her in his 1960 taped interview and reported that she had just passed away in Rocky Mount, N. C., a few months before. Although she taught only one year in Kitty Hawk, Zene Perry had established a friendship with her at that time and had maintained contact with her for sixty years.

There were many other teachers who served the Kitty Hawk school system over the years. Mattie Newbold from Perquimans County taught several years at Kitty Hawk before moving on to Poplar Branch. She married Charles Austin Wright of Currituck County and they had a son, Charles Newbold Wright, who became a doctor and the family physician for many Kitty Hawkers. Margaret F. Wright of Camden County taught in Kitty Hawk in 1910, met a local man, William Franklin Midgett, and married him. Mattie Perry from Pasquotank County was the head teacher in the Down-The-Road School for a number of years. She too met and married a Kitty Hawk man, Arthur Curtis Twiford.

Not all teachers were from other places. Stella Baum, a Kitty Hawk native, returned to teach in her home community after she completed her education at Blackstone College for Girls in Virginia. Two local sisters, Claudia Sanderlin and Mattie Sanderlin Wescott, taught in the Kitty Hawk schools for a few years. There were also teachers from Wanchese and Nags Head, who taught for various periods in the local schools and who had family relations in Kitty Hawk. Each teacher brought a certain talent to the classroom and it appears from this distance in time that Kitty Hawk was blessed with many teachers of special talents and skills.

Teaching Staff

Orville Baum

Tom Beacham

Chapter Six

RELIGION

The Baptist Church and different iterations throughout the decades

Kitty Hawkers have always been proud of their churches and pleased with their religious affiliation, be it Baptist or Methodist. Both Kitty Hawk churches were established in the 1850s and each church represented one of the two most popular religious denominations of the day. Each church was in a different part of the community; the Baptist Up-the-Road, the Methodist Down-the-Road. Not surprisingly, most of the people who attended the Baptist church were from that section of the Up-The-Road community, while the Down-The-Road community residents made up the membership majority of the Methodist church.

Although the Baptist and Methodist held very divergent views on religion, there was no apparent animosity between the two groups within the community, or in their daily lives. In fact, they shared their homes, lodging and food when either was having special church services that brought visitors into the community, and they attended each other's services from time to time. They even married across church lines and usually one spouse would forsake their own church and join their companion's religious order. Usually, their children could join whichever church they pleased.

BAPTISTS

The Baptists were among the early religious denominations to move into eastern North Carolina and the Albemarle area. Shiloh Baptist Church in Camden County, North Carolina, is reported to be the first church of that faith founded in the colony. Others followed and by 1752 there were sixteen General Baptist churches in North Carolina.

With the increasing numbers of churches being formed, groups of churches of the same faith in the same general area began organizing into church associations. The Kehukee Baptist Association was organized in 1765 as the fourth Association of Baptist churches in America, behind Philadelphia (1707), Pennsylvania, and Charleston (1751) and Sandy Creek (1758) in South Carolina.

The Association was formed at a meeting-house called "Kehukee," near the Kehukee Creek in Halifax County, North Carolina. Other churches in the new Association included Toisnot in Edgecombe County, Falls of Tar River in Edgecombe County, Fishing Creek in Halifax County, Sandy Creek in Warren County, Sandy Run in Bertie County, and a church from Camden County.

In the following years, other churches throughout northeastern North Carolina and southeastern Virginia joined the Association and by 1790 sixty-one churches were counted in the Association, including the Coinjock Church in Currituck County, North Carolina and Flatty Creek in Pasquotank County, North Carolina. At the Associations meeting that year, the churches agreed to a division of the Association with nineteen churches in Virginia forming the Virginia Portsmouth Association and forty-two churches in North Carolina remaining in the Kehukee Association. A few years later another division occurred within the Association with the Tar River forming the dividing boundary. Those churches north of the river stayed as the Kehukee Association, while those south of the river forming the Neuse Association.

Even with the formation of associations, there was not a hierarchy of organization within the Baptist church. Each church was independent and free to apply their own religious beliefs and discipline, agreeable to the word of God within their congregation. Not all Baptist churches were affiliated in an association and as more and more churches were formed, the non-affiliated soon outnumbered those of association membership.

The Powells Point Baptist Church did not affiliate with the Kehukee Association when formed in 1801, though some of its members preferred the Kehukee style of discipline over that of the newer General Baptist discipline being promoted in most new churches. The Powells Point Church served the people of the lower end of Currituck County and those Baptist individuals and families on the North Banks from present day Duck through Kitty Hawk. For the bankers, it meant boat rides of some distance crossing Currituck Sound to attend services at the church and returning home, but many made the trip.

Friction within the Baptist church began to grow in the late 1700s and early 1800s, mostly over the issue of promoting missionary work within the church family. It reached a point in 1827 where the Kehukee Association issued a "Declaration of Principles" denouncing these and related items. In their declaration, they stated that they would "discard all Missions Societies, Bible Societies and Theological Seminaries, the practice heretofore resorted to for their support, in begging money from the public." Further they opposed "...any of the members of our church joining the fraternity of Masons or, being members, continue to visit the lodges and parades, we will not invite them to preach in our pulpits, believing them to be guilty of such practices; and we declare non-fellowship with them and such practices altogether."

The Declaration further stated that the Kehukee Association membership believed "these societies and institutions to be the inventions of men, and not warranted from the word of God." The Kehukee Association subscribes to these principles to this day.

In September 1830, a dozen or so members of the Powells Point "Missionary" Baptist Church separated themselves from that church to form the Regular Baptists at Powells Point and petitioned for membership in the Kehukee Association, which was granted. The Regular Baptist held their meeting in the Missionary Baptist meeting-house on a schedule that did not conflict with the others church's use. They continued to share the meeting-house until April 12, 1851, when they moved into their own meeting-house located less than ½ mile away. They renamed the new church Elim.

In the early years Elim Church did not have a regular preacher, or Elder, but was served by visiting Elders from other churches; Malachi Corbell from Coinjock, Samuel Tatum from Bethlehem Church in Pasquotank County, George W. Carawan from Washington County, and Foster Jarvis, probably Coinjock. Sermons were also delivered by congregation members who had been given a letter or license by the church "to exercise his gift by exhortation." Brothers Benjamin Evans, James Melson, Hodges Gallop, Thomas McKimmey, and Caleb T. Sawyer were issued letters and delivered sermons when the Church was without an Elder.

In early August 1854 eight Elim Church members from the North Banks petitioned the church to be set apart for the purposes of starting a church on the North Banks. The letters of "demission" were granted to Hodges Gallop, Thomas McKimmey, Morris Beals, Jasper Toler, Alsey McKimmey, Sally Toler, Peggy Owens and Betsey Beacham. August 26, 1854, was set aside as "a day of fasting and pray for the purpose of constitution a church on the North Banks by the name of Providence Church. Elder Samuel Tatum from Primitive Bethlehem Church, Pasquotank County, and Elder Caleb T. Sawyer from Powells Point Elium Church as presbytery of minister."

Other members of Elim Church participated in the services. The eight members of the new church sat together as a body, presented their faith and covenant, which was read and agreed to and recorded in their Church Book. Elder Hodges Gallop, who had been ordained the previous year, was selected as the first pastor of the new Providence Baptist Church on the North Banks. The Church immediately applied for membership in the Kehukee Association.

The church held its meetings in the school house located at the Sign Post on the Main Road through Kitty Hawk woods. Per information from interviews in 1960 with elderly members of the community, the building was located east of the Main Road and slightly north of the intersection with what was then Turtle Road. That location today is the intersection of Twiford Road with Woods Road. The school house had been built sometime prior to 1848, probably by Hodges Gallop, on his land. Gallop was a person of considerable means and had school age children so he may have constructed the building to serve his family needs as well as those of the community. It was typical for a school district of that day to use a private building for a school.

A.B. Love Tillett

The old school building at the Sign Post served the Baptist Church well for 44 years, but in July 1898 Providence Primitive Baptist Church moved into a new church building at the southeast corner of Turtle Road and the Main Road through the village. The land for the church was donated by A. B. Love Tillett and his wife, Nancy, for church purposes with the provision that should the land no longer serve church purposes, the land would be returned to the original track. Years later that would become a problem for people wanting to secure title to the land.

Providence Primitive Baptist Church

The new wood framed church building was a large structure, 40 feet by 50 feet, simple in its rectangular design and A-framed roof, but functional in purpose. The building had eight 8 ft by 3 ft. windows along the east and west side walls, four windows and a door on the south wall, and three windows and two doors on the north entrance wall. The original chimney was in the north end of the building, but in 1952 a second chimney was added to the south end and became the primary chimney used with their heating stove. The room was initially heated by a wood stove, then a coal stove and in May 1978, gas heaters. The north end chimney was removed recently during a reroofing project.

The exterior of the building was painted white with black trim on the window and door facings, corner boards and roof facer boards. There were no screens at any of the windows. The building was covered with vinyl siding around 1987.

The interior of the building was one large room. It was finished in beaded-board ceiling and painted. The walls and ceiling are white today but there is some ghost mark evidence that the interior may have been painted a different color, or even varnished, at an earlier time. Two rows of 6-inch post, set approximately 12 feet apart, support the roof system and visually divide the room into three long sections. Pews were located between the posts in the center of the building, with shorter section of pews next to the outside walls. There was an aisle on each side of the building between the short wall pews and the center pews. The pulpit was located on a raised platform at the south end of the room. The church deacons normally sat in small pews on the east side facing the pulpit while the choir, if there was one assembled for the services, in pews on the west side, also facing the pulpit.

The building was designed with many windows to take advantage of natural lighting. Truxton Midgett remembered, however, that the Lyons sisters, Hannah, Isabella, and Bertha, from Asbury Park, New Jersey, who had purchased the Hodges Gallop property in 1893, gave kerosene lanterns for lights in the new church. Ghost marks show that there were five wall mounted lanterns; two on the east wall, one on the west wall, one on a post to light the center pew area, and a single lantern on the wall behind the pulpit. Additionally, there was a very attractive and colorful six lantern chandeliers suspended over the center section of the pews near the pulpit end of the room. According to the Church Book the building was initially wired for electricity in

1938 with $40.00 given to the church by Sister Hester A. Lundy for that purpose. The church was rewired in 1968 by Charles Reid and Wally Mathias who were working for a local electrical contractor, Norman "Big Smittie" Smith, at the time. Four single light bulbs hung from wiring extended from the ceiling provided the lighting for the sanctuary and later, four ceiling fans were installed to help with air circulation in the room.

Providence Baptist Church was the official name of the new Kitty Hawk church, but most locals referred to it simply as "the Primitive Baptist Church." The members of the church were proud to be of the "old school of Baptist" and not offended to be called "Kehukee Baptist" or even "hard shell Kehukee Baptist." It confirmed their dedication and faith in their religion.

Providence Primitive Baptist Church was fortunate in having two Elders, Hodges Gallop and Thomas McKimmey, in their congregation from the beginning and other locals, John D. Wicker, Hezakiah W. Beasley, John Rodgers and Avery J. Austin, were appointed within the first 30 years of the church's establishment. With Elders close at hand, the church could maintain a monthly meeting schedule. There were periods in the late 1880s and again in the late 1890s, however, when there was only one Elder around and the pastors for various reasons could not fulfill their duties and there were no church services for several months at a time.

Avery J. Austin, who died in 1902, was the last local Elder to serve as pastor of Providence Primitive Baptist Church. After his death, Elder E. E. Lundy, from the Wilmington, NC, area was selected as the church pastor. With a pastor who lived away from Kitty Hawk and probably had several churches under his charge, Providence Church changed their meetings from monthly to quarterly. The pastor was not paid for his services nor given a travel allowance, but individual church members could, if they desired, help him with his expenses; and they did. Aubrey C. Harris told an interesting story about the expenses of the pastor. In 1911 when he was getting ready to marry Almeda Rodgers he decided he needed to go to Elizabeth City to buy a new suit. After waiting around a week for the freight boat, which did not come because of mechanical problems, Aubrey hired Captain Bill Perry, who has a small gasoline boat, to take him to get his suit. Captain

Perry charged him $3.00 for the round trip, but told him that if he had passengers for the return trip, he would deduct their fee from his fare. They got to Elizabeth City; Aubrey purchased his suit and returned to the docks to meet Captain Perry for the return trip. Sure enough, there were two new passengers waiting for the trip to Kitty Hawk, Elder Lundy and an assistant. Since the clergy did not pay transportation fares, Aubrey had no refund coming. Elder Lundy married Aubrey and Almeda while he was in Kitty Hawk on that trip.

When the church met either in monthly or later quarterly meetings, they were essentially two separate meetings over two days. Saturday meetings were called a "conference meeting" and were the time when the church conducted its business, while Sundays were devoted to preaching, baptism, communion, and feet washing.

Conference meetings opened with a prayer, followed by a sermon usually by the church pastor. The congregation selected a Moderator for the session who usually was the pastor or a visiting Elder, but could be a senior member of the church. Visitors of "like faith and order" were invited to sit with the congregation and the "dore" was opened for new members. Church members were permitted to speak on any subject they wished without interruption "…untell he gives his light on the subject" as allowed in their "Rules of Decorum." The nature of their comments generally was not recorded unless it involved Association business, such as the annual Association contribution or attendance at the annual Association meeting, or behavior of church members. Member's behavior required special attention and often resulted in some action on the part of the conference.

Each member was expected to attend each conference meeting of the church. If "…any being absent two monthly meetings shall be notified to attend the next conference to state to the church reason and cause of his absenting from the monthly meeting." Additionally, "any male members absent at conference it shall be his duty next conference to state to the church the reason for his absents." Usually, two church Deacons were sent to see the member who had missed the church meeting and "site him to the church for his nunattendance." In most cases the member would "come forward (at the next conference) and made confession and was received back in full fellowship;" but not always. Members were dismissed from the church for a number of reasons, usually non-attendance, disorderly conduct, going to another church of a different faith, or as in the case of B. D. Tillett, for joining the Masonic Order. Tillett was later reinstated to the church so presumably he gave up his membership in the Masonic Order. Brother Joshua Guard was called before the conference to "make confession of drinking to mutch strong licquars" and after the confession was received back into full fellowship. Sisters Juley A. McNight and Frances Perry did not fair as well as they were reported to have been seen dancing and playing at Mr. Theoflus Daniels' house on Poor Ridge. The conference removed their names from the Church book. On another occasion, Brother William Wicker was observed dancing and when confronted by a church member he replied that the church must deal with him as they saw proper. Sisters Bethany Harris and Jukey Harris were expelled from the church for misconduct and not attendance without given the opportunity to ask forgiveness. After having been forgiven once for non-attendance, three years later Sister Melissa Green Tillett's name was "rast from church book by motion" of the conference for non attendance.

Misconduct was not limited to the general membership. Sometimes the pastor was involved. In September 1884, Elder John D. Wicker, pastor of the Providence Baptist Church came forward to the church and confesses his disorderly conduct. "He said through the weakness of the flesh and great temptation he went a stray and he ask the church for forgiveness and the church forgave." He also submitted his resignation and reported that he was "moving away off of this place and can't atten to it often." No one else came forward to confess a "weakness of the flesh" so Wicker's transgressions must have been out of the faith. His resignation was accepted and Elder John Rodgers was appointed pastor of the church.

Sunday's services were devoted to baptism, communion, feet washing, and preaching. The Baptist believed for a proper baptism a person had to be fully immersed or dipped in water. For the Elim Baptist Church, baptisms were usually held in Currituck

Sound at Parker's Landing near their church. On at least one occasion, and before Providence Baptist Church was established, Margaret Owens, Harriet Baum, Morris Beals and Josiah D. Perry, all from North Banks, were baptized at John Baum's Landing along Moore Shore on the east shores of Kitty Hawk Bay. Later all Providence Baptist Church baptisms were conducted at Dowdy's Landing, or Sound Landing, normally Sunday morning. The baptism was performed in Currituck Sound in hip depth water where the candidate was immersed by the pastor. After the baptism, the baptism party and witnesses returned to the church for preaching services for the day.

Communion and feet washing occurred on Sundays after preaching. There were no hard and fast rules among the Primitive Baptist about the scheduling of these services. Those churches that had an active congregation and observed the services usually scheduled them quarterly, but that did not always happen at the Kitty Hawk church. In fact, according to records in the Church book, communion and feet washing might not occur more than once a year, if that frequently. On several occasions in the early years of the new church, the communion service had to be canceled because the church did not have all the "elements" of the services, with wine being the principal missing "element." The services would also be canceled if the preacher did not show up on the day communion was scheduled since he was the only person who could perform the services. On several occasions the services had to be canceled because "so many of the Brothering being gone."

Elder A. J. Austin died in November 1902 and Elder E. E. Lundy was appointed as Pastor of the Providence Baptist Church. Shortly thereafter, the congregation established quarterly meetings for the church with conference meetings occurring on the Saturday before the 4th Sunday in March, June, September and December. Sunday preaching followed the Saturday conference meeting. When Elder E. E. Lundy died in 1921, Elder John P. Tingle was named pastor. The church continued the quarterly meeting schedule with the new pastor and established the practice of holding communion and feet washing on Sundays after preaching. That tradition continued for the remainder of the church's history.

The practice of primitive Baptist holding Union meetings dates from a very early period and may even predate the establishment of the Kehukee Baptist Association in 1765. The establishment of "unions" between primitive Baptist churches was not a requirement of association membership but occurred between neighboring churches of the same order and faith in the same general area to promote brotherhood and general fellowship. By 1803 there were four unions within the Kehukee Association: the Eastern, Bertie, Flat Swamp, and Swift Creek. In the Eastern Union was Coinjock in Currituck County, Flatty Creek and Knobs crook in Pasquotank County, Sawyer's Creek in Camden County, Yoppin in Chowan County and Ballard's Bridge, probably Perquimans County. Powells Point Regular Baptist and Providence Baptist had not been formed by 1803 and thus not listed. Through the years as new churches were constituted, and others dissolved, the makeup of the Unions changed or was reformed. Before Kitty Hawk was included as part of Dare County, Providence Baptist Church was in the Pasquotank-Currituck Union, and the union name was probably changed again later.

Most churches held their scheduled Conference Meeting on Saturday before the 1st, 2nd, 3rd or 4th Sunday in a month. Union Meetings were often held on the 5th Sunday of the month, including the previous Friday and Saturday, which occur four times annually Kitty Hawk usually requested that they host their Union Meeting in the June – July time frame.

Hosting a Union Meeting was a special pleasure for members of Providence Baptist Church and they went out of their way to accommodate the visitors. Both church members and non-members opened their homes to the guest and provided them food, lodging and hospitality for the three-day event. Guests came from sister churches in the Union, but old timers remember that people also came from other areas as well. Many of the guests were primitive church members but others were simply supporters of that religious sect and enjoyed the meetings. Getting to Kitty Hawk before Tom Baum's ferry in 1926 or the 1930 Wright

Memorial Bridge was by boat so it was not easy to attend the Union Meetings, but the faithful came. For the Kitty Hawkers, the visits were a pleasant change from the daily routine in the isolated village and it gave them an opportunity to see old friends, reestablish relations and meet new people. Probably the locals looked at these gatherings as much a social event as a religions experience.

The Union Meetings occurred over a three-day period of Friday through Sunday. Breakfast was usually with the host, while other meals were largely supplied by the community, which were served on the church grounds. The day's services included praise, prayers and sermons, and the primitive Baptist Church was noted for long services and particularly long sermons. All visiting Elders were afforded the opportunity to deliver a sermon to the gathering, and most did.

Very little local church business was conducted during the Union Meetings except the occasional receiving of new members. At the June 1909 Union Meeting, five candidates, John Perry, Letha Perry, Elnora Perry, Pussy Perry and Elizabeth Rogers, came forward to join the Providence Baptist Church and were baptized the same day. Occasionally, but not always, communion was offered Primitive Baptist members in attendance at the Union Meeting.

The hospitality and friendship extended by the community to attendees at the Kitty Hawk Union Meeting was more than repaid when Kitty Hawkers attended Union Meetings in sister churches in their communities.

The Kehukee Association held its annual conference in the early fall usually in Martin, Edgecombe, Pitt or Halifax County. All churches were invited to attend and send officially designated "messengers" who delivered a letter from the church on conditions of their church and its work and membership. The "messengers" also delivered a modest contribution, sometimes no more that two dollars, to help the Association with publication cost for the conference proceedings. Kitty Hawk usually designated two "messengers," but in later years included alternates for the meeting.

In 1951, the Kitty Hawk Providence Baptist Church was host to the annual session of the Kehukee Association. This was the first, and would be the only time that the Association would meet on the coast, and among the few times it had met in northeastern North Carolina. Over 1500 people and 30 preachers attended the session during the three-day event of October 5th through the 7th. Ordinarily, housing and feeding that size crowd in Kitty Hawk would have been a problem in the 1950s, but the community came together as they did at Union Meetings to accommodate the guests. Some remember that it took three or four settings of the breakfast table to get everyone fed. For lunch and dinner waist level long plank tables were set up on the church grounds for placement of the food and for people to set their plates. Walter Beacham, who oversaw the food for the session, secured 600 chickens for some of the meals and Caleb Toler and his crew provided fish that was caught fresh for the occasion. Walter Perry served as the chief chef for the fish fry and ladies in the community provided the trimmings for the meals. As was customary at church gatherings visiting guests brought food to help feed the people.

A gathering of the Baptist members, including the long community table

Providing an opportunity for all the preachers to deliver a sermon was probably a bigger challenge for the host than feeding the crowds. Prior to the meeting, the church had the underbrush cleared from the church grounds and neighbors allowed the church to clear adjoining high ground. The cooking facilities were set up across the road from the church and the tables for food placed on the ridge to the east of the church building. While a sermon was going on inside the church building, a second preacher would be delivering a sermon on the church grounds where chairs had been placed for that purpose. Vehicle parking was a premium, but neighbors again provided parking on their property. Despite the food, lodging, and space limitations, those who attended the Kehukee Association Session at the Kitty Hawk Providence Primitive Baptist Church in 1951 consider the meeting a success.

Providence Baptist Church in Kitty Hawk was constituted on August 26, 1854, with eight members. Over the next 100 years more that 140 persons joined the church, mostly from the Up-the-Road community of Kitty Hawk village, but also from Colington Island and the "Northern Neighborhood," which is today the Town of Duck. While these numbers are impressive, in reality there were probably not more than 40 or 50 church members on the rolls at any one time over the 100-year period. There was however very high support for the church within the communities from non-members. In many households, only one adult was a church member, but usually the entire family turned out for church services. Both members and non-members provided lodging for visiting church guests, food for Union meetings, and donations for the upkeep of the meeting house and other church needs.

The popularity of the primitive Baptist religion began to decline in the late 19th and early 20th century. Coinjock Primitive Baptist Church closed sometime in the late 1800s and the last two members of Elim Baptist Church at Powells Point, Hillary Wilson Scarborough and Francis "Frank" Nixon Rogers, moved their membership to Kitty Hawk in May 1925. Providence Church also experienced the decline as the number of new members joining the church did not keep pace with the loss from the congregation of members dying or leaving the church for other reasons. At the time of the Kehukee Association annual session in Kitty Hawk in 1951, Providence Church registered 28 members and that total dropped to the mid-teens in the 1970s. By 1999 there were only two members on the church rolls, Mrs. Nellie G. Perry and Mr. Troy G. Shepard. The last church service at the Providence Baptist Church occurred on May 16, 1999. Elder Henry Jones continued to service the church at meetings in Mr. Troy Shepard's home until Mr. Shepard died in June 2001. Mrs. Nellie Perry, the sole remaining member of the Providence Baptist Church, asked for a home in the Skewarkey Primitive Baptist Church, Williamston, North Carolina, and was accepted in membership.

For 140 years, Providence Baptist Church has served the spiritual needs of Baptist in Kitty Hawk and neighboring areas. For many of those early years it was the most popular church in the area and undoubtedly the social center of the community. Its members extended a hand of friendship and hospitality to visiting Baptist at Union meetings in Kitty Hawk and were likewise received when they visited churches in other communities. But like so many of its sister churches within the Kehukee Association, and across the nation, the primitive Baptist religion could not sustain a congregation to maintain the church. An important cultural element of Kitty Hawk's history came to an end in 2001.

Chapter Seven

METHODISTS

The Growth of the Methodist Church from the 1800s to Present Day

Very little is known about early Methodist activities in the Kitty Hawk community as there are no records at the church on its history, at the Elizabeth City Superintendent's Office or in the Raleigh office of the North Carolina Methodist Conference. When contacted, each office reported that "according to local information the church was established in 1858." Even the Virginia Conference, in which all northeastern North Carolina Methodist churches were members until 1890, has no archival records of the Kitty Hawk church. Maybe there was less formality and record keeping in the early days of the Methodist movement when churches were formed in backcountry isolated areas at the edge of the wilderness.

The Baptist, Presbyterians, Protestant Episcopalians, and Quakers were all well established and long active before John Wesley founded Methodism in England in 1739. Methodism grew rapidly in England and spread with immigration to America in the mid-1700s. As the number of Methodist grew in the colonies their need for organization, structure and encouragement was apparent and at their request John Wesley sent two preachers (Richard Boardman and Joseph Pilmore) from England to America in 1769. The preachers worked principally in New York and Philadelphia and neighboring areas organizing Methodist Societies.

In late summer of 1772 Reverend Joseph Pilmore, while working with the Methodists in Norfolk, took the opportunity to visit northeastern North Carolina. On Sept 28, 1772, he preached a sermon at the Currituck Court House, probably the first Methodist sermon delivered in North Carolina. The following year he traveled overland through eastern North Carolina from Norfolk to Charleston and preached whenever there was a gathering. He used the tour to deliver the gospel, to observe the distribution of the population and assess the opportunities for the spread of Methodism in the region.

The first Conference of Methodist leaders in America was held in Philadelphia in June 1773. An important outcome of that meeting was the appointment of preachers in New York, Philadelphia, New Jersey, Baltimore, Petersburg, and Norfolk. Similar appointments were made at annual conferences in subsequent years for the seaboard colonies south to Virginia.

Of importance for the Methodists of North Carolina, and the origin of their history, was the formation of the "Carolina Circuit" at the General Conference in Baltimore in May of 1776. The new circuit was huge; stretching from the Atlantic Ocean on the east across what became the States of North Carolina and Tennessee to the Mississippi River in the west. At the time of its formation, there were no Methodist preachers working this new circuit although there were a reported 683 Methodists scattered across the region. The Conference appointed three seasoned and able preachers to serve the circuit; Edward Drumgoole for the eastern counties, Francis Poythress in central Carolina and Isham Tatum for the western section. Within a few short years, the Carolina Circuit began to be subdivided into smaller circuits. In 1783 the "Camden Circuit," of which Perquimans, Pasquotank, Camden, Currituck and Chowan counties were parts, was formed. It was renamed "Camden and Banks Circuit" some years later, probably to reflect additional responsibilities of the itinerant preachers working the circuit, and then the name was changed back to Camden Circuit a few years later.

The Treaty of Paris in 1783 ended the American Revolutionary War and recognized the national sovereignty of the United States. With America an independent nation, John Wesley believed that the Methodists of America should be independent from England as well and ordained and appointed Dr. Thomas Coke as head of Methodism in America to affect the change. Coke in turn ordained Francis Asbury after he arrived in America. At the General Conference in Baltimore in 1784, Methodist preachers throughout the nation formed the Methodist Episcopal Church in the New World. Both Coke and Asbury were elected Bishops for the new church.

In the early Carolina Circuit days, the itinerant preachers were from England, Scotland, or Ireland and had worked with John Wesley, or had been circuit preachers in one of the Methodist conferences in America. As Methodism flourished in America, native sons picked up the mantle and chose to be itinerant preachers. Some no more than 19 years of age though most were in their early 20s were given a license to preach and assigned a circuit. On their horse with only their saddle bags, a Bible and a hymnal, they trotted off in the wilderness to save souls and gain converts. At $64.00 a year, if they received their pay at all, they accepted their assignment and went forward. These "soldiers of the cross," as they were affectionately called by the true believers, covered every community, hamlet, crossroad, and neighborhood in their circuit and preached the gospel at every opportunity. When they had covered their circuit thoroughly, they restarted their tour again and again as often as their time in the circuit allowed. Normally itinerants were assigned to a circuit for only a year and then reassigned, usually some distance away to replace another itinerant in another circuit who also was reassigned.

Life was not easy for itinerants. Northeastern North Carolina was an area of relative sparse population, poor roads with some through swamps, bridgeless creeks and rivers, broad sounds with limited transportation for horse and rider, and an environment that could be damp and cold in the winter and then hot, muggy, and hordes of mosquitoes in the warmer seasons. These early Methodist missionaries were strangers in a strange land and were unsure what reception they would get. Finding lodging and food was a constant problem for the preachers as they were totally dependent on the good will and generosity of the inhabitants of the area. It was not unusual, however, for an itinerant to sleep unfed in the woods overnight and hope for better accommodations at the next appointment.

It is unclear when Methodist circuit preachers started serving the barrier banks, but probably quite early since "Banks" was included in the circuit name, "Camden and Banks." A "Banks" circuit was later established for a short time, but then reunited within the Camden Circuit. The North Banks, of which Kitty Hawk was a part, should have been fertile territory for the early Methodist itinerant preachers, if the problem of transportation from the mainland could be managed. In the 1790 census, there were 43 families and 218 people living on the North Banks from Caffeys Inlet through Nags Head, including Colington Island. Another 67 families and over 300 people lived on Roanoke Island. There were no churches structures or active religious denominations in the area at the time.

Kitty Hawk must have been an appointment for the circuit rider in the early days. Two 1808 Currituck County deeds identified the "Methodist Road" as the east boundary of a tract of land that extended from the road to the sound. The names of the adjoining landowners and the property description suggest the tract was on the sound side some distance north of Sound Landing in the Up-The-Road community of Kitty Hawk. Methodist Road was probably the old road which ran from the main Kitty Hawk road near the Austin Cemetery north to the end of Martins Point. The dirt road was used until the new paved road was constructed from the Wright Memorial Bridge to beach in the early 1930s.

Why the road was named "Methodist Road" is a mystery. There were no families living along the road and the people in the Up-the-Road community were mostly of the Baptist faith. The name "Methodist Road" did not appear in any other document after 1808. The road today is commonly known as "Ridge Road." A possible explanation of the name may be that the Methodist itinerant preachers used it to enter the village after coming over from the mainland to the Willis Gallop plantation at Martins Point. Willis Gallop was a man of considerable means, farming both the Martins Point peninsula and land on the Currituck County mainland. His operation probably included boats to ferry supplies, equipment, livestock and personnel between the two locations. He may very well have provided transportation to the itinerant preachers. His family was very active in the local Baptist church and his son, Hodges Gallop, was one of the founders and an Elder of the 1854 Providence Baptist Church in Kitty Hawk.

KITTY HAWK METHODIST CHURCH

Over time the Methodist itinerant ministers developed a following in Kitty Hawk, but mostly in the Down-the-Road community on the east side of the village. Tradition passed down by the congregation through the years has it that the Methodists of Kitty Hawk organized a church for the community in 1858; and that is probably correct even if documentation can not be located. They did not, however, build a meeting house until some years later. Even after the church was formed its members continued to be served by an itinerant preacher and met in private homes or in the open if the weather permitted. Between preacher's visits, lay members of the church family conducted prayer services, exhorted as they felt the urge and led the hymnal singing for the congregation.

On March 8, 1869, Soloman A. Baum, a native of Roanoke Island and a stock raiser in the Nags Head Township, conveyed by deed a one-acre piece of land in Kitty Hawk village to the Trustees of the Methodist Church for $1.00. The deed provided that the Trustees "shall build or cause to be built a house of worship to Almighty God for the use of the Methodist Episcopal Church South and if they should fail so to do in five years this deed is nul and void." Trustees listed in the deed included James Hobbs, Moses Delane, Benjamin Tillett, Dennis (Nichodemus) Best, Jessee Partridge, William Tate, and Truxton Twiford. Eliza Hobbs, Joseph M. Baum and Sophia D. Tate signed as witnesses to the deed and were also probably members of the church. The deed was registered June 15, 1869.

The Methodist trustees built their first meeting house in the village on their deeded land located on the main village road in a field just west of Mingoes Ridge Gut (Creek) near the Great Wading Place. Mattie Sanderlin Wescott, who wrote *A brief History Of The Kitty Hawk Methodist Church* in 1958, described the church as: "...of small dimensions, roughly about the size of the average neighborhood living room. Its frame was hand hewn, enclosed by vertically fastened foot-wide rough boards. The inside was unfinished and it was floored. The pews were long, wide boards resting on three upright blocks cut from a large log."

The site of the church in the field was subject to flooding during hurricane or strong northwest wind storms. In spite of these potential weather-related problems, the meetinghouse served the community for well over a decade.

By the mid 1880s, the church facility had outlived its usefulness and the congregation wanted a larger, nicer church building. Elijah Sibbern, who owned all the land around the first church and had land holdings elsewhere in the village offered the church trustees use of a ½ acre site on Mingoes Ridge on the main road about ¼ mile north east of their church. The ridge was not very wide but high enough to be above any storm tide that might flood the village. The deed for the property was not conveyed to the trustees until 1904, but on the good faith of the personal agreement with Elijah Sibbern the trustees commenced building the new church facility in 1887.

Captain James R. Hobbs, Keeper of the Kitty Hawk Life-Saving Service Station, supervised the construction while Thomas N. Sanderlin, a master carpenter, directed the community volunteer construction crew who had tools, knowledge of carpentry and time to work. The church structure was probably built during the summer of 1887 when the Life-Saving Service crews were discharged for the season.

Mattie Sanderlin Wescott's *History* reports: "This church was somewhat larger than the original one, approximately 24 x 36 feet and a very nicely constructed frame building. It was finished outside with horizontal siding painted white and inside with horizontal sheathing painted white with a medium blue ceiling and window trim. There were 9 windows. Three were in each side; two in the pulpit end, (one at each side of the pulpit) and one between the two front doors in the front end. An aisle led from each front door down to the pulpit. Long pews were in the center between the two aisles, and half-length pews on the opposite sides of the aisles and attached to the sidewalls. The pews were mill made. Four matching oil lamps were suspended from the ceiling. One hung over the pulpit, and the three others hung in line down the center of the room over the long pews. Four bracket oil lamps were on the sidewalls, one between each two windows." She also reported that: "The church's name was chosen as "Boaz" by

Captain Hobbs, inspired by a verse of the Scripture referring to King Solomon's Temple, which reads: 'and set up the left pillar, and called the name thereof Boaz' First Kings, 7th Chapter, 21st verse."

In 1888, shortly after the new church was built, the Methodist Conference assigned Reverend Sanderson Payne as the first pastor of the Boaz Methodist Episcopal Church South and served the four member Nags Head Methodist Church. Around 1900 the Kitty Hawk charge was enlarged to include Currituck Inlet Church, 30 miles north of Kitty Hawk, and the Methodist Church on Colington Island. In 1922 the

Currituck Inlet Church was withdrawn and Duck Methodist Church added to the charge. From 1943 to 1953, Mount Zion Methodist Church and Hebron Methodist Church on Currituck mainland were members of the Kitty Hawk charge. The Nags Head Church also dropped out in 1953, leaving the Kitty Hawk charge, later named the Outer Banks Parish, with only Kitty Hawk, Duck and Colington. The three churches each became independent with their own pastors in 1983.

Singing of hymns had always been an integral part of church services, even in the days when the itinerant preachers visited the communities on their regular circuit visits. In the early years of the church's history and for the first 15 years in the new Boaz Methodist Episcopal Church South, singing was without the benefit of musical accompaniment, but that changed after the turn of the 20th Century.

Again, Mattie Sanderlin Wescott's *History* reports: "In the year of 1902 the Ladies Aid Society of the church purchased by installment plan for the amount of $75.00 a used organ. This organ had the appearance of a small pipe organ, though the pipes were only ornamental." The first organist was Miss Nora L. Baum, assisted by her brother Elijah W. Baum. Following the purchase of the organ for two or more summers, the young people of the community took short courses in music reading, referred to as "singing school." Those musical courses of about 12 lessons each were taught by Mr. Ed Sowers, assisted by his daughter Bernie. Thus, the choir was born. The first choir director was Elijah W. Baum. The used pump organ had been in service in a church in Edenton, North Carolina, then purchased by the Steiff Piano Company of Elizabeth City, North Carolina, and in turn sold to the Ladies Aid Society of the Kitty Hawk church. Captain Franklin Harris Midgett, a church trustee and owner of the freight boat line operating between Kitty Hawk and Elizabeth City, arranged for the purchase and transportation of the organ. The organ was picked up in Elizabeth City in early September 1902 and loaded on Captain Harris' fifty-foot schooner, *Lou Willis*. Because the schooner's centerboard occupied space in the ship's hold and the vessel had a small hatch opening through the deck, the organ had to be lashed on the main deck for transportation to Kitty Hawk. At Kitty Hawk the organ was off loaded, probably first on a barge and then to a pony drawn cart for the final trip to the church.

According to Truxton Midgett, son of Franklin Harris Midgett and mate on the *Lou Willis* and who helped with transporting the organ from Elizabeth City, the organ was first played in the church on September 3, 1902, at the wedding of Oliver O'Neal and Charlotte Midgett, a widower and widow. The organist was Nora Baum, a 15-year-old girl whose legs were too short to pump the pedals. She was assisted by an attendant who pumped a handle on the side of the organ so that she could play. Nora eventually grew to the task and continued as the church organist for well over 50 years. The original organ was later replaced and loaned to the Colington Methodist Church, returned to Kitty Hawk and sold or given to a church in Nags Head. From records in the church files the organ was sold in 1964 by the Nags Head church to a private individual.

The Boaz church was reasonably new when the church members and trustees realized its size was inadequate to support the needs of the congregation. Over the years, the church had experienced an increase in membership, had commenced a church choir and youth musical training programs, and had emerging programs such as the Ladies Aid Society and regular Sunday School classes. The church trustees could not move forward with expanding plans until they had a clear title to the land, which they finally secured in 1904.

Elijah Sibbern had permitted the Trustees of the church to build on a ½ acre lot on Mingoes Ridge in 1887 but had not formally conveyed the property by deed to the church. On January 16, 1904, that transfer was formalized by deed: "Witnesses that for and in consideration of the sum of $1.00 One Dollar to him paid the receipt of which is hereby acknowledged and in further consideration of a certain piece of land deeded to the said Elijah Sibbern by the above named Trustees, the

Elijah Sibbern

said Elijah Sibbern has given, granted and sold and by these present doth give, grant, bargain & sell unto the said F. H. Midgett, T. N. Sanderlin and Edward O'Neal, Trustee, as aforesaid and their successors in office a certain lot or parcel of land being in the State and County aforesaid in Atlantic Township bounded as follows: Bounded on all sides by the lands of James R. Best having a log wood post set in the ground at each corner containing one half acre upon which the said Boaz Methodist Church now stands." In effect, the church purchased the ½ acre site of the Boaz Methodist Church for $1.00 and the conveying to Elijah Sibbern of the 1-acre site that Soloman A. Baum had given them in 1869. Clearing title to the land was important to allow the church to improve their facilities.

The trustees authorized an enlargement of the church building in 1905. A 45 by 25-foot addition, which was slightly larger than the original structure, was added to the south or pulpit end of the building and formed a "T" shaped structure to the church. It was constructed and finished to match the original structure, both inside and outside. Doors were provided in the south end of the sanctuary to access the new addition and a raised platform was built at the right of the pulpit for the seating of the new church choir. The new construction, as well as the remodeling, was undoubtedly performed by volunteer congregation labor again under the leadership of Thomas Nelson Sanderlin.

Boaz Methodist Church, seen here with the 1905 addition attached in the background, and land cleared.

The church with its new addition served the congregation well without additional remodeling for the next 30 years, but by the mid 1930s a new church to replace one that was over 50 years of age was needed. Although the country was just beginning to show signs of recovery from the Great Depression, it was still an uncertain time for the 86-member church to take on such a project. However, they were eager for a new church building and up to the challenge.

The new church was scheduled to be erected on the site of the old one, but since that lot was only ½ acre the old building had to be removed before its replacement could be built. With the disruption caused by construction the congregation would be without a church for worship. To meet this need church Board of Trustees arranged with the local School Committee the use of the Kitty Hawk School auditorium for services. Making these arrangements was probably not difficult since some church Board members were also on the local School Committees.

Rev. Matt. Ransom Gardner, a native of Goldsboro, North Carolina, was assigned as a "Supply Pastor" to the Boaz Methodist Episcopal Church South at Kitty Hawk in 1935. It was his first pastorship and he was undoubtedly "admitted on trial." His trial admission was apparently successful because in 1936 he joined the North Carolina Methodist Conference and was designated the Pastor-in-Charge of the Kitty Hawk church.

His arrival in Kitty Hawk apparently coincided with the Board of Trustees decision to build a new church. Church member Jesse Etheridge Baum, Jr., a local general store merchant, offered $200 donation to the new church building fund. He was promptly appointed to the Building Committee and named its chairman. Mrs. Nellie Caldwell, Mrs. Mary F. Best, Mr. Elsworth J. Baum, Mr. Edward N. Baum and Mr. Elijah W. Baum were also appointed to complete the committee.

The church did not have a building fund reserve so fund raising was one of the first orders of business for the new committee. The fund-raising program allowed for basically three types of gifts: building fund, furniture, and hymnals. Over time they expanded the appeal to include donations of labor, sale of salvageable materials, sponsorship of church windows, and contribution to a church bell. In addition to donations from church members, contributions were received from many former church members, former residents of Kitty Hawk, non-Methodist including staunch Primitive Baptist in the community, residents of Colington Island and Duck, community leaders throughout Dare County, businessmen in Elizabeth City, and individuals who simply wanted to support the congregation. To encourage beach summer residents to participate, Mrs. Rosaline Hayman Swain, her daughter, Mrs. Oma Pearl DeLaune Tillett, and Mrs. Gardner, the Pastor's wife, canvassed the beach community for donations to the building fund and the church bell. Reverend Gardner personally canvassed his friends, family and associates in his home town of Goldsboro, NC, for funding for church furnishings. Most, if not all the furnishings for the new church came from this unselfish effort. Donations were also received from Methodist churches in Goldsboro, Wilmington, Henderson, and Elizabeth City. The fund-raising program proved successful and with a contribution from the Duke Endowment Fund, the building committee met its objectives.

Removal of the old Boaz church commenced in May 1938 and was completed within a month. Some materials were salvaged for reuse in the new structure and some sold publicly. The new church was designed by Architect H. N. Haines of Durham, N. C., with the Duke Endowment who also served as project supervisor for the construction. Construction of the new church commenced June 13, 1938. Elijah W. Baum was head carpenter with Adolphus Lee Hines his principal back-up. William "Will" M. Midgett and Andrew J. Scarborough also worked as carpenters some of the time. Most of the other local workers during the construction were listed as laborers, although they undoubtedly did much of the carpentry work as well. A brick mason crew headed by Irvin and Leon Overton were brought in to lay the brick for the church. The visiting crew boarded with Mrs. Mary M. Best, while electrician P. H. Watson and gutter worker Ray Tillett boarded at the Carlos Dowdy home. The church paid all boarding fees. Holland Furnace Company furnished and installed the furnace for the new church.

A new feature, which the Boaz church did not have, was a church bell to call the congregation to worship. The Building Committee arranged to purchase a surplus bell from the First Methodist Church in Elizabeth City. The bell's history is unknown but it probably served in the 19th century Elizabeth City First Methodist Church building which was replaced in 1922. The price of $250.00 for the used bell was probably considered a good buy compared to what the committee might have had to pay for a new cast iron bell.

When completed the church had cost about $9,500, of which the Duke Endowment Fund had provided about half the cost.

Seated at the Kitty Hawk Methodist Church - Front row- Bill Harris, Edna B. Harris, Roy Harris. Row 2-Tommy Sande-lin, Hettie Baum, Nora Baum, & unknown parishioner

In addition to the main sanctuary, the new brick veneer church had electrical service, a warm air heating plant in the basement, a tall spire and belfry for the bell, new oak furniture, four class rooms and a pastor's study. It was the first brick church in Dare County and one of the few brick churches in rural North Carolina at the time. The first service in the new structure was held November 13, 1938, just five months after construction began. Dr. D. E. Earnhardt, President of Louisburg College, delivered the first sermon and Bishop Clare Purcell of Charlotte, N. C., and Presiding Elder Rev. B. B. Slaughter were in attendance. The church's Ladies Aid Society served chicken dinner on the grounds.

While the first service in the new church was in November 1938, the new facility was not formally dedicated until November 25, 1939, a year later. At that service, Dr. J. M. Ormond, School of Religion, Duke University, Durham, N. C., delivered the dedicatory sermon. Methodist District Superintendent Rev. B. B. Slaughter, outgoing Pastor Rev. Matt. R. Gardner and incoming

Pastor Rev. Thomas Merriman participated in the dedication. In his final building committee report Reverend Matt. Ransom Gardner offered these remarks:

May God bless this church to stand for many years and grant that the full Gospel of our Lord and Savior Jesus Christ may be so faithfully taught and preached in the power of the blessed Holy Ghost that many souls will be saved and edified. May the grace and love of Christ so fill the hearts of this people that they will obediently serve God and greatly advance the Kingdom of God. In Christ's name and for the Glory of God.
    -Matt. Ransom Gardner

The new Kitty Hawk Methodist Church was the pride of the congregation, and the only brick structure in the community. By local standards, with a warm air furnace, electricity, and new furnishings, it was the most modern building as well, even though it lacked restroom facilities. In size, however, it was probably not much larger than the wooden Boaz church structure it replaced.

The Kitty Hawk Methodist Church experienced a sizable increase in membership starting in the late 1930s and continuing into the 1950s, and undoubtedly an increase in attendance. It soon became apparent that the church needed to be expanded to accommodate the needs of its ever-increasing congregation. Mrs. Fanny Brothers Perry's Intermediate Sunday School Class of teenagers was the first to act on the expansion program. In 1953 her class

Elijah Baum served as head carpenter for the education building. He worked as carpenter at the Wright Bros. site as well.

initiated a building fund drive for an Education Building addition and at Christmas presented the church with an $18.00 donation toward the program. The Church Trustees appointed Mrs. Perry as the Secretary-Treasurer for the building fund on the Board of Stewards. The fund-raising program was off and running and for the next several years church membership actively sought donations toward the Education Building fund. By 1958 the fund had grown to $22,000, work pledges of $5,000 were committed, and a grant from the Duke Endowment Fund of $5,000 received for the project. The Board of Trustees were satisfied that they could raise the remaining funds or arrange funding for the $50,000 project. They authorized a ground-breaking ceremony at the site during the church's 100th Anniversary services on October 25, 1958. The cornerstone was laid a month later when construction began. As with the construction of the brick church in 1937, Elijah W. Baum was appointed head carpenter to supervise the project and direct the work of both the paid and volunteer workers. Bishop Paul N. Garber and District Superintendent Robert L. Jerome formally dedicated the new Education Building in 1960.

The 1958 Kitty Hawk Methodist Church Centennial was a grand affair which occurred over two days, Saturday, October 25th, and Sunday, October 26th. The centennial planning board, chaired by Mrs. Josephine Partridge Twiford, billed it as two days of "worship, fellowship, and spiritual gratitude." For some visiting guests, it was a homecoming to the church that nourished their youth.

Kitty Hawk United Methodist Church, 1960.

Saturday was a day of fun, food and fellowship. Basketball, baseball and children's games were scheduled at the Kitty Hawk School playground. Horseshoes and "Spin-A-Hoop Contest" were offered on the church grounds, as was a midday lunch and an evening fish fry. A special Homecoming Convention was held from 2:00 to 4:00 p.m. Saturday at the church with Rev. Louis A. Aitken from the Manteo Methodist Church as guest speaker. The Educational Building Committee reported on funding progress to date. Saturday's program ended in the evening with community and folk singing and vesper service.

Sunday's activities were more in line with traditional church services with a Sunday School hour, Morning Worship and an afternoon Memorial Service. A chicken dinner on the grounds was served to the congregation and visitors following the morning services.

Dr. C. W. Robbins, President, Louisburg College, Dr. Vergil E. Queen, pastor First Methodist Church in Elizabeth City, and District Superintendent Rev. C. Freeman Heath, were special guest's speakers for the day's activities. The centennial program concluded with a Communion by Candle Light Service Sunday evening.

The Methodist parsonage in 1964, next door to the church.

In 1953 the trustees of the church purchased from Mrs. Mary M. Best 210 feet by 26 feet strip of land between the church's west boundary and the Jessie E. Baum tract. This was the first land purchase since the church originally acquired the ½ acre church site from Elijah Sibbern in 1904. The trustees acquired additional lands east of the church property in 1963 from Clavis Wyatt and Buena H. Baum and in 1976 from Francis D. and Elizabeth P. Hemilright to increase the church campus to 2 ½ acres, as it is today. A parsonage was built on the former Baum track in 1964.

In 1973, for the second time in its history, the church lost a major church facility to fire. The first fire destroyed the church parsonage in April 1928; the second in 1973 destroyed the 1937 built church.

Rev. William S. "Willie" Teague had moved his family into the parsonage next to the church on June 14, 1973, and retired for the evening after a very busy day. He was looking forward to his new pastorship and charge. A little after midnight the family dog's barking aroused Rev. Teague who arose to investigate the cause of the dog's agitation. He smelled something burning and then saw smoke coming out of the roof of the church building next door. He immediately called the Kitty Hawk Volunteer Fire Department who responded within five minutes. The fire was well advanced by the time the volunteers arrived and Fire Chief Sidney

Toler summoned assistance from the Kill Devil Hills, Nags Head, and Manteo fire departments. In all 125 firemen fought the blaze and while the main church building was destroyed the firemen did manage to save the Educational Building addition, though it sustained some heat, smoke and water damage.

With the loss of the sanctuary and damage to the Educational Building, the church Trustees had to act quickly to provide for continuing church services. The June 17th service, just a day and a half after the fire, was held at The Circus Tent, a summer Christian outreach program the Kitty Hawk United Methodist Church has sponsored since 1968. An alternative site for church services was soon found through the cooperation of Jap Richardson at the Colony House movie theater. In the meantime, work commenced on repairing the Educational Building while congregation volunteers helped with cleaning the building and its furnishings of smoke and water damage. With repairs and cleaning completed, church services were moved to the Educational Building although the cramped quarters were not ideal.

The Kitty Hawk Methodist Church after the fire. The nave and sanctuary were completely destroyed, with the roof caving in during the fire.

Replacing the burned-out church was more of a challenge than originally expected. Initially, the Methodist Conference strongly recommended that the Trustees seek a new church location with a minimum 5-acre campus for current and future expansion needs. A committee was appointed to seek a location and reported back that a site near the Kitty Hawk Elementary School in Southern Shores would meet the requirements and could be acquired. The Trustees, most of whom who had grown up in the old church, studied the report but voted to keep the church in the village rather than move it 2 miles north of the community.

The architect retained by the Conference to assist the church with architectural drawing submitted a plan that was considerably more modern in appearance than the old church structure. Some in the congregation wanted a larger structure but also wanted to retain the appearance of the old church. After much consideration, the Trustees accepted the architect's design and received architectural drawing for the new structure.

The Conference recommended that the Trustees offer the building for a bidder's contract, but again the Trustees stepped in and elected to have the church built on a cost-plus basis by a local builder, as they had done on all previous church construction. Builder Shelby Hines was selected for the construction and retired U. S. Coast Guard Chief Warrant Officer, Clavis Wyatt Baum, a master carpenter and church member, offered his services to the building team. Construction commenced and proceeded on schedule.

The new $225,000 church was finished and dedicated July 27, 1975. An insurance policy of $100,000 on the former church initiated the building fund and a Duke Endowment helped support the construction cost, but individual contributions from members and church friends as well as businesses in the area, plus many types of fund raisers by the congregation secured the completion of the project. Bishop Robert M. Blackburn formally dedicated the new sanctuary on January 17, 1977, and delivered a Certificate of Dedication, signifying the sanctuary free of all debt.

The Kitty Hawk United Methodist Church was once again fully serving the village and the larger beach communities.

During the period from the mid 1960s to the present, the beach communities and the older Outer Banks established villages experienced an increase in population due to the influx of retirees and service personnel to support their needs. Likewise, an increase in church attendance and membership followed. Although the new Kitty Hawk United Methodist Church sanctuary was larger than the one it replaced, the remainder of the church facility still dated from the needs as seen in late 1950s. It soon became apparent that the new church needed more classrooms and service areas. Accordingly, the Trustees authorized another expansion of the church and a Fellowship Hall was constructed in 1985 to meet the ever-increasing needs of the congregation. Otis Meekins, a Chesapeake, Va., architect, designed the addition and Wimco Corporation of Washington, NC, was the construction contractor for the $295,322 expansion. The Fellowship Hall was the last major construction project for the Kitty Hawk United Methodist Church facility although in time other construction needs will undoubtedly be identified and undertaken.

Chapter Eight

THE PARSONAGE

How The Methodists Provided a Home for their Pastors

The residents of Kitty Hawk have had a long history of sharing their homes with boarders, particularly with teachers who had come to the community to work. When those workers had families, it was difficult if not impossible to provide that same level of support and living accommodations. Such was the case for pastors who came to the Kitty Hawk Charge; there simply were not many if any vacant homes for the pastor, or the church, to rent for short time use. Realizing this difficulty, Captain James R. Hobbs and his wife Eliza Murphy Hobbs donate a lot at what is now the southeast corner of West Kitty Hawk and Moore Shore Roads "for the use and benefit of a site for a parsonage in Kitty Hawk Mission." T. N. Sanderlin, F. H. Midgett and Edward O'Neal, trustees for the Methodist Episcopal Church South in Kitty Hawk, accepted the gift on July 1, 1896. J. A. Ketcham, B. J. Hines, and M. L. Sanderlin were deed witnesses.

Building a parsonage in Kitty Hawk had some practical advantages for the community. Kitty Hawk had by far the largest population of Methodist on the North Banks and the church needed and could support an assigned pastor. Having a parsonage greatly facilitated the placement of a pastor in the community when rental accommodations were all but non-existent. Although the pastor may be assigned to serve other churches in his charge, by living in the village he would more often be at or near his residence instead of at one of the other churches or neighborhoods. It was a good deal for the Kitty Hawk church community to provide their pastor with a parsonage.

The trustees built a parsonage on the property donated by the Hobbses, which Mattie Sanderlin Wescott described in her church history as:… "L shaped. A front porch extended down the west side its full length. A center hall opened from the front porch and led through to a back porch which extended eastward along the north side of the back wing of the house. The dining room and kitchen opened on the porch. On the left of the center hall was a living room, on the right was a bedroom, and leading from it was a second floor consisting of two bedrooms." The furnishings of the parsonage were a gift from Mrs. Hannah Lyons. The same team of builders who built the second church also built the parsonage under the same working arrangement. Three Lyons sisters from Asbury Park, New Jersey, had purchased the Gallop property on the Banks in 1893 as a vacation site. The property extended from Kitty Hawk village north to the "Northern Neighborhood" (Duck), all of what is today the Town of Southern Shores and the Martins Point peninsula, the sisters apparently got to know their new neighbors very soon after they purchased the property and because they were people of some financial means the Lyons assisted the local people in their community projects. The Lyons women are known to have provided the kerosene lamps and chandeliers for the Providence Baptist church in the Up-the-Road community when it was built in 1898. They may also have furnished the kerosene lamps for the Boaz Methodist Church, though that has not been documented.

The 1928 Tate Home and Methodist parsonage.

In 1919 the Kitty Hawk church had the opportunity to improve their church property by purchase the William J. Tate home place on Moore Shore Road. Both the Tate home and the parsonage were of the same approximate age, but the Tate home was much larger and included 3 acres rather that the one quarter acre at the existing parsonage. With the blessing of the congregation Church Trustees, F. H. Midgett, Fields O'Neal and T. N. Sanderlin, concluded the purchase of the Tate place for $800.00. The deed was registered on September 14, 1920.

The "Kitty Hawk Circuit Parsonage of the M. E. Church South", which was the Hobbs donated property and first parsonage site, was sold to James Raleigh Best for $10.00, and registered June 2, 1920. It was reported, but not documented, that lumber salvaged from the original parsonage building was used in the construction of the Baum and Baum Store, which was built that year in the village diagonally across from the Methodist Church.

In 1927 the citizens of Kitty Hawk decided to erect a monument to Wilbur and Orville Wright in the front yard of the parsonage where Wilbur Wright had begun the assembly of his 1900 glider while living with the Tates. This monument would be the first marker erected in America to the Wright brothers and would be a testament to the brothers of the community's appreciation of them and for the fame they had brought to Kitty Hawk. Dedication of the monument was set for May 2, 1928. On April 7, 1928, in preparation for the event, Rev. W. A. Betts and his two sons, Bill and Henry, started clearing the weeds, briars and brush from around the property and the monument site. They piled the vegetation debris in a heap and set it afire. Unfortunately, cinders from the fire ignited the parsonage and burned it to the ground. In short order the church lost its parsonage with its furnishings, whatever church records were in the building, and possibly their communion set. Reverent Betts and his family lost everything, including his personal religious library and genealogical files. The community quickly removed the fire debris from the site and the monument dedication ceremonies went on as planned.

Soon after the fire the church moved forward with building a replacement parsonage. Funds for the new parsonage were received from people in the community, Elizabeth City merchants, Duke Endowment Fund, and individuals who wanted to assist the church. Elijah W. Baum, a devoted member of the church and a Kitty Hawk merchant, led the construction crew and had the parsonage finished by the end of 1928, the year of the fire.

The rebuilt 1929 parsonage with the Wright monument in front.

The new parsonage on Moore Shore Road served the church needs for the next 36 years, until it was replaced by a new brick parsonage on land adjacent to the church in 1964. The 1964 single story ranch style parsonage was planned and designed by Edgar Perry, a church Trustee, and Shelby Hines. The Board of Trustees approved the sketch plans and asked Shelby Hines and his crew to build the new parsonage. It was built on a cost-plus basis.

The old parsonage and property were sold to Nellie C. Van Vleek for "...ONE HUNDRED ($100.00) DOLLARS and other good and valuable consideration..." Trustees for the Kitty Hawk Methodist Church signing the deed selling the parsonage included: Hallet F. Perry, Jesse E. Baum, Herbert Van Vleek, Jackson S. Twiford, Carlos C. Dowdy, and Maxine T. Evans. Since the Colington Methodist Church and the Grace Methodist Church of

156

Duck were parties in the Kitty Hawk charge their trustees signed the deed as well. Trustees signing for the Colington Church were Charles Beasley, Henry Dean Haywood, Fred Haywood and Manie Haywood. Andrew J. Scarborough, Elmo Whitson, Solomon Whitson, Sam D. Tate, P. A. Tillett and Emmanuel "Hap" Santo signed for the Grace Methodist Church. The financial note for the 1964 parsonage was formally retired in a 'Note Burning" ceremony in front of the new parsonage in 1981.

The 1964 parsonage building was a vast improvement over the 1928 constructed building, but the 1928 building has also been an improvement over the earlier Tate house parsonage which was probably constructed in the mid 1890s. Both earlier structures were built during periods when there was no electrical service in the community and thus no running water or bathrooms in the residences, insulation of the building was an amenity to be realized in the future, and closets were not a personal requirement when movable clothes hampers could accommodate the minimum wardrobe of the residents. These early buildings lacked many of the amenities we take for granted today, but for their time they were standard accommodations, at least in this community.

Constructing the 1964 parsonage on the campus grounds next to the main church seemed an appropriate action for the trustees. It was certainly convenient for the pastor to be next door to his church and only a short walk to the sanctuary. However, over time the closeness of the parsonage to the church proved to be an inconvenience for the pastor and his family. It was too easy for someone to pop in on the preacher for an unscheduled meeting, or simply to ask for the keys to the sanctuary. The location also limited the pastor and his family their personal privacy. It was not a desirable situation.

The North Carolina Methodist Conference also recognized that across the state there were many problems with housing for pastors and no standards to address the problems. Providing housing for pastors was a critical need for recruiting, assigning and retaining pastors. The Conference considered its responsibilities in this area and developed standards that would apply to new housing. The Kitty Hawk United Methodist Church trustees acknowledged the need to improve their pastor's housing and began the process of securing better housing. A new parsonage residence was built in Southern Shores in 1990 and the 1964 brick parsonage building next to the church was designated to serve as the Church Office.

Having a parsonage for their preachers has served the community well over the years and reflects the foresight of the early church leadership in providing this very necessary service in support of the church.

Chapter Nine

SANCTIFIED

The Traveling Sanctified Holy Church Visits Kitty Hawk

For about 4 weeks in the late summers of 1896 and again in 1897, members of the Christ's Sanctified Holy Church of Camden County, NC, came to Kitty Hawk to share their religious beliefs and experiences and to spread the message of sanctification. They arrived in a sailboat towing a flat barge with a house on the deck, which they called, "The Ark", or "the float house," or simply "the float." The housing portion of the float was built on a barge of approximately 20 feet by 40 feet in size and covered most of the deck. It was one big open room which could serve as a church tabernacle, but removable partitions were provided to allow for a few individual rooms for privacy. Some church members slept aboard the sailboat but others shared the living space on the float house.

The Christ's Sanctified Holy Church was formed at Chincoteague, Virginia, in February 1892. Its initial membership was almost exclusively from the Chincoteague Methodist Episcopal Church congregation. That membership had become disillusioned by the new direction and "modernization" of Methodism in general and especially the leadership provided by the district conference office. The congregation was incensed when the conference bishop rejected their signed petition to replace their church minister, who they considered an unholy man. The bishop not only rejected the petition but removed all 52 petition signers from any leadership role in the church. The rejected petitioners walked out of the church to seek religious satisfaction from another source.

Joseph Lynch had held a long-term belief, which he shared with others that the only path to salvation was through the blessing of Sanctification by the power of the Holy Ghost. As a leader of the petitioners who left the church, his views were soon endorsed by others and became the guiding principle for the new religious sect who established the first Christ's Sanctified Holy Church. The church installed Lynch as its first minister.

The Sanctified Church attracted a good following very early on in its history, but Chincoteague Island was a comparatively small island with a limited population and at least three other protestant churches to support. The Sanctifieds looked for additional audiences and soon were traveling back to their former home towns and communities throughout the Eastern Shores of Virginia, Maryland and Delaware. They also reached out to settlements around the Chesapeake Bay and its tributaries. By splitting their congregation into smaller units they could cover more territory and contact a greater number of potential members.

By 1895 the Sanctifieds had expanded their range of contacts and had reached Eastern North Carolina. To accommodate their ever-growing numbers of travelers, they had a couple of float houses built in Elizabeth City and made the town their base of operation for a few years. From there they could easily travel the Albemarle and Currituck Sounds to Cannon's Ferry, South Creek, Powell's Point, Nixonton, Old Trap, Jarvisburg, and other waterfront communities. The villages of Kitty Hawk, Colington and Duck were also visited, but not as regularly as the others.

The Sanctified church had its best successes in attracting new members in North Carolina from its work with the people of Camden County, especially those from the Old Trap community. Leary, Forbes, Riggs, Parker, Burgess, and Needham, all popular Camden County family names, are just a few of the families they attracted and the family names that were appearing most frequently in the early history of the Sanctified church. The Sanctifieds also attracted followers from Currituck County who joined with their Camden neighbors and traveled with the main Church body as it moved south into South Carolina, Georgia, Florida, Alabama and Louisiana. Many of these members stayed on and traveled with the group as it moved further west to

Mississippi, Kansas, Texas, and even Colorado and California. After much wandering the Sanctifieds finally settled in Perry, Georgia, in 1938 as their permanent home.

Typically, when the Sanctifieds arrived at the place where they had planned to offer their services, they took advantage of any location to preach; be it a street corner, school house, store building, city park, courthouse, mission hall or any other building they were allowed to use or even a private home if that was the only choice. If there were no accommodations, they used the tabernacle of the float house.

In the 1890s Kitty Hawk was one of the largest villages in population on the Outer Banks, and surpassed some mainland Currituck County community totals. There were two churches in the community, a Methodist and a Primitive Baptist. A former residence served as the village school but there were no other public buildings in Kitty Hawk. Although there were wide gaps between the Methodist and Baptist regarding religious beliefs and practices, the two religious sects came together to share food and accommodations whenever either group was having any type of special services such as Union Meetings for the Baptist or revivals by the Methodist.

The community population appeared to be about evenly split between Methodist, Baptist and those unaffiliated with either church. The community probably welcomed the Sanctified with open arms since they did not pose a threat to community values, and besides, new visitors in the community represented a change from a rather routine rural lifestyle.

Resident Caleb Hobbs Toler is thought to have invited the Sanctifieds to Kitty Hawk. He was a young man with a young family of mostly pre-school aged children and was a leader in the community. How he contacted the Sanctifieds is unknown, but in rural America like northeastern North Carolina, everyone knew new people when they came in the area and certainly as soon as they entered the village. The Sanctifieds arrived in Kitty Hawk and set up their church operation at Poor Ridge Landing on the west side of Kitty Hawk Bay. Although the bay is a very large body of water it is basically shallow with the only deep-water channel into the village at the end of Poor Ridge. The church group of approximately 15-20 people arrived under the leadership of Joseph Lynch and Samuel Leary. Except for the churches and the lone school building, Kitty Hawk did not have any of the public places found in towns or cities, so their religious services had to be presented in an open field, at a private residence or on the float houses.

One of the Sanctified preachers when delivering his sermon on the float house liked to talk about Jesus "walking on water". To dramatize his presentation, he had a short wharf built with its surface just below the normal tide level. When he came to the part about "walking on water" he would step off the float and simulate walking across the surface of the water. It was an impressive presentation which punctuated his sermon and was enjoyed by the congregation. Some of the local boys, however, thought it would be funny if while "walking on water" the wharf gave way and the preacher was dunked into Kitty Hawk Bay. One night under the cloak of darkness, Fonnie Tillett and several of his boyhood friends got under the wharf and sawed a couple of stringers to the point where a person's weight would cause the structure to collapse. The next time the preacher presented his sermon of "walking on water" he had a wet experience before he could finish his presentation.

Depending on the opportunities available to them, the traveling Sanctified men would work in the community they visited. Kitty Hawk did not offer much in temporary work so the Church men fished the surrounding bays and sounds to support their ministry and families. Probably the women helped by tying and mending nets, but the daily feeding of 15 to 20 people was always an issue. The visiting traveling church members were well liked but they also had a very healthy appetite. Locals helped with food, but after a few days or weeks, the community food supply began to dwindle. Encouraging the group to move on was not a rejection of their religious message, but a need to return to normality in the community.

Weddings and funerals were part of the rituals practiced by the Christ's Sanctified Holy Church. As a demonstration of the acceptance of the Church in the community, Pastor Sarah Collins, who was one of the original church founders and the second pastor appointed to the church, performed marriage ceremonies for four Old Trap couples in 1895. The couples included Mary and Jordan Brown, Lou and Fred Forbes, Angie Bell and Evan Leary and Annie and Isaac Riggs.

Although there was no formal ceremony and the incidences of the occurrences probably somewhat exaggerated, the Sanctifieds did allow the practice of their members taking "Spiritual wives and husbands" while engaged in Sanctified events and in travel. In some cases, members in the group helped with selecting the "Spiritual companion" for the church member, but that did not always work out to their mutual satisfaction. On at least one occasion a woman was selected for a man but he rejected the choice since the woman was much older than he and did not have a tooth in her head!

While the Sanctifieds spent a couple of seasons in Kitty Hawk they apparently did not make much of a lasting impression on the community. It is not believed that anyone from Kitty Hawk joined the group or took a "Spiritual wife or husband" because of their visit. Without the memory of those few Kitty Hawkers who lived in the community around 1896-97 and saw the Sanctifieds in the village, their presence there would probably not even be a memory today.

Caleb Hobbs Toler and his wife Mandy. Toler is thought to have invited the Christ's Sanctified Holy Church to Kitty Hawk Village.

Section Four

A Side Trip Up And Down The Road

Chapter Ten

ROAD DAYS

The Locals Keep Up The Roads On Their Own

Until the state took over the public roads in 1931, the maintenance of roads within a community was a local responsibility. Work on public roads was performed by the resident males of the communities under the general supervision of a "Road Overseer." He was appointed by the county commissioners, and was responsible for deciding what work needed to be done, setting the time and place for the work, making sure that all scheduled people were present and accounted for, and working and supervising the work detail. In Kitty Hawk the overseer was sure to set the road work date for either June or July, when local Life-Saving Service personnel would be home from their station due to their seasonal break in service.

Except for road realignments, which had to be coordinated with landowners and constructed by the residents without State or county funds, annual road days were not complicated, nor necessarily time consuming. Generally, it involved removing encroaching vegetation, filling holes and washouts, removing roots in pathways and repairing bridges. In low areas with fill or across marshy areas or swamps, logs were laid parallel to the road to keep storm water runoff from eroding shoulders. At least one short section of a Kitty Hawk road across a very swampy area was a "corduroy road" with logs laid in the swamp to form a base to support fill for the driving surface. Regardless of the amount of work to be performed, the residents were responsible so the quality of their roads depended on their interest and work ethic. This community road maintenance system was a carry over from the early days of settlement. The colonial government required each able-bodied white freemen of sixteen years and older and all able-bodied slaves of twelve years and older to work one day a year on the public roads. After slavery was abolished, the law was changed to require each able-bodied man between the age of 18 and 45 to work one day a year on maintaining public roads. The law did allow for a scheduled worker to send a substitute if he could not be present on the assigned workday, and many a young son substituted for his father, and older men over 45 covered for a friend. Failure to show up for work without sending a substitute incurred a $1.00 fine.

In a series of 1960s interviews with Kitty Hawk old timers the men invariably mentioned the road days. Truxton E. Midgett recalled a humorous, if not very serious, incident concerning a substitute filling in on a scheduled road work day. Sometime in the 1890s Truxton Midgett's father, Franklin Harris Midgett, needed to be away from the village during the period of scheduled public road work. His sons were too young to substitute so he asked his best friend and step brother-in-law, George Washington Baum, to take his place. George Baum was over 45 and did not have to work for himself. He was in good health and still active in the U. S. Life-Saving Service. George agreed to be the substitute and Harris Midgett offered to pay him $1.00 for his services. The community roads were worked as scheduled.

When Harris Midgett returned to the village, he visited George Baum to pay him the promised $1.00, but George would only accept 50 cents. He told Harris that the crew had only worked one-half a day on the roads, thus he would only accept one-half the pay. Harris accepted the explanation and paid George fifty cents.

Sam Sutton, who was living and working in the village at that time, failed to show for the scheduled road work. Oliver O'Neal, as the road overseer went to see Mr. Sutton to advise him of the $1.00 fine for not appearing for work or sending a substitute. Sutton said to O'Neal, "Captain Midgett did not send a dollar, he sent a man and the man charged him fifty cents. He worked only half a day and everyone knew that. Now I will give you half-a-dollar." Oliver replied, "Mr. Sutton I can not do that and you know I can't. The law says if you don't come, you send a man or a dollar, and you didn't do either one, so I have to have a dollar." Sutton replied, "You won't get it!"

The men who had worked the roads were upset with Sam Sutton and advised Oliver O'Neal that if he did not collect the $1.00, or indict Sam, they would put the law on him. Finally, Oliver took the issue to court and won - and Sam Sutton paid his fine.

Many men served as road overseers in Kitty Hawk over the years, but a full record of their names or the times they served has not survived. The identity of a few overseers was, however, reported in the minutes of the Currituck County Court of Pleas and Quarters from 1799 to 1868, but absent in the Board of County Commissioners minutes after 1868. Dare County Commission minutes list some road overseers, but Kitty Hawk did not become a part of Dare County until 1920.

In the minutes of the August 28, 1804, Currituck County Court of Pleas and Quarters, the Court ordered "…that Asa Walker be appointed overseer of the publick road on the North Banks from Jaycoxes Beach to the head of Jane Gyte Creek and that he act therein agreeable to law." The location of Jaycoxes Beach is something of a mystery, though it may have been an early local name for Moore Shore. In its May 25, 1812, meeting the Court ordered "…that John Luark be appointed overseer of the public road on Kitty Hawk banks for the ensuing year in the room and stead of (instead of, or in place of) Asa Walker, the late overseer." Two years later, on June 2, 1814, John Luark was replaced by the Court when it "…ordered that Hugh Gallop be appointed overseer of the public road on Kitty Hawk, North Bank…in the room and stead of John Luark, the late overseer."

The public record does not indicate how long Hugh Gallop served as overseer, but on February 27, 1821, Edmond Best was "…appointed overseer of public road from Currituck Sound at John Partridge's to the main road." To the "main road" would be to the Sign Post at what is now the intersection of Twiford and Woods Roads. In the unusual and only such report in the minutes, there was a listing of the workers who formed the road crew with Edmond Best. They were: Frederick Perry, Joseph Best, Zebulon

Beacham, William Tillett, Thomas Gallop, Mathias Gallop, Elijah Wicker, Mathias Best, Urias Best, Jesse Best, and John Perry.

Two years later Thomas Curles was "...appointed overseer in the room of Elijah Wickeman (Wicker) of the road leading from J. Patridge, Esquire, to main road." In August 1824, William Simpson replaced Thomas Curles, who had died. Others served as road overseer in succeeding years including: Jehue Gamell (Gamiel), William Keys, Jasper Toller (Toler), Samuel Tillett, George W. Patridge (Partridge), Joseph B. Owens, Jackson Sanderlin, William Curls, Joseph Baum, and undoubtedly others not recorded.

Communities both north and south of Kitty Hawk had road overseers appointed by the Court of Pleas and Quarters. For Nags Head, James Hackett, Norris Baum, Louis Mann and Josiah H. Tillett, among others, served as road overseers between 1799 and 1868. To the north in what was known in early days as the "Northern Neighborhood" before the Postal Service established the Duck post office in 1909, many residents held the post of road overseer. Their assigned road was from Caffeys Inlet south to the Sign Post, or "Headquarters" as it was also known, on the main road in Kitty Hawk; today's Twiford and Woods Roads intersection. William Rogers, Joshua Gamewell, John Rogers, Robert Harris, Barnabee Beasley, James Brinson, Mashack Sawyer, George Stow, Willis Patridge (Partridge), Kimbly (Kimberly) Rodgers, and George Scarboro (Scarborough) were recorded in the minutes as being appointed as road overseer, but because of the small population of the area most of the men served more than once.

After Kitty Hawk became a part of Dare County in 1920 and before the State took over responsibilities for the roads, Zenith F. Perry, Callie Parker, Elijah W. Baum, William D. Rogers, William Ivey Dowdy, Cal Perry, Ezekiel D. Midgett, Clarence Beasley, Herbert L. Perry and undoubtedly others served as road overseers for various periods of times in the two Kitty Hawk communities of Up-The-Road and Down-The-Road.

The early original roads in Kitty Hawk apparently simply evolved over time rather than as a planned design. Probably, the roads followed the path of least resistance through the landscape, crossing waterways and swamps at their most narrow and shallow spots and traversing open fields and woods where passage would permit. Originally waterways were not bridged as evident by notations in early deeds to "the wading place," "the horse wading place," "the great wading place," and similar terminology. There is also a 1778 reference to a "...large lying down tree in the footway" over Northern Gut for foot traffic. References to wading places or footbridges did not occur in deeds after about 1820, which suggest that these wet areas had been bridged or otherwise improved for travel.

The early main road serving the northern Outer Banks started in the Nags Head community, proceeded north through Nags Head woods, passed west of the Kill Devil Hills, continued near the shores of Lemores Bay, a place name that has been lost to history, along Kitty Hawk Bay over what was later called the Moore Shore Road, and then entered Kitty Hawk village. The road proceeded through the village to the Sign Post. One branch of the road turned west to the Up-The-Road Kitty Hawk community and the main branch continued north towards the Northern Neighborhood.

Note map points refer to the four part map at the front of this book.

As could be expected, the road alignment through Kitty Hawk village today is not the same as it was originally - but there are more similarities than differences. The earliest map of Kitty Hawk was prepared as part of the U.S. Coast Survey, 1848-49. It shows the Kitty Hawk road system at that time with the road entering the village from the east at about where the current road crosses Bull Ridge Creek (map point A), just down the hill from the Catholic Church, proceeding west along the existing alignment across Kitty Hawk Ridge, which was called High Bridge at its intersection with Elijah Baum Road, and then to Mingoes Gut creek (map point B). The Mingoes Gut creek complex was a very extensive swamp and wetland area, which was called "the Great Wading Place" in early deeds. At Mingoes Gut the road turned south along the east bank of the gut over a corduroy road of logs for about 200 yards and then turned west, crossing the gut and proceeding along the south side of Elijah

Sibbern's open farm field. At the end of the field the road turned north along the west edge of the field and connects with what is today Midgett Road. At the north end of Midgett Road, where it intersects West Kitty Hawk Road (map point C), the village road turned west again and followed the present road alignment to Duck Pond Creek (map point D).

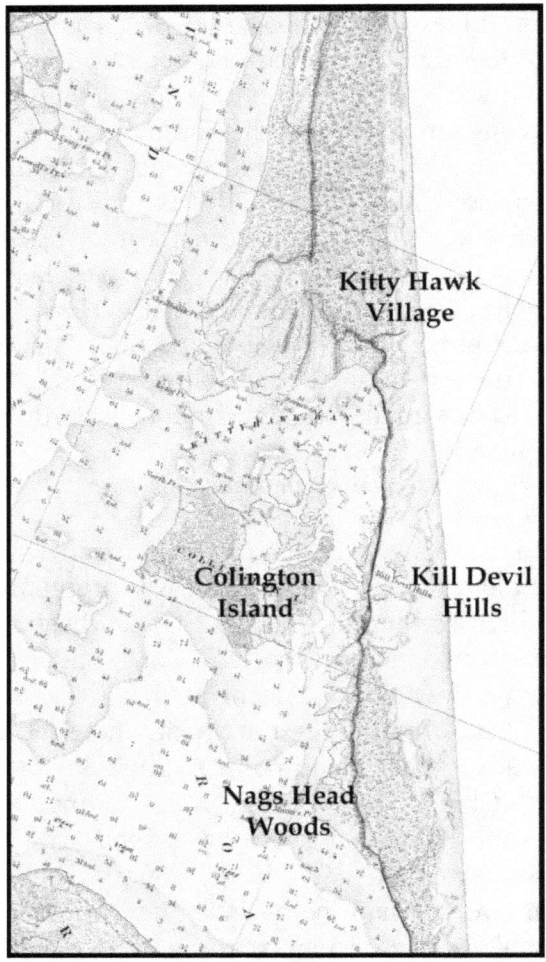

An 1860 map showing the original road system of the Outer Banks, running from Nags Head in the south, through Nags Head Woods, along the sound side of Kill Devil Hills, past Kitty Hawk Bay, and into Kitty Hawk Village. The village roads would link up to a wooded road running north into Duck.

The early road forked just east of Duck Pond Creek with the left fork proceeding west across the creek and then turning south down Poor Ridge (map point E), though it was not called Poor Ridge until the 1870s. The right fork proceeded on the current alignment to the Sign Post (map point F), where it forked again. The right fork continued north to the other communities on the North Banks (map point G), while the left fork turned west and followed Twiford Road (map point H) to West Kitty Hawk Road and continued along the present alignment to the area of Austin Cemetery and Sound Landing (map point I) on Currituck Sound. In very early days Sound Landing was known as "...the road leading from John Partridge," and after 1838 "...Doudey (Dowdy) Landing." For several years in the 1850s and 1860s, what we know today as Twiford Road was called "Turtle Road," probably because swamps lined both sides of the road, favorite habitat for turtles.

The Kitty Hawk road system we know today began to evolve in the later part of the 1800s. That portion of West Kitty Hawk Road from the old 1926 school house to the Baptist Church did not appear on the 1897 Coast Survey Chart, but the Up-the-Road School was built around that time and most likely the road was constructed before the school opened. A portion of that section of the road was in place earlier as a private road from the turnoff to Poor Ridge to the several home places. The road was upgraded and continued west across Sedge Swamp and north along a small ridge to Turtle Road. The resulting road was a shortcut for the Up-the-Road residence to the rest of the community (map point J).

Another major road improvement occurring in the 1890s was the construction of a road across Mingoes Gut, through Cypress Swamp, to the present Midgett Road/West Kitty Hawk Road intersection (map point K). This road today passes in front of the new fire house. The new road bypassed the U-shaped trail which crossed the Great Wading Place and passed around Elijah Sibbern's farm. No doubt the present section of Herbert Perry Road from West Kitty Hawk road to Midgett Road was opened about the same time.

In the late 1800s, after a hundred years of open livestock grazing, principally sheep, which denuded the sand hills east of

Kitty Hawk village of vegetation, the migrating sand hills threatened to block the entrance road to the community. The locals referred to the emerging sand hill at the entrance as "Shot Beach Hill," probably because of the difficulty in getting over the hill to the road going south along Kitty Hawk Bay. Around 1895, to bypass this sand obstacle, the community road crew built a causeway across the marsh from Bull Ridge to Moore Shore, and bridged Bull Ridge Gut. This road, the Moore Shore Road, became the principal entrance to the village until the paved road was built in the 1930s (map point L).

Kitty Hawk Village Road passes by the Methodist church

With the completion of bridges across Roanoke Sound by Dare County in 1928 and Currituck Sound by a private company in 1930, the State of North Carolina assumed responsibility for construction of a hard surface road connecting the two bridges. The project, completed in 1931, included hard surface spur roads to Kitty Hawk village, the Wright Memorial, and access to the Nags Head sound side community. The Kitty Hawk spur extended for a mile from the Virginia Dare Trail (the beach road) opposite the Kitty Hawk Coast Guard Station to Mingoes Gut next to the Kitty Hawk Methodist Church. Beyond Mingoes Gut the road continued as sand trails through the village to Sound Landing on Currituck Sound for a few more years.

Paving a road across the sand hills east of the village did not eliminate sand migration problems for Kitty Hawk travelers. A moderate nor'easter would frequently cover the roadway with loose sand causing vehicles to become stuck in sand on top of a paved road. Tom J. King, from Duck, the lone highway employee in the area, had the responsibility of clearing the roadway, usually with nothing more than a shovel, truck and backbreaking labor. Jesse Calvin Perry joined him in later years and together they worked to keep both the paved and unimproved roads passable, ditches functioning properly, and bridges and signs repaired.

In the late 1930s a Works Progress Administration (WPA) project extended the Kitty Hawk main road west another mile to the Kitty Hawk School. The final segment of the main road to Austin Cemetery was paved after World War II. Side roads, including parts of Moore Shore, Elijah Baum, Herbert Perry, Poor Ridge and Bob Perry, were improved in the 1960s with county allocated state funds from the fuel tax. US 158 Bypass was also completed in the early 1960s. The improvement and paving of Woods and Twiford Roads were completed in the early 1990s. Subdivision development accounts for most of the other improved roads in the Town.

The Kitty Hawk road system has evolved slowly over two centuries from little more than sand trails. While there have been some minor changes in alignments and today roads approach national uniform standards of construction and maintenance, there is an element of historic Kitty Hawk within the road system, if one would only stop a moment, look and reflect on the past. Kitty Hawk's history is right there, even if under pavement.

Kitty Hawk Road Construction

Kitty Hawk Village Road

Section Five

Federal Initiatives

Chapter Eleven

FEDERAL INITIATIVES

The Federal Government Helped Growth Around Kitty Hawk

Several Federal Government initiatives in the 1870s had a profound impact on the growth, development and lifestyles of the people of Kitty Hawk and adjoining communities. During that period, the U. S. Life-Saving Service established a series of life saving stations along the North Carolina coast including a station at Kitty Hawk in December 1874. The U. S. Army Signal Corps established a Weather Bureau Station at the Cape Hatteras Lighthouse Keeper's Quarters and a second weather station at the Kitty Hawk Life-Saving Station in January 1875. On November 11, 1878, the U. S. Postal Service expanded its Services on the Outer Banks with the establishment of the Kitty Hawk post office. Each initiative in its own way contributed to improving the quality of Life for Kitty Hawkers and guided the development of the area, but the Life-Saving Service probably had the greatest overall impact through the humanitarian services it extended to mariners and locals alike and in providing employment through the years to many Kitty Hawkers.

THE GRAVEYARD OF THE ATLANTIC

The North Carolina coastline has long been known as "The Graveyard of The Atlantic," but what might surprise a great many locals of coastal North Carolina is that other areas also claim that descriptive title, including the coastline around Sable Island off the coast of central Nova Scotia. One of the most obvious differences, however, in describing the two areas is that North

Carolina's "Graveyard of The Atlantic" has upper case letters, while Nova Scotia's "graveyard of the Atlantic" is most often shown in lower case. For a shipwrecked mariner on either coast, the letter case size and style would make no difference. What they wanted was rescue assistance in the event of a stranding. However, in North Carolina the first organized rescue crews did not arrive until 1874, after the formation of the United States Life-Saving Service.

From the time of European exploration in the 16th and 17th century, mariners have sailed north along the North American coastline for their return to Europe. This route was favored because of the strong flow of northerly ocean current of better than 5 miles per hour that shortened their sailing time from the New World to a European home port. The Gulf Stream, so named in the late 1700s, passes through the Florida Straits and flows northward along the coast to the area of Diamond Shoals off Cape Hatteras, and then proceeds northeasterly to form the North American Drift. Nearing the European continent, the drift splits with a northern branch forming the Norwegian current and a southern leg, the Canary current, flowing south along the West African coast and used for sailing to the New World. Another ocean current of significance to sailing interest along the North American continent was the Labrador Current, which originates in the Arctic Ocean. It flows south along the coast between the continental mainland and the Gulf Stream, and dissipates in the Diamond Shoals off the Outer Banks of North Carolina. Although not as strong as the Gulf Stream, when the two currents collide, as they do on the Grand Banks off Newfoundland near Nova Scotia and the Diamond Shoals of North Carolina, the collision causes turbulent seas and the formation of ever-changing shoals which are a menace to navigation.

WRECK COMMISSIONERS

In spite of its reputation, most vessels successfully sailed the North Carolina coast in either direction without mishap or misfortune. There were, of course, strandings and wrecks, but they were for the most part the exception rather that the rule. Any wreck, however, was a significant loss to the owners and shippers and could result in the loss of lives, both sailors and passengers, and destruction of cargo. By 1808, the State of North Carolina had established the office of Commissioner of Wrecks in the counties bordering the Atlantic Ocean and authorized the appointment of Commissioners. Willis Gallop, who lived at Martins Point, was one of the first if not the first appointed Commissioner for the section of beach that included Kitty Hawk. The importance of the Wreck Commissioner's appointment was significant as a surety bond of 1,000 pounds was required just for the appointment. He served as a Wreck Commissioner for many years and in 1840, at age 73, decided to give it up and his son Hodges Gallop was appointed as his replacement. By then the bond requirement had increased to $15,000 and the area covered was called District 3. The records show that both John Partridge and son Willis Gallop Partridge also each served for several years as a 3rd District Commissioner of Wrecks, however, it is not known if they were in addition to or in place of one of the Gallops.

Undoubtedly the Commissioner of Wrecks assisted stranded people on any wreck event he happened upon, however, his official responsibility was not rescue but protection of ship cargo and property when grounded or wrecked in his district. When that happened, he took charge at the wreck scene and arranged with residents for assistance in gathering property washed ashore. He also engaged them to off-load cargo if the vessel had not broken up and removal of the cargo possible. The Commissioner also contacted the owner, shipping agent or insurance underwriter to arrange disposal of the salvaged materials. In many cases the owner made appropriate restitution to the Commissioner of Wrecks and had the salvage items picked up and transported to a convenient storage facility, most often in the Norfolk, Virginia, area. When moving expenses of salvage materials was more expensive than its value, the Commissioner would arrange a vendue, or public sale on site, of the salvaged property. Many early homes in Kitty Hawk and surrounding communities were built or improved with lumber purchased at a shipwreck vendue on the Kitty Hawk Beach, and a few residents still have furniture from shipwreck vendue sales.

EARLY MARITIME ASSISTANCE EFFORTS

It took the Federal Government a long time to involve itself in the business of assisting mariners in distress. Though not Federal, the first organized effort to give aid and comfort to mariners was initiated by the Massachusetts Humane Society in 1785. Their early involvement included building houses of refuge, or huts, stocked with food, candles, firewood and related provisions, as shelters for shipwrecked mariners who might wreck along the Massachusetts coast. The huts were a welcome aid for survivors who successfully reached the shore and could find the huts. Unfortunately, the shelters were unattended and some or most of the supplies and provisions were stolen or vandalized before they were of service to survivors. Later the Society experimented with the use of special built lifeboats and expanded their service to lifeboat stations, but they still depended on volunteers to help with any rescue effort. The work of the Massachusetts Humane Society worked well for the State of Massachusetts. However, it was not a national program and did not involve other states with dangerous shorelines. In 1848 a New Jersey congressman supported a successful appropriation bill for federal funding for rescue equipment and services to be used along the New Jersey coast. Subsequent appropriation extended the coverage to the New York coast. The funding helped, but the effort of providing rescue service was still the responsibility of volunteers and they were not always available, or properly trained for the task.

THE LIFE-SAVING SERVICE

Following the Civil War, the Nation's maritime traffic increased with larger vessels, increased cargo, and more passengers, and when wrecks occurred there could be correspondingly greater losses, both in goods and human life. In 1870 Congress responded in part to these problems and appropriated funding to address the issue of improving life saving programs along the nation's coastline. Additional federal funding in 1873 authorized the establishment of the first life saving stations with crews along the North Carolina coast. In all, seven North Carolina stations were constructed during 1873-74, including: Jones Hill (later named Whale's Head and then Currituck Beach), Caffeys Inlet, Kitty Hawk Beach (later just Kitty Hawk), Nags Head, Bodie Island (later called Oregon Inlet), Chicamacomico, and Little Kinnakeet.

Additional stations were authorized, constructed and manned before the opening of the 1878 active season, including: Wash Woods, Old Currituck Inlet (later Penny's Hill), Poyner's Hill, Paul Gamiel's Hill, Kill Devil Hills, Tommy's Hummock (later called Bodie Island), Pea Island, New Inlet, Gull Shoal, Big Kinnakeet, Cape Hatteras, Creed's Hill, Durant's, and additional stations south of Hatteras Island. Initially the stations had been about 12 to 15 miles apart, but with the newly constructed stations they were normally within 5 to 6 miles of each other, and close enough for foot beach patrols between stations at night and in inclement weather.

ARTICLE OF ENGAGEMENT KEEPERS & SURFMEN

In an official memorandum of February 11, 1875, to the Secretary of the Treasury, Inspector of U. S. Life-Saving Stations, Captain J. H. Merryman, U. S. Revenue Marine, transmitted a list of Keepers and surfmen employed within the 6th Life-Saving Service District. The Kitty Hawk Beach Life-Saving Station, Number 6, and crew included: Keeper A. L. Follett, and surfmen William B. Flannagan, William H. Neal, George D. Newbern, James R. Hobbs, George W. Lyon, and Jeremiah Morgan. James R. Hobbs was the only Kitty Hawker in that first crew.

The enlistment date of the Keeper was not given, but all surfmen signed their "Article of Engagement" on December 1, 1874, which would also date the official opening of the Kitty

Hawk Life-Saving Station. Interestingly, all other North Carolina Stations also showed their crews as enlisting on December 1, 1874, but none give a date for when the Keeper joined the Life-Saving Service. The crews for the three 6th District Virginia Stations, which opened in 1874, enlisted on December 5, 1874, indicating that those stations opened a few days later than the ones in North Carolina. There was a new crew at the Kitty Hawk Station for the 1875-76 season that included Keeper William Douglas Tate and surfmen: William Perry, Benjamin Dough Tillett, Edward "Ned" Baum, Lemuel Tillett Hines, William James Baum, and Samuel Avery Tillett, Jr. – all Kitty Hawkers. Having an all Kitty Hawk crew was important to the community because the employment of local men meant economic investment in the community. Benjamin D. and Samuel A. Tillett were brothers and Keeper Tate had to justify their employment to Charles Guirkin, the 6th District Superintendent of Life-Saving Stations in Elizabeth City, NC, and ask for forgiveness, which apparently was given. The appointment of William D. Tate as Keeper at Kitty Hawk was special in that the U. S. Government had originally secured the land for the station from Tate and he was the nearest neighbor to the new station. Tate left the Service in 1877 for other pursuits. He was replaced by James Raleigh Hobbs as Keeper, another nearby neighbor. In January 1892, Samuel J. Payne of Currituck County was appointed Keeper and was followed on January 14, 1902, by Avery Benjamin Love "Be Love" Tillett of Kitty Hawk. Tillett was the Keeper when the Life-Saving Service and Revenue Cutter Service merged to form the United States Coast Guard in 1915.

THE SURFMEN

Being a surfman was a choice profession for these early Kitty Hawkers and a much sought after appointment by the adult males in the community. To be a surfman the applicant had to be at least 18 years of age, although most were much older, could read and write, and physically fit. In 1874, when selected they had to sign an "Articles of Engagement for Surfmen" for a one-year appointment, but they were only required to serve "an active season" at their assigned station from December 1st through March 31st, unless called out for special duty by the Keeper. The pay was $40.00 per month, but if called out for special duty they receive $3.00 per day for their time spent. With the $40.00 monthly pay the surfmen were expected to furnish their clothing and food. Later they received an allotment for uniforms, and in 1908 they were given 30-cents a day food allowance. Initially the Keeper was employed for the full year at an annual salary of $200.00. He was expected to check on the Station and its equipment during the non-active season and respond to emergencies should any occur.

An Act of Congress of June 18, 1878 formally established the U. S. Life-Saving Service within the Department of the Treasury. Sumner I. Kimball was appointed its General Superintendent and served in that capacity until the Life-Saving Service became part of the U. S. Coast Guard in 1915. The 1878 act also increased the length of the active season for Atlantic Coast Stations to 10 months, August 1st through May 31st, and increased Keepers salaries to $400.00 per year. Keeper's salaries incrementally increased to $1,000 per year by 1900 while surfmen salaries also increased from $40.00 to $60.00 per month. In 1908, surfmen salaries were set at $65.00 per month with the #1 surfman receiving $70.00 per month.

Unfortunately, the Life-Saving Service did not have a retirement program so when a surfman, or Keeper, left the Service they were on their own and hopefully had planned for their old age. With the merging of the Life-Saving Service and Revenue Cutter Service into the U. S. Coast Guard in 1915, a retirement program was granted and it significantly improved the lot of the retirees.

Most people have a romantic vision of the Life-Saving Service Mission and work, but the life of the surfman was usually anything but romantic. Typically, the surfman spent their time training and drilling for stranded vessel rescues, standing watch on the lookout platform atop the station building, and walking beach patrols at night or in inclement weather to warn ships away from the beach or to secure help if there was a ship ashore.

Maintaining the station in good order was also part of their duties. The surfmen were allowed one "home day" a week, from sun-up to sun-down, but they had to be back at the station each night.

Although there are stories of spectacular and famous rescues up and down the North Carolina coast, none except for possibly the wreck of the schooner *Luola Murhison*, occurred at Kitty Hawk. That vessel grounded on a sand bar abreast the station and was stuck fast there for weeks. The crew and their personal effects were saved. A wreck steamer from Norfolk came to the *Luola Murhison* with the expectation of refloating the vessel, but was unsuccessful and the hull and cargo was a total loss just offshore from the station.

Probably the more important service rendered by the Kitty Hawk Station crew and the U. S. Life-Saving Service, other than an actual rescue, was warning mariners away from the coast. Typically, a surfman on the beach patrol upon seeing a ship dangerously close to the shore would ignite a Coston Light flare to warn the ship of the danger. The flare also served to alert them that help was at hand should they need it. There is no telling how many U.S.S *Huron*, *Metropolis*, *Priscilla* or similar wrecks were avoided by the simple act of the foot surfman signaling with his Coston Light.

Life around the station was often repetitious and most likely boring to the seasoned surfman, but the routine was required and necessary if the crew was to remain ready for the next rescue should it occur. The routine schedule included: Monday, clean station and repair and polish equipment; Tuesday, surf boat drill; Wednesday, signal flags practice, Thursday, beach apparatus and breeches buoy drill; Friday, first aid and resuscitation practice; Saturday, laundry and personal work; and Sunday, rest and religion. The following week, and each week thereafter, the same routine repeated itself. The training, practice and drills were not wasted, however, as quarterly the District Inspector would visit the stations to check the crew on their training and observe the surf boat and beeches buoy drills. A breeches buoy drill of less than 5 minutes was considered satisfactory and the time of 3 minutes, 50 seconds, by the crew under Keeper Samuel J. Payne on August 20, 1900, would undoubtedly have been considered excellent.

Kitty Hawk Lifesaving Station Crew, 1900. From left to right, Robert Lee Griggs, Robert Fulton Sanderlin, Thomas Edward Hines, Joseph Baum, station cook, Samuel J. Payne, James Riley Best, Thomas Nelson Sanderlin. The station dog, Brown, is at bottom center.

The Life-Saving Service did not provide a cook at the station, thus each surfman was responsible for his own meals. At most stations the crew hired a cook and in the case of the Kitty Hawk crew, they pooled their funds and hired Joe Ed Baum to do the cooking in the years before and after 1900. At times Joe Ed also served as a substitute surfman for a regular surfman who had to be away from the station for health or personal reasons. He was paid by the Government as a substitute surfman, but the Service docked the pay of the regular surfman for not being present.

NEW LIFE-SAVING STATIONS

In the late 1800s the Life-Saving Service began a program of upgrading some of their stations along the North Carolina coast. Caffeys Inlet and Oregon Inlet were among the first new stations constructed, both in the 1897-98 periods. A new Kitty Hawk station was built in 1911 and served as the main station building thereafter with the earlier structure serving as a boathouse. In the 1920s the Kitty Hawk station was placed in a caretaker status with a crew of two Coast Guardsmen, Kitty Hawkers Silas Davis Guard as Officer-in-Charge, or Keeper, and Sylvanus Valerious "Vene" Harris, as surfman. The station probably closed in the late 1930s During World War II, the station was reactivated for national defense purposes, but closed after the war and the property sold in 1945. The 1911 building

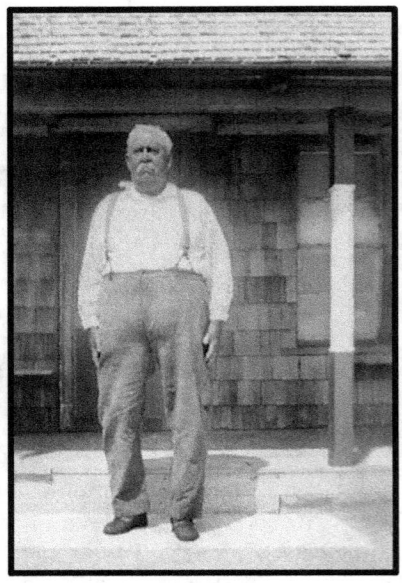

Vene Harris

has since been moved west across NC 12 and south about .03 mile and serves as a summer residence and rental. The original 1874 building was also moved and relocated to the southwest corner of NC 12 and East Kitty Hawk Road, with modifications and expansions to serves as a restaurant.

KITTY HAWKERS

Over the years, a high number of Kitty Hawkers served in the U. S. Life-Saving Service and U. S. Coast Guard and some were assigned to the Kitty Hawk stations. Probably the one person who spent the most time at the Kitty Hawk was Thomas Nelson Sanderlin who enlisted there in 1877 and retired there on April 2,

1915. He advanced through the ranks and retired as the #2 Surfman, a position the record shows he held from at least 1897, and probably longer. At the time of his retirement, he was 66 years of age and over the mandatory retirement age for the new U. S. Coast Guard, so he became one of the first former Life-Saving surfmen to retire from the U. S. Coast Guard. It is reported that on his last day of service, he walked his beach patrol one last time, returned to the station, turned in his gear, and left the station for his Kitty Hawk village home and retirement, having completed nearly 40 years of life-saving service for the nation at one duty station.

Thomas N. Sanderlin was more than a surfman in the community. He was an outstanding carpenter and was reported to have helped build the Boaz Methodist Episcopal Church South in the village, the Methodist parsonage, and the Down-the-Road school house and its remodeling over the years. He also kept a supply of lumber on hand for special needs and one of those special needs was to build a coffin when someone passed away.

Thomas Nelson Sanderlin

Some in the family report that occasionally the Wright brothers called on him for small pieces of wood to repair their glider, but that association is not documented. The Wright brothers knew Thomas N. Sanderlin as he appears in two of their 1900 Kitty Hawk Life-Saving Station crew member pictures. Also, his home was near the Kitty Hawk post office where the Wrights were frequent patrons. Grandson Bob Wescott reported that Orville Wright came to Thomas Sanderlin's house and visited on the porch on one of his return trips to Kitty Hawk. Two of the Sanderlin daughters were teachers in the village schools, so the

Sanderlin influence in the community trickled down through the ages. Also on April 2, 1915, Kitty Hawk Surfman George Washington Baum, like Thomas Sanderlin, retired due to age. He had enlisted on April 6, 1881, under Keeper Jessie Partridge, his former step-father, at the Kill Devil Hills Life-Saving Station and signed on as the #7 Surfman. The #7 Surfman did not work the full season but was on duty from the first of December through March, the usual period of unstable weather and heavy surf conditions. George Baum preferred that schedule because it gave him an opportunity to work his garden in the spring and be a member of a fishing crew at other times if he wished. Neighbor and cousin Truxton Midgett said George Baum, though small of stature, was as strong as "whet leather", and he jogged wherever he went. He could jog from the Kill Devil Hills Station to his home in Kitty Hawk village in about an hour's time. Once on his way home he met a man in a horse and cart on the road and was asked if he would like a ride. He thanked him and said, "No, I'm in a hurry!" George Baum transferred to the Kitty Hawk Station in January 1901 and finished his career there. The Kitty Hawk Station did not carry a #7 surfman position so he fulfilled the #6 position and was a full time surfman from August 1st through May 30th for years until he retired.

KEEPER JAMES RALEIGH HOBBS

One of the best-known Keepers, at least by the locals, and maybe the most controversial of the Kitty Hawk Keepers was James Raleigh Hobbs. He was born on Dews Quarters Island in Currituck Sound to Noah Hobbs and Elizabeth Lewark. Elizabeth had previously been married to a Beacham in Kitty Hawk and James Raleigh Hobbs most likely inherited Kitty Hawk land from his mother. However, he also purchased 100 acres of land from the executor of the Thomas Twiford estate where he built his house and lived from the mid-1860s until he moved in 1916 to the Masonic Home for elderly members in Greensboro, NC. The Hobbs property of 100 acres was located on the east side of Kitty

Hawk village and ran east from approximately Bull Ridge Gut to the ocean. Property lines were not perpendicular to the beach but rather ran in a north east/southwest alignment. Thomas Nelson Sanderlin owned approximately the same size track of land north of Hobbs, and William Douglas Tate owned similar land south of the Hobbs track that included the site of the later Kitty Hawk Life-Saving Service station.

People who knew James Raleigh Hobbs as an old man when they were only teenagers reported that Hobbs had been a sea captain before he returned to Kitty Hawk in the 1850s. That may be true, but that period of his life has not been documented. However, there is no question that he was an ocean-going sailor. On May 12, 1944, the *Dare County Times* printed a November 7, 1909, letter from James Hobbs to Thomas T. Toler of Skyco, NC, in which he reminisced about their being shipmates in 1852 on the clipper ship, *Winged Racer*. They left New York on the ship on December 10, 1852, and it took 53 days to sail to Cape Horn and another 55 days to get to the Golden Gate in California. Apparently, the *Winged Racer* worked out of New York where he probably met Elizabeth C. "Eliza" Murphy of London, England. They married June 6, 1855, and moved to Kitty Hawk.

In the 1860 Census for the North Banks, Currituck County, which included Kitty Hawk, Hobbs listed his occupation as "waterman," with property holdings of $50.00 and $100 in personal worth. By August 1864, Hobbs was serving as a civilian "pilot" in the Service of the Union Navy aboard the USS *Chicopee* operating in the inland waters of Eastern North Carolina. Hobbs joined the ship in New Bern, NC, and left there with the ship as the pilot for the Albemarle Sound region on July 13, 1864. In a September 6, 1864, letter to his wife he reported his wages were $100 per month, but in a later letter he thought that his wages would be $125 a month.

The *Chicopee*'s principal duty in the Albemarle Sound was to keep the CSS *Albemarle* from leaving Plymouth, NC, or if it did venture out the mouth of Roanoke River, to engage her. That did not become necessary as a commando type raid delivered a torpedo that sunk the ironclad on October 28, 1824. The *Chicopee* stayed in the Plymouth, NC, area after the sinking of the

Albemarle to support Union Army troops serving in eastern North Carolina. Hobbs probably left the *Chicopee* when the vessel went into the Norfolk Navy Yard for an overhaul in early 1865.

In the 1870 Census, James Raleigh Hobbs listed his occupation as a farmer and his real property valued at $300 and personal estate at $200. Apparently, he made out well during the Civil War. James and Eliza Hobbs had several boarders in their home in the 1870 census, including Susan Best Partridge and her son, Nicodemus, school teacher Alfred Jones, and Caleb Hobbs Toler, whose parents were apparently deceased. Susan Best Partridge's husband, George Partridge, had died in a Union prison during the Civil War and she and her son later became wards of Currituck County. The Branson's North Carolina Directory 1884, lists James R. Hobbs as operating a boarding house in Kitty Hawk, so the boarders of the 1870 census may have been there as paying customers for a business rather than a benevolent accommodation on the part of the Hobbs.

James Raleigh Hobbs enlisted as a surfman on December 1, 1874, on the first Kitty Hawk Life-Saving Station crew, but no one from that crew returned the second year and Hobbs must have returned to farming. On May 8, 1878, however, he was appointed the third Keeper of the Kitty Hawk Life-Saving station and served in that capacity until dismissed on December 24, 1891. The cause of the dismissal has not been discovered, but throughout his Service as Keeper he seemed to have been at odds with someone most of the time.

Even before his Life-Saving Service days he had conflicts with people in the community. In a September 6, 1864, letter to his wife while serving on the USS *Chicopee* he expressed concern for her safety because of a conflict with neighbor William Douglas Tate and he advised her to get someone to live with her while he was away. That conflict must have continued because he was not reappointed in the Life-Saving Service after Mr. Tate became Keeper of the Kitty Hawk Station in 1875.

After Hobbs became Keeper in 1878, he seemed to have a running feud with the Signal Service officer assigned to Kitty Hawk. He accused the officer of returning to the station drunk and disorderly and "...using most profane language disturbing everybody…and calling my wife all kinds of names for discharging him from the house for drunkness."

Hobbs wanted the Signal Corps office removed from the station, but that could not be accomplished quickly because the Signal Corps did not have the funding to build or lease another site. Hobbs also had conflicts with members of his crew as reported in a letter from Daniel M. Tate, Jr., to USLSS General Superintendent Sumner Kimball: "Daniel M. Tate Jr., Kitty Hawk NC, April 28, 1884 to Kimball. In reply to your communication of the 22nd inst. I beg leave to say that the circumstances connected with my having left the Life-Saving station on the 20th of Dec. last, have been erroneously stated to you. The facts in the case are simply these - on the above date; i.e., Dec. 20th, Capt. J. R. Hobbs, Keeper of the station, sent myself and another surfman away from the station on private business for himself and during our absence we drank two or three drinks of liquor, but neither of us were under the influence of it to any extent. Neither before nor after returning to the station on said day, we had no orders to return immediately, and were absent about three (3) hours, and when we returned Keeper Hobbs abused me for being absent so long and I after some words, asked him for my discharge. He replied that he would not give me a discharge that I might take my traps and leave, which I did. On another occasion during April 1883, Keeper Hobbs and myself and the No. 3 man from the station during a thick northeaster for several hours plowing in his field, we were paid by the government to perform duty in the Life-Saving Station under Keeper Hobbs, and he took us away from that duty and used both of us for several hours on his own private work. At that time he found no fault with our absence." An investigation conducted with impartiality would disclose many other important facts in connection with the management of this particular station.

Keeper Hobbs' most celebrated conflict occurred July 7, 1884, as reported by Assistant Inspector E. C Clayton, 6th Life-Saving Service District: "July 9, 1884. E. C. Clayton to Kimball. Nags Head NC (Have gone to Kitty Hawk LSS to inquire into charges made by Theoflus L. "Theof" Daniels against Hobbs for using the station paint in painting a boat belonging to Hobbs.) On my arrival at the station Daniels in a very insolent manner asked me if I was going to put Keeper Hobbs out of the station on this charge, or if it would only amount to the same as the other made by him for plundering the wreck schooner "*Murchison*." I replied to Daniels, it was the General Superintendent's right to deal with these matters as he saw fit, and I did not come to the station to be bullied by anyone. We then went into the house. I requested Daniels to produce his witnesses. Capt. Hobbs then came into the boat room, where we were holding the investigation, as soon as Daniels saw Hobbs, Daniels commenced to use blasphemous language, and squared off as if he was going to strike Hobbs, Hobbs remarked to Daniels: "if you strike me, I will hit you with a heaving stick." I stopped them from quarreling, and said to Daniels if he did not behave himself in a proper manner, I would have him put out of the station. Capt. Hobbs also remarked to Daniels, "We came here to do Gov. business and not to quarrel, and for him Daniel to keep quiet," Daniels replied to Hobbs, "he be G- d- if he would shut up for him Hobbs, but eluate (to) do so for the Lieut."

"After getting them quiet and down, I then commenced the investigation, and Captain Hobbs left the boat room, when I got though with the second witness, Hobbs again came in to question the witness on his appearance. Daniels commenced at Hobbs again. Daniels remarked to Hobbs, "If you ever draw as much as a penknife on me, I will kill you." Hobbs answered "I do not carry anything to defend myself with, not even a small knife, but you Daniels have a pistol in your pocket." Daniels replied, "I have no pistol and if you say I have one, you are a dam liar." During this conversation I was sitting at the desk writing down the evidence of one of the witnesses in the case and doing all in my power by words to keep Hobbs and Daniels apart, when Daniels made the remark to Hobbs "If you say I have a pistol in my pocket you are a dam liar." Daniels placed his hand behind him if in the act of drawing one, and walked backwards towards the place I was sitting. As Daniels retreated, Capt. Hobbs went to the closet in the room and took from it a double barrel shot gun. When Daniels came towards me and Hobbs took the gun from the closet every man that was in the boat room ran out, leaving me alone with

Hobbs and Daniels. I was powerless to prevent the shooting, with no one to assist me, had I tried to hold one the other would have shot. Hobbs took the gun from the closet with his left hand, letting the stock rest on the floor, when Daniels saw the gun, he got down alongside of me with his left arm around my neck and with his right hand trying to draw his pistol, and said to Hobbs, "Don't shoot me," as soon as I saw what Daniels was doing. Concluding the moment he got his pistol in a position to use it, he would shoot Hobbs over my shoulder thinking Hobbs would not fire while I was between them. I then threw Daniels from me and walked backwards towards Capt. Hobbs, keeping my eyes on Daniels for fear he would fire, when I arrived in about 3 feet from Hobbs. Hobbs rested his gun on my right shoulder and fired at Daniels the shot taking effect in Daniels' left arm about 4 inches below the shoulder, making a frightful wound. As soon as Daniels was shot, he ran toward Hobbs and myself, Hobbs keeping behind me all of the time. When Daniels arrived opposite to me, Hobbs, with the barrel of his gun, shoved Daniels and myself to one side, which caused Daniels to stagger into the closet. When Daniels recovered himself, he turned towards me, then Hobbs fired the second shot, which took effect in the same arm about 4 inches from the first wound through the fleshy part entering apparently Daniels's lungs and heart at that shot Daniel fell and died almost instantly.

"I had Daniels placed on a stretcher and taken outside of the station, then sent one of the men who had run away from the room, but returned after the shooting, to notify the authorities. When the men picked up the body of Daniels to move him, we found a pistol in his right hand loaded and cocked, and the pocket it was taken from turned wrong side out. If the pistol had not caught in Daniels' pocket, he would certainly have shot Hobbs or myself before Hobbs did him.

"Before my arrival at the station Daniels remarked to a boy that was there, "Good by Billy and take care of yourself for I may never see you again." Showing by the remark he had gone to the station for the purpose of causing trouble. From what I can learn Daniels has threatened to take Capt. Hobbs' life more than once. It was only a few days ago, he remarked to one of the ex-surfmen that he, Daniels, "would Kill Hobbs or go into his own box."

"Daniels for years has done all in his power to injure and annoy Capt. Hobbs. He was a man that had no character, and was feared and despised by all who knew him. I am confident from what I witnessed, had Hobbs not killed Daniels, Daniels would have killed Hobbs. If there had been anyone in the boat room to assist me, we could have probably prevented the shooting, but being alone with the belligerents, I was powerless to do anything. I placed the No. 1 surfman in charge of the station. After the inquest, whose verdict was self-defense, Capt. Hobbs was placed under arrest and sent to the Currituck jail. Hobbs' trial comes off on the 1st Monday in September...."

After the incident, Keeper Hobbs was escorted to the county jail at the Currituck Court House. He was issued a summons and released. At his trial, he was cleared of all charges on the bases of self-defense and returned to his Keeper duties at the Kitty Hawk Life-Saving station.

Over the years there have been stories about how the hard feeling developed between Jimmy Hobbs and Theoflus Daniels, but no good explanation has been forthcoming. One of the most repeated stories was that Theoflus Daniels was riding in a cart with Jimmy Hobbs and his wife and when he spit out his tobacco juice it sprayed Mrs. Hobbs. That is a quick and easy but undocumented explanation of their conflict. It is believed that both men were so hard headed and strong willed that there must have been other conflicts in their personal contacts. Theoflus Daniels was a fish buyer who lived on Poor Ridge and maybe he thought that he was a better waterman and should be the Keeper of the Kitty Hawk station, or as he charges in his letter to the Life-Saving Service, he thought Jimmy Hobbs was taking advantage of his position by using government equipment and supplies for his personal use. At any rate, Jimmy Hobbs was an interesting and colorful Keeper at the Kitty Hawk Life-Saving station.

In the community, Jimmy Hobbs was maybe less colorful, but still very much a leader. He supervised the construction of the new Methodist Church in the village in the late 1880s and suggested the name for the church which was accepted by the trustees: Boaz Methodist Episcopal Church South. Jimmy Hobbs and his wife, Eliza, gave land at the southeast corner of the old main road through the village and Moore Shore Road for the first church parsonage.

James Hobbs and his wife Eliza in later days at their house.

After his Life Service days, he retired to the community and worked his farmland. By this time his health and that of his wife's was becoming an issue. She died in December 1909 and was buried in a small plot next to the Methodist church. Jimmy Hobbs lived on for a while but signs of dementia began to appear. One day Mattie Twiford, who lived on Moore Shore Road, saw Mr. Hobbs walking towards Kitty Hawk Bay. She called to him and asked where he was going. He reported, "To the bay to drown myself!" She said, "OK" and went on about her work. In a little while she saw him walking back from Kitty Hawk Bay and called to him, "Captain Hobbs, I thought you were going to drown yourself?" He responded, "The water is too cold!" Some of the local Masons arranged for Hobbs to be taken in at the Masonic Home in Greensboro, NC. He moved there on August 20, 1916, and stayed on two years until he died. He was buried in the Masonic Home Cemetery; probably because he had no close family in Kitty Hawk to have his body returned to be buried with his wife.

After the brick Kitty Hawk Methodist Church burned in 1976, it became necessary to build a new and bigger church. To accommodate the sanctuary building the remains of Mrs. Eliza Hobbs and others buried on the church grounds were disinterred and reburied in the Austin Cemetery. The reburial of Eliza Hobbs closed an interesting chapter of Kitty Hawk history on two very important and contributing residents of the community.

LIFE SAVERS: AT SEA AND HOME

Another Kitty Hawker who became Keeper of the Kitty

A. B. 'Love' Tillett

Hawk Life-Saving station was Avery Benjamin Love "Be Love" Tillett. Be Love Tillett enlisted as a surfman in the Life-Saving Service under Keeper Jesse Partridge at the Kill Devil Hills station on Dec. 1, 1880. He advanced as a surfman and by the late 1890s, was the #1 Surfman at the station. He must have been a well-respected and liked surfman because he was named Keeper of the Kitty Hawk Life-Saving station when Keeper Samuel J. Payne left the Life-Saving Service to return to his farm at Point Harbor, NC. Be Love Tillett reported to his new Keeper's position on January 14, 1902. In a newspaper article on the changes at the Kitty Hawk station, the *Elizabeth City Tar Heel* recorded: "HARBINGER - Capt. S.J. PAYNE, who was Keeper of Kitty Hawk L.S.S. #12, a resident of this place, has resigned his office after a term of about 20 years in the Service. Mr. A.B. Love Tillett, who was first man in #13 L.S.S., is promoted to Captain of #12. We congratulate him.

He is worthy of the position and we feel quite sure he will make a good Captain."

The Kitty Hawk station was not the most active station regarding wrecks on the North Carolina coast during Keeper Tillett's time, but it had its share of emergencies for which the crew responded and their work was recorded in an annual report of the U. S. Life-Saving Service. The 1906 annual report gave the following account of the rescue of the Schooner *Aragon* conducted by the Kitty Hawk station crew December 5, 1905:

"The patrol, discovering this vessel perilously near the beach, hastened to the station to report her situation to the Keeper; but before he could reach the end of his beat she struck the beach about 3/4 miles SE of the station. The Keeper of Kill Devil Hills station, being notified by telephone, the beach apparatus was taken to the wreck, the Lyle gun set up, and a line fired over the stranded craft. The crew from Kill Devil Hills now arrives upon the scene and aided in the work of rescuing the shipwrecked people. The hawser was successfully run off and twenty-one persons, with their baggage, were safely landed on shore in the breeches buoy and taken to the station and succored for four days. On the 13th instant the wreckers arrived and began operations to float the vessel; their efforts proving successful, she was towed to port."

Other assistance to people was less dramatic such as recovering an unidentified body on the beach and after removing valuable for safekeeping buried the body. They later learned the identity of the drowned person, disinterred the remains and delivered it to the responsible parties, along with the valuables. The Kitty Hawk station assisted in saving the personal property of Mr. Walter W. Best, whose house was approximately a mile west of the station and totally consumed by fire. There were numerous reports of the surfmen from the Kitty Hawk station helping refloat stranded vessels in Kitty Hawk Bay or Roanoke Sound.

A most unusual assistance given by the surfmen in 1918 was helping round up a herd of steers driven from their range by a storm and storm tides. On August 5, 1919, 11-year-old Orville Lee Baum, fell overboard into Kitty Hawk Bay from his sailing skiff in front of the E. W. Baum Store and Kitty Hawk post office.

He was taken from the water by an unidentified person and resuscitated by Surfman Robert Lee Wescott, Sr., who just happened to be at the Kitty Hawk post office picking up the station's mail.

Very few people know, in fact virtually no one knows, that Keeper Be Love Tillett was a distant witness to the Wright brothers 1903 powered flights. In a footnote in *The Papers of Wilbur and Orville Wright* edited by Marvin W. McFarland, he stated "In a letter to Carl Dienstbach, written Nov. 17, 1905, but not included in this work, the Wrights stated: 'The flights near Kitty Hawk were seen by nearly all the men at the U. S. Kill Devil Hill Life Saving Station, who were present, and by Captain [S. J. Payne] of the Kitty Hawk Station [four miles away], who viewed the flights through a glass." McFarland was mistaken in identifying and inserting S. J. Payne as the witness and Keeper of the Kitty Hawk Station in 1903. Keeper Be Love Tillett had replaced Keeper S. J. Payne in January 1902 and would have been the observer of the flights in 1903.

In addition to his service in the U. S. Life-Saving Service, Be Love Tillett and his wife, Mary Frances Sibbern Tillett, were contributors to their community. They conveyed to the Providence Baptist Church the use of land next to Sedge Marsh for the site of their church if there was a church need for the property. The Providence Church structure still occupies the land although the church is no longer active and the land ownership issue has been resolved. Be Love Tillett and wife also made a similar conveyance for the use of land next to Northern Gut creek for use of the Up-the-Road school. A school at that site was active until a consolidated school was opened in Kitty Hawk in 1926. The re-conveyance of that land back to the Tillett estate has never been formally documented, but current ownership may have been established by adverse possession. Keeper Be Love Tillett stayed on with the Life-Saving Service at Kitty Hawk through the transition to the U. S. Coast Guard. His wife died in 1912 and he sold his homestead on Kitty Hawk Bay in 1919, and probably retired soon after that date. In retirement, he stayed in Kitty Hawk with his good friend George Washington Baum and family part of the time and with the Clarence Leroy Twiford family in Elizabeth

City other times. Be Love and his wife, Mary Frances, raised Clarence Twiford after Clarence's mother became sick and was confined to a hospital in Raleigh, NC. Their daughter had died young and Clarence became their son, though not formally adopted. There does not seem to be any question that Avery Benjamin Love "Be Love" Tillett lived up to the prediction made in the 1902 *Elizabeth City Tar Heel* newspaper which stated: "He is worthy of the position and we feel quite sure he will make a good Captain."

COAST GUARD CARETAKERS

In the early 1920s, the Kitty Hawk Coast Guard Station was placed in a caretaker status with just two men assigned as crew; Silas Davis Guard as Keeper, or Captain, and Sylvanus Valerious Harris as surfman. Silas D. Guard had entered the Life-Saving Service around 1906 at the Caffeys Inlet Life-Saving Station as the #6 Surfman under Keeper Thaddeus M. Snow and worked his way up over the years to #1 Surfman. He probably transferred to the Kitty Hawk Coast Guard Station after Keeper Avery B. Love Tillett retired in the early 1920s.

Keeper Silas D. Guard with wife Nancy and son Julian

When vehicles began to appear in Kitty Hawk, they were driven and pushed - mostly pushed through the soft sand - down the beach from Virginia. Silas D. Guard was among one of the first, if not the first, Kitty Hawker to bring a vehicle to the village by barge. He borrowed a flatboat, or barge, from William Charles "Will" Perry to move his new vehicle from mainland Currituck County to Kitty Hawk. He also hired Captain Bill Perry to use his power boat to move the barge and car across to Sound Landing on the Kitty Hawk side of Currituck Sound. Transporting the vehicle went so well that Captain Perry decided to build a bigger barge and offer ferry service as a business. He even recruited his friend and neighbor, William Ivey Dowdy, who also had a power boat to assist him with the ferry service. The ferry traffic flourished. In 1926, Thomas Azarah Baum bought out Captain Perry and furnished a larger powered boat, named the *Rebecca*, outfitted as a ferry. He soon established a scheduled service across Currituck Sound from Point Harbor to Kitty Hawk and a connection to Roanoke Island. Although the ferry service would have probably developed anyway, it is interesting that it appeared to begin with Captain Silas D. Guard wanting to ferry his vehicle across Currituck Sound instead of having to bring it down the beach from Virginia Beach, which could have meant pushing it through the soft sand as much as riding in the new car.

Captain Silas Guard's assistant at the Kitty Hawk Coast Guard Station was Sylvanus Valerious "Vene" Harris. He owned a cottage across from the station. "Vene" Harris had enlisted in the Life-Saving Service at Penny's Hill Life-Saving Station under Keeper Thomas Jefferson Tillett, his 1st cousin. Maybe that kinship was far enough removed not to constitute nepotism, but Tillett also enlisted at the same time Decatur "Cade" Beacham, his nephew, an even closer relative, but still no one ever officially raised the earlier issue of nepotism with these enlistments. When Sylvanus Harris signed his papers for enlistment, he left the middle name blank. Keeper Tillett asked him for his middle name, but Sylvanus stated that he did not have one. "Well then," stated Keeper Tillett, "I will give you one." And he gave him the name "Valerious", most likely for Valerious L. Knight who was the #1

Surfman at the Penny's Hill Life-Saving Station at the time, and later Keeper of the Wash Woods Life-Saving Service Station.

Sylvanus Harris served as a surfman at the Penny's Hill station for about six years and then moved to the Caffeys Inlet station. In another couple of years, he transferred to the Kitty Hawk station. He may have been stationed at the Kill Devil Hills station for a short period but the records are incomplete. He ended his 31-year military career at the Kitty Hawk Coast Guard Station.

Truxton Midgett, who was Officer-In-Charge of the Caffeys Inlet Coast Guard Station at the time, was familiar with the circumstance of Sylvanus Harris' retirement. The U. S. Coast Guard had advised Sylvanus Harris as he approached his 64th birthday that he would be retired when he reached that age. Sylvanus advised the Coast Guard that he was in good health, doing his job, and did not wish to retire. The Coast Guard advised him that there were no alternatives because age 64 was the mandatory retirement age for all Coast Guard personnel. Sylvanus Harris was not very happy with the response from the Coast Guard and as he left the Kitty Hawk Coast Guard Station on February 04, 1927, with his retirement papers in hand, he jumped up and kicked the door facing and said, "Take that!" and walked out of the building, never to return.

At the time of his retirement Sylvanus Harris was 64 years of age, but his wife, Lizzie Tillett Harris, was only 31 years old. She was his second wife after his first wife, Ellen Beacham Harris, had died. Sylvanus "Vene" Harris died in 1940 and widow Lizzie T. Harris, drew her widow's subsistence check from the Coast Guard for the rest of her life. She lived until 1993, 53 years after "Vene" died. The U. S. Coast Guard had to "Take that" after all.

The Life-Saving Service maintained stations along the north coast for just over 40 years. They drew most of their surfmen and keeper appointments from the nearby communities and during that period the Life-Saving Service appointed over 40 Kitty Hawkers as surfmen and named nine as Station Keepers. At least 12 other Kitty Hawkers, but probably many more, served as station cooks or substitute surfmen when the regular surfman had to be away for medical, personal or business reasons. A few of the surfmen only served a few years, but the majority recorded 10 years or more, and some stayed 30 years and retired under the U. S. Coast Guard program. Although the population of Kitty Hawk in the late 1800s and early 1900s was not high, many men from the village served in the U.S. Life-Saving Service. It is fair to say that Kitty Hawkers made a significant contribution to the success of the service on the Outer Banks. A hallmark of the Life-Saving Service was that they trained and prepared for a quick response to a ship in distress, and they were well prepared for that service. The ability of the Life-Saving Service crews to respond to any emergency may have been the inspiration for the U. S. Coast Guard motto: SEMPER PARATUS -Always Ready.

The 1911 Kitty Hawk Lifesaving Station

The 1911 Kitty Hawk Lifesaving Station

Chapter Twelve

AND THE HIGH FOR THE DAY WAS

U. S. Army Signal Corps Weather Service

The Weather Bureau Station at Kitty Hawk will forever be linked to the Wright brothers and their work at Kitty Hawk; first, because it was the station operator who first advised the Wrights of the land and wind conditions at Kitty Hawk, and secondly, from the Kitty Hawk Weather Bureau office Orville sent the message of their December 17th, 1903 successes to their father, Bishop Milton Wright.

In an 1870 Act of Congress, the U. S. Army Signal Corps was directed to establish a weather observation and forecasting program. Some of those observation platforms needed to be along the coast, so shortly after the enactment of the Act, officers of the Signal Corps and the U. S. Life-Saving Servicemen agreed to a plan for the Signal Corps to share space in some of the newly established or planned Life-Saving Stations along the Atlantic Coast. Under the arrangement of sharing space, the Signal Corps would permit the Life-Saving Service the use of their telegraphic equipment to improve their communication between stations and with their reporting offices. In the late 1880s, the telegraphic service was supplemented with telephone service at each station, which significantly improved their communication and coordination operations. The Signal Corps also had a similar arrangement with the U. S. Lighthouse Service. The Signal Corps established the first weather observation station in North Carolina in the keepers quarters at the Cape Hatteras Light Station on August 16, 1874. Their second station opened in the Kitty Hawk Life-Saving Station on January 2, 1875. Since the telegraphic lines came down the coast from Virginia Beach, the first operating station in North Carolina was the Kitty Hawk office. Normally there were two Signal Corpsmen assigned to each station: a sergeant, who was the telegraph operator and officer-in-charge of the post, and a private, whose primary job was to keep the telegraph lines up and in good working order. The relationships between the personnel of the Signal Corps and the Life-Saving Service were generally good throughout their joint operation, including Kitty Hawk. However, in April 1881, Keeper James R. Hobbs of the Kitty Hawk station complained about Sergeant Leonardi who was the Corps Station officer. Keeper Hobbs believed that Sergeant Leonardi drank too much and used foul language. After some seeming reluctance on the part of the Signal Corps to relocate Sergeant Leonardi because his work for them was very satisfactory, they did transfer him to another post in May 1881. Two years later, April 1883, the Life-Saving Service, probably prompted by Keeper Hobbs, encouraged the Signal Corps to remove their office from the Kitty Hawk Station building. The Signal Corps reported that they did not have funding to move the station at that time, but would make other arrangements after July 1, 1883. On June 12, 1884, the Signal Corps secured from – of all people – James R. Hobbs and wife Eliza, a 99-year lease for a one-acre site about 150 feet north of the Kitty Hawk Life-Saving Station and built a new station building with quarters for their operator. The new building was approximately 24 feet by 40 feet, single story with quarters in the north end of the building for the sergeant-observer and family and a weather service office on the south end. The outside entrance doors to both the quarters and office were protected by wind break walls. The building was equipped with a chimney in both units. A platform on the roof with an outside stairway held several weather instruments for recording temperature, relative humidity, wind velocity and direction, and barometric and wind pressures. Weather recordings were made several times a day and relayed by telegraph to the Chief Signal Officer in Washington, D. C.

THE CIVILIAN WEATHER BUREAU AND THE WRIGHT BROTHERS

The Weather Bureau Station in 1903

On October 1, 1890, the Congress transferred the Weather Service from the U. S. Army Signal Corps to the Department of Agriculture. The physical transfer of all weather stations, telegraph lines, apparatus, and personnel, if they so choose, occurred on July 1, 1891, and formed the new civilian Weather Bureau. Wilbur Wright's letter of August 3, 1900, to the Kitty Hawk Weather Bureau office has not survived so we do not know precisely what he asked, but Weather Bureau observer Joseph J. Dosher's reply gives us an insight into Wilbur Wright's inquiry. In his letter Dosher said: "...the beach here is about one mile wide clear of trees or high hills, and islands for nearly sixty miles south. Conditions: the wind blows mostly from the north and northeast September and October which is nearly down this piece of land." Dosher also shared his incoming letter from Wilbur Wright with Mr. William James "Bill" Tate, probably the best-read person in Kitty Hawk at the time. Bill Tate also wrote to Wilbur Wright saying: "...I would say that you would find here nearly any type of ground you could wish; you could, for instance, get a stretch of sandy land one mile by five with a bare hill in the center 80 feet high, not a tree or bush anywhere to break the evenness of the wind current. This in my opinion would be a fine place; our winds are always steady, generally from 10 to 20 miles velocity per hour. He further wrote: "If you decide to try your machine here & come, I will take pleasure in doing all I can for your convenience & success & pleasure, & I assure you will find a hospitable people when you come among us." On the strength of the two letters, the brothers decided to take their machine to Kitty Hawk for their experiments. Wilbur and Orville arrived at Kitty Hawk two weeks apart in September 1900, spent about a month as boarders with the Tate family. On October 4, they moved to their tent camp which they had setup on the sand dunes about midway between Kitty Hawk village and the site of the Life-Saving Station and Weather Bureau buildings. The Wright brothers maintained a friendly relationship with the weather station operator, Joseph J. Dosher, throughout the four separate trips to Kitty Hawk from 1900 to 1903. During their 1900 trip Joe Dosher loaned the brothers a hand-held anemometer so they could confirm wind speed when conducting their tests. When a telegram was received for the brothers, Dosher would make a special effort to send word by whoever was going their way that he had a telegram for them to pick up at his office, and the brothers would also see Dosher when they had telegrams to send to others. The most important telegram they sent from Kitty Hawk by far was the one to their father, Bishop Milton Wright, on December 17, 1903, announcing their successful powered flight that day, and that they would be home by Christmas.

Some years later after the Wright brothers' accomplishments had been generally acknowledged, many news reporters and writers began identifying Alpheus W. Drinkwater as the person who relayed the telegraph message to Virginia Beach, which in turn was transmitted by Western Union to Dayton and Bishop Wright, and was picked up by the press. Without discounting the fact that the message was sent from the Kitty Hawk Weather Bureau Station, some writers reported that Drinkwater was working the telegraph line north of Kitty Hawk to report on the stranding of the U. S. Navy submarine, USS *Moccasin*. They theorized that he received the message and then relayed it on. The problem with that theory was that there was no reason or cause for him to interrupt the transmission and he never made that claim himself personally. Instead, in a November 18, 1932, news article in the Elizabeth City, N. C. *The Daily Advance*, he reported that; "I didn't send the first telegram announcing that the Wright brothers had made a successful flight," says Alpheus W. Drinkwater. "Joe Dozier,

Alpheus Drinkwater

who is dead now, did that." The confusion of Drinkwater's involvement probably resulted from the fact that in 1908, five years after the 1903 flights, as the telegraph operator in Manteo, NC, Drinkwater did send out hundreds and hundreds of lines of text reporting on the Wright brothers further experiments at their Kill Devil Hill camps in preparation for test flights for selling an airplane to the U. S. Government.

The Weather Bureau established the Manteo Weather Station on November 10, 1904, and closed the Kitty Hawk Weather Station. Alpheus Drinkwater, who had been for years a lineman servicing the telegraph lines along the northern North Carolina coast, was placed in charge of the new station. Joseph J. Dosher is reported to have left the Weather Bureau and was working for the Marconi Company, a private telecommunications and engineering company. The fate of the Kitty Hawk Weather Bureau building is unknown. In an interview with Truxton Midgett in 1977, he expressed that he spent several nights in that building while with a beach fishing crew after the Weather Bureau moved out.

Since the U. S. Signal Corps had acquired the property under a long-term lease, the property and improvements thereon probably reverted to the lessor when the lease was no longer needed. In this case the property would have reverted to James R. Hobbs, who was still living in 1904. He could have sold the building and the lumber salvaged for other construction purposes, but there is no documentation available to that effect. The structure did not appear in a series of Kitty Hawk Coast Guard Station photographs in 1917, so the structure was removed sometime between 1904 and 1917, and it could have been removed to allow the construction of the 1911 Kitty Hawk Life Saving Station. The loss of the Weather Bureau Station closed another chapter in Kitty Hawk's history.

The Second Kitty Hawk Lifesaving Station was constructed on the site of the Weather Bureau Station. It still stands and is currently a private home.

Chapter Thirteen

THE MAIL BOAT IS HERE

The US Postal Service and Who Served in Kitty Hawk

Kitty Hawk has one of the best-known place names in America, if not the world. Its notoriety of course is attributed to the publicity associated with Wilbur and Orville Wright's aviation experiments here in the early 1900s, the many books written about the brothers and their successes, and the annual celebrations that bring special attention to the birth of aviation. There have been other celebrations, events and activities that have also publicized the Wright brothers and Kitty Hawk such as several first day stamp issues and yearly special Kitty Hawk postmarked envelopes and cachet cancellation from the "Birthplace of Aviation." Kitty Hawk did not start out with any degree of notoriety. In fact, it was not until the 1850s that the community name of Kitty Hawk came into general use. Up to that time Kitty Hawk, like all other communities on the banks with maybe the exception of Nags Head was simply referred to as North Banks. In the early 1800s the postal department established the "Norfolk" post road to serve the northeastern corner of North Carolina. The route started in Norfolk and proceeded south with stops at the Currituck Court House, Camden Courthouse, Elizabeth City, Hertford, and terminated at Edenton. There were different names for other post roads that served other parts of North Carolina from cities in Virginia. The Currituck Court House post office was opened in 1808 and was followed with post offices at Coinjock and Poplar Branch in 1829 and one at Powells Point in 1833. All three of the new post offices were served by contract mail carriers from the Currituck Court House post office. Since there was no delivery service at that time, the post masters held the mail until the addressee, or their agent, called for the mail. Mail service was certainly not fast, but correspondence between people and businesses could succeed, if one was patient.

The person who applied to the postal department for an office at Kitty Hawk has not been identified, but most likely it was William Douglas Tate, or possibly his wife, Sophie D. Tate. She was appointed the first postmaster for Kitty Hawk on November 11, 1878, and operated the post office out of her home. The Tate home site location appears on an 1848-49 U. S. Coast Survey map as being near the northeast shores of Kitty Hawk Bay approximately 200 yards north of the bay and 200 yards south of where the Catholic Church is today. Son Bill Tate demolished the home around 1900 to salvage the lumber because the structure was rapidly being covered by blowing sand. The site of the former home is probably under 30 feet or more of sand today.

Selecting a name for the new post office probably was not a problem. The community name of Kitty Hawk had been in use a few years by the 1870s and the newly established Life-Saving Station and Weather Bureau Station had each incorporated "Kitty Hawk" in their station's name. During the first 75 years of its existence, the Kitty Hawk post office had 6 postmasters, and each one was either a Tate or a Baum. That suggests some type of political influence in the appointment of the postmaster, but neither family was very much involved in politics. The criteria for being a postmaster appears to have been that the person had to be qualified for the job, had an office facility that had space enough to conduct postal business, be convenient to the public and near enough to Kitty Hawk Bay for mail boat

Elijah and Hettie Baum in front of the Kitty Hawk Post Office

214

delivery and pick up. The first six postmasters were: Sophia D. Tate, November 11, 1878, Joseph M. Baum, November 22, 1879, William J. Tate, January 6, 1892, Addie M. Tate, February 3, 1898, Elijah W. Baum, Jan 10, 1914, Hettie M. Baum, February 14, 1929.

With one exception, when each new postmaster was appointed the location of the post office changed as well. In the early days, the post office was generally in the home of the postmaster, but during the period of 1892-1896, William James "Bill" Tate operated the Kitty Hawk post office out of Daniel M. Tate's

Hettie Baum sorts mail in the Kitty Hawk Post Office

store at the head of Kitty Hawk Bay. After he married and built his own home on Moore Shore Road, he relocated the post office to his home for the next 18 years. When Elijah W. Baum was appointed postmaster in 1914, the post office was again relocated to within the Baum general store. Though the post office stayed within his store, the store operation itself moved several times before 1944. In spite of the changes of postmasters and post office location, the post office was always within ½ mile as the crow flies of its original 1878 location near the head of Kitty Hawk Bay. Being established as an official U. S. post office did not initially put the office on the established mail distribution route. When the Kitty Hawk post office opened in 1878, William Douglas Tate was contracted by the postal department to sail across Currituck Sound to Powells Point to deliver and pick up Kitty Hawk mail at the "California post office." The name "California" may confuse some people, but from December 5, 1872, to December 7, 1881, the name "Powells Point post office" was changed to "California post office," but then changed back to its original name. The reason for the name change is unknown. Although his wife gave up the post office and died in January 1880, William D. Tate apparently continued as mail carrier until he died on December 8, 1880. His death was either the result of a boating accident or medical problem in Currituck Sound, presumably while performing his postal contract duties. In a December 11, 2001, letter to historian David Stick, great grandson Daniel Grady Tate reported that his great uncle, William Douglas Tate, died of hypothermia on his overturned sailboat in Currituck Sound. In addition to handling mail for the residents of Kitty Hawk, mail for the Kitty Hawk, Paul Gamiels Hill and Kill Devil Hills Life-Saving Stations and the Signal Corps Weather Bureau Office was processed through the Kitty Hawk post office. Around 1900 William Avery Perry bought the Samuel B. Dowdy property at Sound Landing on the west side of Kitty Hawk, tore down the old Dowdy home place, built a new house and moved his family from Colington to Kitty Hawk. He also built a small store for his new wife, Frances Holland Crank Perry, and applied to the postal department for a post office for the Up-The-Road community of Kitty Hawk. He offered "Sound" or "Atlantic" as possible names for the post office, but both were rejected. Then he suggested "Otila", which happened to be the middle name of his youngest daughter, Hattie Otila Perry, and that was acceptable to the postal department.

The Otila post office was established on 20 September 1905, with Frances Holland Perry as Post Master. Within a few years, the Up-The-Road community was being referred to as "Otila" Instead of Kitty Hawk and official documents, including birth and death certificates, were listing Otila as the place name. Initially the Otila office served as a satellite of the Kitty Hawk post office and Lloyd Owens was the first mail carrier connecting the two post offices. The postal department then offered a 2-year mail carrier contract, and Zene Perry was the successful bidder at $195 per year. His routine was to pick up the outgoing mail from Postmaster Frances Holland Perry at 7:00 a.m., walk to the Kitty Hawk office to deliver the mail, pick up the incoming Otila mail, which was usually in and sorted by 8:00 a.m., and return to the Otila office. He was normally home by 9:00 a.m. At the time, he was the mail carrier. Mrs. Maggie Sibbern Cogswell, sister to

Postmaster Addie Sibbern Tate, was running the post office for her sister. By 1909, the regular mail boat operator offered a bid and received a contract for delivering and picking up the Otila post office mail, and a Sound Landing stop was included in his regular mail delivery schedule. It was no longer necessary to have a mail carrier to deliver and pick up Otila mail at the Kitty Hawk post office Down-The-Road. The Otila post office experienced several postmaster changes after Frances Holland Perry gave up her appointment in 1913. William Avery "Captain Bill" Perry replaced his wife as postmaster on August 29, 1913, William James "Bill" Tate became postmaster April 6, 1914, and "Captain Bill" Perry was again reappointed on July 20, 1914. The Otila post office was discontinued on May 15, 1918 and the people in the Up-The-Road community again began receiving their mail through the Kitty Hawk post office thereafter and the name Otila faded into history. The date when the contract mail boat began serving Kitty Hawk is unknown, but probably around 1884 when Nags Head opened a post office and Manteo became the mail hub for communities in Dare County. In his August 18, 1900, letter to Wilbur Wright, William J. Tate reported that the mail boat from Manteo, 12 miles away, arrived in Kitty Hawk on Monday, Wednesday and Friday. He also reported that he could book passage on the mail boat if he wished; otherwise, he would have to make private arrangement to get to Kitty Hawk. In the early days, the mail boat was a sailing vessel and sometimes it took more than a day to make the route deliveries so the three days a week delivery was determined more by weather that any other scheduling event. Jessie E. Meekins of Colington, NC, was the last mail boat carrier for the route from Manteo to Nags Head, Colington, Kitty Hawk, Point Harbor and Duck. His son, William Lewis Meekins, sometimes ran the route for him, and some of his other children assisted him from time to time. His last mail boat was a powered vessel named *BOB*, but the origin of that name is unknown.

With the opening of the Wright Memorial Bridge across Currituck Sound in September 1930, the mailboat delivery was replaced by truck delivery. Mr. Meekins fulfilled that responsibility for a time, but the route was eventually taken over under contract by the Virginia Dare Transportation Company after they incorporated in 1931. For the first fifty years of its existence, the Kitty Hawk post office, like probably most rural offices across the nation, was not a very active place. There were probably few regular customers, except for the several Life-Saving Service Stations in the area. How frequently the residents use the mail service is unknown, but most likely not very often as no one has ever come forth with a treasure trove of letters. For the 1900 Kitty Hawk residents, most of them had probably been born in the village and would stay in the community for the remainder of their lives. Thus, locals had very little need to send letters because their relatives and the people they knew were neighbors, who they could see at any time. But activities at the Kitty Hawk post office took a sudden increase in 1928 and has continued through the years, at least for a few days each year.

The Kitty Hawk mail boat ties up at the dock for deliveries and pickups

Chapter Fourteen

KILL DEVIL HILLS MEMORIAL ASSOCIATION

The Post Office Serves a Growth in Collectibles with the Wright Brothers Anniversaries

Kitty Hawk as the birthplace of aviation was historically established on December 17, 1903, with the four flights Orville and Wilbur Wright made near the base of Kill Devil Hill. But, without some type of formal recognition of those feats, the flights would have been little more than a footnote to history. The formal recognition came on March 2, 1927, when President Calvin Coolidge signed an Act of Congress establishing the Kill Devil Hills Monument National Memorial and authorizing the erection of a monument atop the massive sand dune. That Act and with the preservation of the site of the first flights and the construction of the memorial shaft gave official recognition to the Wright brothers and their inventive accomplishments. These developments and later improvements gave a destination for people to visit, the site where flight began. The passing of legislation to establish the Kill Devil Hills Monument National Memorial prompted civic and community leaders in northeastern North Carolina, particularly those in Elizabeth City, to get involved in promoting the construction of the Memorial and provide access to the site. The Kill Devil Hills Memorial Association, formed on August 16, 1927, took the lead in getting political leaders both at the Federal and State level to commit to getting the project moving. After acquiring the property, which they donated to the Federal Government, the Memorial Association served as co-sponsors with the National Aeronautic Association in developing the December 17, 1928, ceremonies for the 25th Anniversary of Powered Flight. The ceremonies included the erection of a memorial boulder marking the site of the first flight and the laying of the cornerstone for the larger Wright Memorial atop Kill Devil Hill. In ensuing years funding for the memorial was secured through the U. S. Congress and the monument built. The memorial was dedicated November 19, 1932. The Memorial Association had enjoyed good success with their plans and programs and while all their initial objectives had been reached with the dedication of the memorial shaft, they elected to stay organized to further assist and promote the park and the newly opened beach resort.

DECEMBER 17TH CELEBRATIONS

From 1933 until today the Association and its successors, the Kill Devil Hills Memorial Society and the First Flight Society, have annually celebrated the anniversary of powered flight at the site on December 17th, weather permitting. Many of the celebrations, particularly the early ones, were rather low-key events, but there were major celebrations which attracted many visitors and major news coverage. The 40th anniversary ceremonies were planned as a grand affair to occur over several days, but an early winter snow blizzard blanketed the area and the ceremonies were canceled.

Although cold winds with sporadic rains occurred throughout the four day 50th anniversary services in 1953, all programs were presented and there was a steady stream of news reports sent throughout the nation and around the world The 60th anniversary in 1963 was a special occasion with cool but pleasant weather and a good public turnout and press coverage. This anniversary

The replica Wright Flyer is delivered to the memorial building hangar

included the placement of a reproduction of the 1903 Flyer in the visitor center and the opening of the First Flight Airstrip. All branches of the military were represented and for the first time ever all five military services participated in the aerial tribute to the Wrights over the park. The 75th Anniversary was well attended in spite of cold weather, but no rain. A highlight of that celebration was an attempt at flight by a young man, Ken Kellett, who had built a modified reproduction of the 1903 Flyer. His attempted flight did not achieve his objectives, but the crowds did not appear to be too disappointed. He tried, but the elements did not cooperate. The biggest celebration ever at the park was the 100th anniversary of powered flight. Over 200,000 people attended the five days of activities which ranged from educational exhibits, static display of vintage aircraft through the years, aerial flybys and aerobatics, visits of historic aviation pioneers and heroes and a visit by President George W. Bush. It was a celebration not likely to be duplicated at the birthplace of aviation any time soon.

STAMP COLLECTING AND CACHETS

The connection between the Wright Brothers National Memorial annual celebrations and the Kitty Hawk post office is linked by the public hobby of collecting stamps and postal cancellations. The first special cancellation from Kitty Hawk was, however, initiated by the dedication of the Wright monument in the village by the local citizens on May 2, 1928, before the Kill Devil Hill Monument National Memorial became operational. *The Dare County Times* of May 2nd reports on that first special cancellation: "Letters have come in daily enclosing air stamped mail with the request that it leave here on the day on which the marker is dedicated to Aviators Wilbur and Orville Wright." F. F. Donahue of Newton Falls, Massachusetts, also enclosed letters which had been mailed on the first air mail trip from Atlanta to New York with the request that they too be stamped at Kitty Hawk, the birthplace of aviation, on May 2. Hundreds of cards had come in also for the Kitty Hawk cancellation postmark. On many of the cards was a picture of the monument and an airplane. The news article did not give the number of cancellations processed, but they were probably only in the hundreds and well within the capacity of the local postmaster. The exercise was useful for Postmaster Baum, however, in preparing for a forthcoming major cancellation program later that year.

The 1928 cancellation

In December 1928, the Federal Government sponsored the International Civil Aeronautics Conference to commemorate the twenty-fifth anniversary of the first successful airplane flight. The first three days of the conference were held in Washington, D. C., followed by a day of travel and a visit to the research laboratories of the National Advisory Committee for Aeronautics at Langley Field, Va., and then another day's travel and programs at the site of the first flight at Kill Devil Hill near Kitty Hawk. Just prior to the conference, the Postal Department issued two commemorative stamps of two cents and five cents each in recognition of the Wright brothers' contribution to aviation. They were not air mail stamps, however. With this special stamp issue and the 25th anniversary of flight celebration with its weeklong program prompted stamp, cachet collectors and hobbyists who participated in philately wanted the December 17, 1928, Kitty Hawk post office postmark cancellation. The December 21, 1928, edition of

The Independent, an Elizabeth City, NC, weekly, reported on the activities at the Kitty Hawk post office: WHEN KITTY HAWK P. O. HAD A RUSH "Stamp collectors and souvenir hunters kept the Kitty Hawk post office busy this week when 5,700 Air Mail letters had to be canceled. Postmaster Elijah Baum turned the living room of his home, which adjoins the post office, into a business office for two officials from the Post Office Department in Washington who were sent down to help take care of the avalanche of Mail."

The international importance of the twenty-fifth anniversary of the Wright flights and the celebration there on Monday made the stamps valuable in the eyes of collectors of rare stamps. The cancellations were all done by hand, which in itself is a very labor-intensive job. In addition to the Washington workers, Postmaster Baum enlisted the volunteered help of his family, who offered their services graciously. There were no special cancellations for several years while the Wright Memorial Monument was under construction, but a new round of cancellations occurred with the November 19, 1932, dedication of the new memorial shaft. *The Daily Advance*, of Elizabeth City, NC, carried a story of the postal event for those dedication activities in its November 25, 1932, edition: STAMP COLLECTORS RUSH KITTY HAWK POST OFFICE Manteo, Nov. 23 – "Postmistress Mrs. Elijah Baum at Kitty Hawk has mailed out to almost every section of the globe envelopes bearing the cachet of the Wright Memorial Monument and the Kitty Hawk postmark. The total number having reached the astounding sum for a Dare County post office of 11,200 at noon yesterday. Requests are still coming in both to the Dare County Chamber of Commerce here and to the Kitty Hawk post office asking for the favor to stamp collectors scattered here and there and everywhere. Mrs. Baum says the total will top 12,000 within the time she is permitted to hold her postmark stamp to the date of November 19, the date of the dedication."

The Kitty Hawk post office volunteers in 1938 on a break for a photo while they were canceling 12,000 stamps.

After the 1932 Wright Memorial dedication there were no big postage cancellations. Each year a small number of stamp and philatelic collectors would contact the Kitty Hawk postmaster for a few cancellations but nothing out of the routine.

In 1938, another significant postmark/cancellation program occurred. Postmaster General James A. Farley declared the week of May 15-21, 1938, National Air Mail Week to commemorate the 20th anniversary of regular Air Mail Service and asked the public to actively participate in the celebration and many communities across the nation did. Most of the communities had their own special designed cachets and they use an air mail stamp to mail their letters. A new 6 cents eagle multi-colored air mail stamp was issued by the Postal Department in Washington, DC, Dayton, OH, and Saint Petersburg, FL, for the celebration. Kitty Hawk was also one of the focal points of the celebration and had its own authorized official cachet to be used at their post office. Over 43,000 letters were stamped and canceled by the 6 visiting postal officials and 10 local temporary workers employed to sorting the letters for distribution. The letters were placed in large postal bags, loaded on Elijah Baum's truck, transported to the Kill Devil Hills Monument National Memorial and loaded on a National Park Service airplane and several corporate aircraft to be flown to Dayton, Ohio. The paved road on the west side of Kill Devil Hill connecting to Colington Island was used as the runway.

Everyone seemed pleased with the public response to National Air Mail Week and Kitty Hawk's fame in aviation history was further enhanced. After 1938 there was a lull in special postmark cancellation at Kitty Hawk except for the regular philatelists who came by every December 17th to have their envelopes stamped. Activities picked up, however, in 1949 when the Post Office Department issued a new air mail stamp commemorating the return of the Wright brothers' airplane from England. The Kitty Hawk post office was selected to handle the First Day Issue of the new air mail stamp and the eyes of the nation focused on that post office that day. The First Day Issue of the

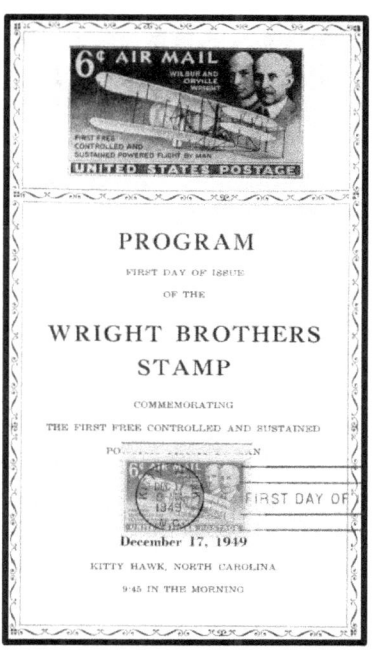

new stamp program at Kitty Hawk was included as one of the scheduled programs of the annual Wright brothers celebration for 1949.

The Elizabeth City high school band performed at the special ceremonies at the Kitty Hawk post office. Congressman Herbert C. Bonner, who had been instrumental in having the stamp issued and released at Kitty Hawk, was in attendance to serve as Master of Ceremonies and to offer a special welcome to those in attendance. The Honorable Robert E. Fellers, Deputy Assistant Postmaster General from Washington, D. C., spoke at the ceremonies and presented a stamp album for the 6 cents Wright brothers stamp to Dr. C. C. Crittenden of the North Carolina Historical Commission for the State of North Carolina. A special event during the Kitty Hawk post office program was a Kitty Hawk canceled letter that was delivered to the Wright Memorial, placed on a U. S. Coast Guard helicopter, delivered to their Elizabeth City Air Station where it was transported to an Air Force jet and flown to Dayton, OH. At Dayton, the letter was hand canceled and returned to Kitty Hawk by jet and helicopter. The total time for the flight from Kitty Hawk to Dayton and returning was 3 hours and 3 minutes, over 900 miles. This Is a far cry from the 120 feet in 12 seconds flown by the Wrights in 1903.

December 17, 1949, was a busy day indeed at the Kitty Hawk post office with over 500,000 first day covers processed that day. Many of the letters had been stamped in Elizabeth City but delivered to Kitty Hawk for cancellation. At Kitty Hawk, post master Mrs. Hettie Baum removed her living room furniture and dedicated the space as a postal work room for two electric cancellation machines to speed the work. Additionally, approximately 19,000 stamps were sold at the post office that day, taken to a local hotel were 12 people were employed in stamping cachets and then returned the letters to the Kitty Hawk post office for cancellation and mailing. December 17, 1949, was a long day and probably by far the busiest day ever in the history of that post office, but in spite of the heavy workload the first day issue of the Wright brothers air mail stamp at Kitty Hawk was an overwhelming success.

After 1949, the Kitty Hawk post office continued to receive requests each year for December 17th cover cancellation, but the bulk cancellations experienced in the 1930s and 1940s were greatly reduced. In 1953, the 50th Anniversary of Powered Flight should have been a major year for postal cancellations at Kitty Hawk, but the State of Ohio was successful in convincing the Postal Department that a stamp honoring the Wright brothers should be released in Dayton, Ohio, their home town. Their rationale was that Dayton was the real Birthplace of Aviation because the Wrights had planned and developed their Flyer there. That was reasonable rational for Ohio since they could not claim the Wright brothers as native sons nor demonstrate that the original Flyer ever flew in Ohio. Additionally, their Congressional representatives succeeded in having a resolution passed by the U.S. Congress designating Dayton, Ohio, as The Birthplace of Aviation. While this may make the citizens of Ohio feel good about their contribution to aviation, it is not possible nor practical to "legislate" history, and no resolution like this fools historians, or changes history.

Chapter Fifteen

A COLD WINTER

When Duty Overrode The Cold For the Local Postmaster

Record breaking cold temperatures engulfed the Atlantic eastern and southern seaboard states during the period of December 1917-January 1918. Spencer Midgett, who had just joined the U.S. Coast Guard at Caffeys Inlet, reported that the temperature dropped to 5 degrees on December 30, 1917, and never got above 12 degrees for 10 days, and apparently remained below freezing for an additional extended period. All the bays and sounds in the area were frozen solid and it was reported that Miles Clark drove his Model T Ford on and maybe across Pasquotank River at Elizabeth City.

At that time the mail came on the steamer *Trent* from Elizabeth City to Manteo through the Skyco, NC, steam line terminal and then delivered from Manteo by mail boat to communities along the banks. Since the sounds and rivers were frozen over there was no mail delivery during that period. The postal department did not have a motto or creed, but an inscription on the James Farley post office in New York City was often quoted as the postal creed; " Neither snow nor rain nor heat nor gloom of night stays these couriers from the swift completion of their appointed rounds." During the big freeze of 1917-18, Postmaster Elijah Baum placed his outgoing mail in an open skiff and with the help of Carthy Perry and another young man from the village pushed, shoved and pulled the skiff across frozen Currituck Sound from Sound Landing on the Kitty Hawk side to Point Harbor on the Currituck County mainland side. In his later life, he never stated why he made the trip across the sound so we can only surmise he felt duty bound, like the inscription on the

James Farley post office building, to dispatch the mail from his post office.

At the time the Kitty Hawk post office processed mail for three Coast Guard Stations; Paul Gamiels Hill, Kitty Hawk and Kill Devil Hills, so Postmaster Baum had the responsibility for federal government mail as well as any generated from the community. Whether there was any return mail for Kitty Hawk is unknown, but it is possible that there was at least a contingency plan to deliver Coast Guard mail to Point Harbor should the normal mail service be interrupted. The trip across frozen Currituck Sound was a success and normal mail service returned with the welcomed thaw in February.

Chapter Sixteen

A LOCAL LEGEND - COLORFUL CHLOE

Chloe Jarvis Midgett Finds a Way to Financial Success Through the Mail

Few people in the history of the Kitty Hawk community have ever left a more interesting and notorious legend than Chloe Jarvis Midgett, though that legend is fading fast with the passing of time and old timers. She was not rich, not famous, not a political celebrity and probably not known outside her circle of friends, but she created a legend by living a different lifestyle. Chloe and her sister, Sadie, lost their mother at a young age. Their father could not provide and care for the young girls and made arrangement for them to be enrolled in an orphanage in Richmond, Virginia. As the girls grew older, they wanted to move out of the orphanage and return to their family, but they could not be released unless they had a sponsor to look after and supervise them. Their first cousin, Mary Frances Meekins Best of Kitty Hawk, agreed for the girls to come live with her family with the understanding that they would work in the community to support themselves. Chloe, at 16 years of age, was about 2 years younger than her sister when they came to Kitty Hawk. "Miss Mary," as she was affectionately known by her friends and neighbors, had arranged housekeeping work for both girls. Chloe was to work with an Up-The-Road family who had 4 small children. Her work routine included washing, ironing, folding and storing clothes, keeping the house straight, and cooking. With a family of six it was hard work and long hours, and not what Chloe wanted to do at all. She complained to her sister that the work was too hard and that she was not going to do it. Sadie reminded Chloe that if she did not work, she would be sent back to the orphanage, but Chloe insisted that she would find an alternative - and she did. Chloe was not long in catching the eye of the most eligible widower in the community, even if he was 21 years her senior. And it was not too long before she was with child and starting her own family. The young family of William Weatherington "Will" Midgett and Chloe Jarvis Midgett were further blessed with a second daughter within a few years. It was said that Will Midgett was totally smitten with his young bride and would do anything to keep her happy. Early on he secured a cart and pony for her exclusive use and she would be seen frequently at the local post office and store, and probably visiting neighbors elsewhere in the community.

Chloe's fame and notoriety resulted from a mail order business she started in 1928. A letter announcing her enterprise has survived and was printed in the January 1, 1938, edition (pages 20-23), of *The New Yorker* magazine. It read: "We know you will be surprised to receive a letter from us so we will first introduce ourselves to you. We are two girls 18 and 20 years old and our father is a local minister here. As father's salary is very small and there is no way of earning money here, we are writing to ask, if you have ever eaten any real southern yam, sweet potatoes? We have some that are so-sweet the syrup stands in the pan where they are baked. Won't you please allow us to send you some when we dig the new ones in September? It will help us out so much, and we will be pleased to send you a nice hamper for five dollars or a barrel for ten dollars (a-barrel weighs 165 1bs.) If you don't care for the yams, perhaps you will allow us to send you a large box of fresh holly and mistletoe by P.P. prepaid for five dollars at the coming Christmas holidays. And if you don't care to send us the money, we will appreciate-very much any clothing you may send us that you will no longer use for mother is used to making over garments. A friend of yours gave us your address but asked us not to mention her name. Please write to us real soon. With all good wishes, your friends, Nannie Mae and Thelma Irene Midgette."

It Is not known who the "friend" was who gave out the address as similar letters were sent to other affluent people in both New York and Philadelphia. Most likely Chloe copied the names and addresses of people in the affluent sections of the cities from telephone directories and took the chance that the recipient would be charitable and interested in helping the minister's family. True to her word, when the sweet potatoes were harvested in the fall those who had placed orders with the Midgetts received their order. Not everyone wanted as many yams as was offered in the order and a smaller supply was provided as requested even though most people had paid the full price, or simply sent money as a donation and declined any yams. Chloe's enterprise was off and running with a good start for her new business. Chloe's business prospered even though her daughters moved on to other locations after they married. Other young people in the community were recruited, including niece Mary Frances Stetson Perry and her husband Edgar Perry, to assist with the letter writing and gathering items for the Christmas boxes. The Midgetts sent out many letters so Chloe must have recruited a small army of young letter writers to meet her needs. The themes of her letter never changed much over time: low waged rural Methodist minister who became an invalid, no opportunity for local employment, health problems of family members, and helping to raise their granddaughter and later orphans from an institution in New York. These problems had an element of truth, but Chloe was an early proponent of not letting facts interfere with a good story and she was a master at telling her story. The holiday boxes were very popular with her clients and she realized a healthy income with the enterprise even during the depression of the 1930s. The line of items offered expanded over time to include "golden rod" honey, home-cured hams, fruitcakes, barrels of pine cones and lightwood splinters, native fig preserves, bed pillows made from home-picked goose and duck feathers, and similar home crafted items.

Unfortunately, Chloe's marketing success contributed to her downfall. Her story and troubles were outlined in a 1936 local newspaper article. The article from *The Daily Advance*, read: Thursday, March 19, 1936 Strange Racket Comes to Light at Kitty Hawk Aid Society in Philadelphia Tells of Mythical "Orphan Children" Manteo, March 19 - "The smoothest racket to come to light in this section in years was uncovered this week through a routine inquiry from a welfare society concerning the condition of a family at Kitty Hawk. Trading on the fact that her husband is a retired minister, Mrs. W. W. Midgett, as revealed in the inquiry, has been posing as a near pauper, sending small gifts to families with money and receiving in return many times the value of the gifts." In the summer of 1935, she bought a new Buick sedan, trading in a 1935 Ford sedan. Yet county officials received the following letter early this week from J. Lawrence Solly, executive secretary of the Traveler's Aid Society, Philadelphia, Pa. "We are interested in learning whether assistance can be or is granted to the above-named family who live in Kitty Hawk, N. C. (referring to Rev. W.W. Midgett, wife and four children). We are writing at the request of Miss Huston, 219 School Lane, Philadelphia." For several years Miss Huston has been assisting this family, although she never met them. They wrote to her several years ago requesting funds which she sent them. Miss Huston did not know how the Midgett family had obtained her name, but felt that a friend of hers may have given it to them. Mrs. Midgett has sent Miss Huston rugs, bed spreads, honey, etc. and Miss Huston sent money for these. "Recently, Miss Huston received a letter from Mrs. Midgett telling her that the family had an outstanding grocery bill of $410 and would Miss Huston send something toward this bill. Mrs. Midgett said they had to give up the four children which they had in their home several years ago because they were financially unable to keep them. During this time the grocer had let them have things on credit. Now the grocer has a boy and a girl in school on a scholarship. They feel that if they can pay the grocery bill that this will enable the grocer, Mr. ---- to keep his children in school. Miss Huston has received letters signed by Rev. Mr. Midgett and believes that he is a minister in Kitty Hawk, although she does not know." Several other inquiries that have been received by county officials reveal that Mrs. Midgett accompanied her gifts with letters, many purporting to have been signed by her husband, telling imaginary tales of grief and often sent the letters without the gifts. So far as can be learned there never were any four children and Mrs. Midgett lives in one of the best homes in Kitty Hawk. All the letters that have been received express some wonder at how Mrs. Midgett obtained the names of the persons contributing money to her "support" and that of the supposed four orphan children she and her retired husband were taking care of. To add to her growing troubled reputation, the Dare County Sheriff reported that he had repeatedly brought charges of bootlegging again Mrs. Midgett, but had never gotten a conviction.

The inquiries into her affairs must have become too troublesome as she left Kitty Hawk in August 1936 for an extended automobile tour and a visit with a daughter in Washington, D.C. The Washington visit was eventful because she purchased a home in the city and after moving in converted it to a boarding house, and a new occupation. The move to Washington offered a new beginning for Chloe. Chloe's holiday business venture had not added appreciably to the postage sales of the Kitty Hawk post office, but the number and size of her holiday packages increased the bulk of the outgoing mail, and the work load of the postal staff. Shortly after Chloe ceased her mail order business, Mrs. Rosaline Hayman Swain started a similar business using the same general operating model. She too included family members and school age students from the community to help with gathering the native holiday decorations. One person who was interviewed for this story reported that as a small girl of nine or ten years of age she was hired by "Miss Rosaline" to gather the red berry fruit of the Partridge berry plant. The herb grows as a woodland creeper on the ground in a dry or moist area of the woods and can only be picked by a person on their hands and knees. The young girl spent the better part of a day gathering berries and putting them in a glass jar to turn in when she had finished. "Miss Rosaline" gave her 25 cents for her day's work. The young worker was disappointed with the pay and figured that she could con her grandmother, who ran a local country store, out of more than 25 cents worth of candy, drinks and ice cream in a day's time, so she did not return for a second day of work. "Miss Rosaline's" business venture continued for several years but it never attracted the clientele or received the notoriety of the Chloe Midgett holiday decorations enterprise.

Chloe's move to Washington was not in the best interest of her marriage to Will Midgett. While he held out for several years hoping Chloe would have a change of heart and return to Kitty Hawk, he finally consented to a divorce. He never remarried, but

Chloe reestablished contact with some of her old friends from the Richmond orphanage and married a fellow orphan from that institution in 1943. He had served in the US Army in WWI and was employed as an x-ray technician at an Army hospital in San Francisco, California. Chloe sold her Washington boarding house and moved with her husband, Russell M. Hooper, to California. Chloe never completely severed her ties with Kitty Hawk and even maintained correspondence contacts with a former neighbor and friend, Hettie Baum, and probably others. When Will Midgett died in 1952, Mrs. Russell M. Hooper, as the former wife of Rev. Will Midgett had the following memorial, which she reportedly wrote, published in the Coastland Times:

IN MEMORIAM Rev. W. W. Midgett I cannot say, and I will not say that he is dead. - He is just away! With a cheery smile, and a wave of the hand, He has wandered into an unknown land. And left us dreaming how very fair it needs must be, since he lingers there. And you-O you, who the wildest yearn for the old-time step and the glad return--Think of him faring on, as dear in the love of there as the love of here; Think of him still as the same, I say; He is not dead-he is just away!

Many years later this writer was attending a funeral at the Austin Cemetery in Kitty Hawk and heard this poem recited at the graveside service. After the services, I spoke with the minister conducting the service about the poem and was told it was written by James Whitcomb Riley [1849-1916] and is read often at funerals! Even on this solemn occasion, Chloe could not resist telling her story to her advantage.

Chloe's contacts continued for a few more years. Sometime in the early 1950s she wrote to Hettie Baum and enclosed a photograph of she and husband Russell with TV host Warren Hull on the set of "Strike It Rich," when they were contestants in the program. Chloe had submitted an entry letter outlining her financial needs and her entry was accepted. She answered all the questions and received a check for $500, a $400 round trip airfare, and a week's stay in the Sheridan Hotel in New York City. A month later they won another contest and were given a week's vacation at a hotel in Acapulco, Mexico, and were given the bridal suite. Chloe died in 1958 and is buried in California. Chloe's story in a section under "FEDERAL INITIATIVES" may seem out of place. She was never a federal employee and had nothing formally to do with the postal service in Kitty Hawk. However, no one in the history of the community utilized the services of the post office to the extent that Chloe Jarvis Midgett did, nor attracted the notoriety of her enterprise to the level she achieved. For a time, she carried on a land office type business during holiday periods that was very lucrative for her time and effort. She was certainly a one-of-a-kind type of person and had a certain flair about her life and work. She may have stretched facts on occasions and did not let the truth get in the way of a good story, but she made an impact in the community and added a special twist to its history. May her memory rest in peace in California.

Chloe Jarvis Midgett Hooper, with second husband Russell, on the TV show *Strike It Rich*

Section Six

Kitty Hawk And The Wright Brothers

Chapter Seventeen

…FROM THIS SPOT…

Marking the Wright Brothers Achievement With the People That Were There

The story of marking the site of the December 17, 1903, first flight has been told several times but each storytelling is slightly different from the others. A recently located letter in the Meekins Collection at the Outer Banks History Center from Rupert E. West of Moyock, NC, to Victor Meekins of Manteo, NC, sheds additional light on the background of how and when the site was first marked. Rupert West and Captain Bill Tate traveled to Kitty Hawk in May 1927 to visit the site of the Wrights 1903 camp where the first powered flight occurred. They invited Elijah W. Baum, Kitty Hawk, NC, Post Master and Tate's lifelong friend, to accompany them. Rupert E. West described the visit to Victor Meekins in his May 23, 1927, letter.

"While at Kill Devil Hill it occurred to me that there has never been a marker of any kind to commemorate the site used by the Wright brothers in their experiments. As I was accompanied by two men who were familiar with facts concerning these experiments and great admirers of the Wright brothers, we decided that it was an opportune moment to mark the spot which in the near future will be the mecca of thousands of people who will come to pay homage to the inventive genius of mankind.

"Exhibit (A) is a photograph of the marker erected out of time worn boards and rusty nails, the same used in the first camp built and used by the Wright brothers in their experiments. Standing by the marker are; Capt. W. J. Tate, in whose home the Wright brothers lived when they first went to Kitty Hawk and who is credited by the Wright brothers with assisting them in their experiment, and Elijah W. Baum, the first man to greet them when they landed at Kitty Hawk. I believe that this is the first marker ever erected to them and I am proud of the fact that I proposed and aided in its erection."

Captain Willaim J. "Bill" Tate and Elijah Baum with the original First Flight marker they constructed out of scraps from the Wrights encampment

Neither of the three, Rupert E. West, Capt. William J. Tate, nor Elijah W.Baum, were witnesses to the first flight so neither of them had personal knowledge of the location of the flight. Capt. Bill Tate was, however, familiar with a January 13, 1920, deposition Orville Wright had given regarding a patent infringement claim in which he described the four flights of December 17, 1903. In the deposition, Orville stated that: "These flights started from a point about 100 feet to the west of our camp. The ground was perfectly level for a mile or two in every direction except those toward the big and smaller Kill Devil Hills. The ground was level in the directions toward these hills for a distance of a quarter of a mile. The machine was launched from a monorail track…"

The west, Tate and Baum party were able to locate remnants of the old Wright camp building and hanger and from those remains were able to identify the approximate take off site of the first flight of December 17, 1903. Elijah Baum told this writer that they drove a metal stake in the ground at the site of the first flight and then built a pyramid over it with old timbers salvaged from the camp buildings. The metal stake was placed in the ground to facilitate relocation of the site in the event the old timbers were later removed or displaced. Rupert West took a few pictures that day including one of Captain Bill Tate and Elijah Baum standing next to the wooden pyramid and a second picture of just the pyramid alone. He reportedly took other photographs that have not been found or identified. The picture of Bill Tate and Elijah Baum next to the temporary wooden pyramid was printed on the front page of the June 3, 1927, edition of *The Independent*, a weekly newspaper in Elizabeth City, N. C. The news media would later refer to the temporary pyramid as the Tate marker. Identifying and marking the site of the first flight proved to be very timely considering events that would evolve in 1928 for the 25th anniversary of the Wright brothers' first flights. Earlier in March 1927, President Calvin Coolidge signed legislation authorizing the erection of a memorial on Kill Devil Hill commemorating the first successful power-driven airplane flight. Funding of the memorial was not a part of the authorization which prompted the formation of the Kill Devil Hills Memorial Association to lobby in part for funding of the monument at the first flight location.

In September 1928, at their annual convention in Los Angeles, the National Aeronautic Association authorized the erection of monument on the spot of the first flight, which had been identified by Tate, Baum and West the previous year. To further authenticate the location of their boulder, the National

Aeronautic Association asked Captain Bill Tate to have the site verified by the surviving witnesses of the first flight. John T. Daniels was unavailable to meet with the group, but Tate assembled the other witnesses at the site on November 4, 1928, and sent the following certification to the National Aeronautic Association:

Kill Devil Hills N. C November 4th 1928

"To Whom it may concern. This is to certify that W. S. Dough, A. D. Etheridge, and John Moore who are all three eye witnesses of the first flight made by Orville Wright at Kill Devil Hills on December the 17th 1903, assembled at Kill Devil Hills on this date at the request of W. J. Tate (acting for The National Aeronautical Association) for the purpose of agreeing upon and marking for the Association, the spot where the Wrights aeroplane first began to move along the ground when this first flight was made. We understand that this was required so as to enable The Association to erect a memorial upon the place where the First Flight actually began, and to prevent the possibility of any future dispute as to the right location.

Beginning with the site of the building which housed the Wrights' plane at the time, distinctly remembering the wind direction at the time, and that the track was laid directly in the wind, corroborating our memory on these facts by the records of the Weather Bureau, remembering that we helped bring the machine from the building and placed it on the tract, referring to distances laid down in feet in Orville Wright's article "How We made our first flight" we proceeded to agree upon the spot, and we individually and collectively state without the least mental reservation, that the spot we located is as near correct as it is humanly possible to be with the data in hand to work from after a lapse of twenty five years. We marked the spot with a copper pipe driven into the ground. We further state, that W. S. Dough, A. D. Etheridge and John Moore are the only persons living who were present on Dec 17th 1903 when Orville Wright made that first flight, except J. T. Daniels (who resides in Edenton, N.C.) and who it was impossible to have present at the time, and Orville Wright Himself.

Respectfully submitted. Attest (s) W. J. Tate (s) A. D. Etheridge (seal)Acting for the (s) W. S. Dough (seal) National Aeronautic (s) J. T. Moore (seal) Association."

In addition to having the site verified, the National Aeronautic Association also contracted in October 1928 with the firm of Ziegler & Duke, a monuments and markers company in Elizabeth City, North Carolina, to secure a granite boulder for the first flight site and to make arrange for its transportation and installation at the authorized site near Kill Devil Hill. Zeigler & Duke in turn contacted the North Carolina Granite Corporation of Mt. Airy, North Carolina, for the boulder.

The granite boulder when delivered would measure approximately 7 feet high, 7 feet wide at the base, and 4 feet thick through the center of the base. The boulder finish was of a rough cut except for a smoothed area to attach a 21 ½ inch by 28-inch bronze plaque. The inscription on the plaque read:

THE FIRST SUCCESSFUL FLIGHT OF AN AIRPLANE WAS MADE FROM THIS SPOT BY ORVILLE WRIGHT

DECEMBER 17, 1903 IN A MACHINE DESIGNED AND BUILT BY WILBUR WRIGHT AND ORVILLE WRIGHT THIS TABLET WAS ERECTED BY THE NATIONAL AERONAUTIC ASSOCIATION OF THE U. S. A. DECEMBER 17, 1928 TO COMMEMORATE THE TWENTY-FIFTH ANNIVERSARY OF THIS EVENT

The boulder that marked the first flight originally stood on a raised mound with a stone path to it. It was located over the spot marked as the take off site.

The boulder was shipped by rail in early December 1928 from Mt. Airy, N.C., to Shawboro, NC, the nearest railroad siding to Kitty Hawk. Zeigler and Duke did not have the equipment to move the seven-ton (sometime identified as ten ton) boulder to its destination at Kill Devil Hills so they hired Daniel Ray Leary to move the stone. Daniel Ray Leary was a friend of Claude Zeigler and a store merchant in Grandy, NC. He also owned and operated a commercial REO Speed Wagon truck with a heavy-duty trailer which he used to deliver farm produce and fish to Tidewater Virginia markets.

The boulder for the Wright marker is offloaded onto a barge for transport across the Currituck Sound.

Moving the boulder, the last 45 miles to Kill Devil Hills was more of a task than had been anticipated. The state road between Shawboro and Point Harbor was in the process of being upgraded and paved and there were detours around some of the construction sites. According to the newspapers of the day at one site near the Currituck Court House the truck capsized and it took considerable work to get the truck and its load back on the road. At another site the truck sank up to its axles in soft soil and had to be pulled through the site with great difficulty. Their luck did not improve any when they got to the ferry landing at Point Harbor. When the truck with its load moved out on the approach ramp to the ferry, the piling began to sink under the load and the truck and trailer had to be moved back to the shore bluff.

A revised plan of transporting the boulder across Currituck Sound involved offloading the boulder from the truck trailer, move it to a barge and offloading from the barge on the Kitty Hawk side of the sound and reloading the boulder back on the truck and trailer. A channel had to be dredged before the barge could be brought close enough to the shore bluff for the transfer of the boulder. It took five days to affect the transfer and have a favorable tide to move the barge across the sound and reload the boulder on the truck trailer.

Moving the boulder from Sound Landing on Currituck Sound at Kitty Hawk to Kill Devil Hill was another time-consuming task. There were no roads in Kitty Hawk, just sand trails with very soft sand over most of the trails. Because of the weight of the truck with its cargo, 2 by 12 inch planks had to be laid down under the tires for the truck to move through the soft sand. When the truck came to the end of the planks another set of planks had to be placed for the truck to move forward. This constant movement of planks from back to front required two days for the truck to reach its destination.

Sound Landing is prepared to receive the boulder

Daniel Ray Leary's REO Speedwagon loaded with the seven ton marker. Note the planks under the wheels to allow the truck to pass over the soft sand of the Outer Banks.

Before the boulder had arrived at its final location a crew had erected a concrete pad approximately 8 feet long, 4 feet wide, and 3 feet high to serve as the base for the boulder. The area where the boulder was placed was subject to periodic flooding from rainwater and by placing the boulder on a raised mound, they could avoid that unsightly display. The boulder was finally placed on the concrete pad on December 14, 1928. Orville L. Baum of Kitty Hawk, NC, was awarded the contract to bring in the sand to form the mound around the base of the monument. He also placed beach grass on top of the sand to keep it from being eroded by wind. With a platform around the monument and a small set of bleachers built by a local U. S. Coast Guard crew, the National Aeronautic Association First Flight Boulder was ready for dedication.

The delegates from the International Civic Aeronautics Conference arrive at Kitty Hawk Landing

   While the folks in northeastern North Carolina prepared for the biggest celebrations to occur on the Outer Banks up to that time, the delegates at the International Civic Aeronautics Conference in Washington, DC, were finishing their meetings and preparing for a two-day pilgrimage to the Birthplace of Aviation in North Carolina. The Conference has been called by President Calvin Coolidge to review accomplishments in aviation over its first 25 years, to consider further developments in the industry and most importantly to honor the Wright brothers for their achievement of flight on December 17, 1903. The Conference was cosponsored by the National Aeronautic Association. The pilgrimage to North Carolina provided the opportunity to honor the Wright brothers and to set the corner stone for a national memorial to their first flight and to dedicate a boulder at the site of that achievement.

   The pilgrimage of approximately 200 International Civil Aeronautics Conference delegates left Washington, DC, Saturday evening, Dec. 15, on the steamer *District of Columbia*, and arrived at Old Point Comfort, Hampton, Va., Sunday afternoon, December 16. They toured the research laboratories at Langley Field, Va., and returned to the steamer for the evening. They left Norfolk by buses Monday morning for Kitty Hawk. At the

Currituck courthouse, they were met by North Carolina delegates and continued their trip by private vehicles. At Point Harbor, many of the delegates crossed Currituck Sound to Kitty Hawk by ferry and transported to Virginia Dare Shores near Kill Devil Hill by private cars. Part of the delegation went directly from Port Harbor to Virginia Dare Shores by private or Coast Guard vessels. A ham, barbecue and turkey luncheon with all the trimmings awaited the delegates at the Virginian Dare Shores pavilion, complements of the Kill Devil Hills Memorial Association.

Following the luncheon, the delegates ascended Kill Devil Hill for the 2 o'clock laying of the corner stone for the Federal monument to be erected atop the historic sand hill. The Honorable Dwight F. Davis, Secretary of War laid the stone for the monument. Following the corner stone ceremonies, the party proceeded down Kill Devil Hill to the site of the first powered flight for the dedication of the National Aeronautic Association boulder. The presiding officer at the boulder dedication was John F. Victory, Secretary of the National Advisory Committee for Aeronautics and Chairman of the Committee on Kitty Hawk Trip.

W. O. Saunders, President of the Kill Devil Hills Memorial Association welcomed the delegates and public to the ceremonies on behalf of citizenship of the State of North Carolina and the Association and pledged the "association will consider itself an unofficial but loyal guardian of this monument and the sacred ground on which it reposes." In his remarks, Captain William J. Tate reported on the authentication and certification of the site by the original witnesses to the flight. He also expressed his personal pride in his contacts with the Wrights and association with them while they were conducting their experiments in Kitty Hawk.

W. O. Saunders leads the welcome on the stand where the boulder
monument would be unveiled

Senator Hiram Bingham was the principal speaker at the
First Flight Boulder. He spoke in reverence of the site and what
happened at this location on December 17, 1903 when he said:

"So this great American, who is with us to-day, climbed
aboard the strange craft. He warmed up the motor. He released the
wire that held the machine to the track from which it was to be
launched. The machine moved forward into the wind. His brother,
Wilbur Wright, ran at the side, holding a wing to help balance the
airplane on the track. And the machine left the ground. It
answered to the controls. Man was flying! Twelve seconds later a
landing was made 120 feet from the point at which the machine
rose in to the air. For thousands of years man had watched and
envied the flying birds. At last he had conquered the secret. He
too could fly."

Senator Bingham officially unveiled the memorial boulder
with the help of Miss Mary Byrd Saunders and Miss Florence
Ballard of Elizabeth City, N. C., who were holding the cords
which held the silken folds of a parachute over the boulder. At
that moment, the U. S. Navy Band played The Star-Spangled

Banner, carrier pigeons were released, circled the crowd and flew toward Norfolk.

Chapter Eighteen

ON THIS SPOT...

The People of Kitty Hawk Erect the First Wright Brothers Monument

Few communities have the opportunity to stage a celebration of national importance, but Kitty Hawk did on May 2, 1928. On that date the citizens of Kitty Hawk dedicated a monument to Wilbur and Orville Wright on the site in Kitty Hawk where the brothers began assembling their first glider which led to the world's first powered flight four years later. The significance of the Wright Brothers Memorial Marker on Moore Shore Road in Kitty Hawk is the fact that it was the first marker erected in the United States to honor the Wright brothers and their accomplishments in aviation. Eight years earlier, in 1920, the French had erected a monument in La Mans, France, to be the first nation in the world to recognize the Wright brothers as the inventors of the airplane. A second United States monument dedicated later in 1928 at the Kill Devil Hills Memorial National Monument would also honor Wilbur and Orville Wright and serve to mark the actual first airplane flight.

The first monument dedicated to the Wrights, erected in Kitty Hawk Village

It is not surprising that William James "Bill" Tate was the Kitty Hawker who proposed a monument to the Wright brothers for the village. He had been their friend from the first days they arrived in Kitty Hawk; Wilbur on September 13, and Orville on September 28, 1900. Since there were no boarding houses in Kitty Hawk, the Tate's invited the brothers to board at their home until they could set up their tent on the sand hills east of the village, which they occupied on October 4, 1900.

During their time with Bill Tate he became an enthusiastic supporter of the Wrights and a valuable asset to them in securing supplies, meeting people in the community and arranging logistics and support. He continued to offer his services in succeeding years when they returned to Kitty Hawk for additional experiments. His enthusiasm for the Wrights never wavered during his and their lifetime.

His proposal for a monument to the Wrights, made shortly after learning of Wilbur Wright's May 30, 1912, death from typhoid fever, did not initially gain much local support. The proposal had been for a monument in what had been his front yard where the Wrights had begun assembling their 1900 glider. Although he still owned the house and the Kitty Hawk post office was still in the building, the Bill Tate family was living at a caretakers' house at Martins Point. He had taken the job in late 1901 as caretaker for several thousand acres of woodland owned by three sisters from Asbury Park, NJ; Hannah Lyons, Isabelle Lyons and Bertha Lyons. His wife, Addie Sibbern Tate, was still the Kitty Hawk postmaster of record in 1912, but Addie's sister, Margaret "Maggie" Sibbern Cogswell, maintained the day-to-day operation of the post office and lived in the house.

Bill Tate's neighbors were somewhat skeptical of his motive for proposing a monument on property he still owned so they did not jump at the opportunity to honor the Wrights. Probably also in the minds of the locals was the thought that the future of aviation was not assured as it had been less than ten years since the first flight and flying was not commonplace, at least not around Kitty Hawk. Bill Tate's proposal was before its time, but the seed for a future monument was planted

The Lyons sisters sold their property in 1910 to the Currituck Timber Corporation, organized for that purpose by three Norfolk, Va., lawyers named Beard, Beaman and Martin. Bill Tate stayed on with the new owners for a couple of years, but in 1913 moved to Norfolk so that his daughters could attend high school. In 1914 he returned to North Carolina as raft inspector on the Coinjock Canal. In 1915 he was appointed Keeper of the North Landing River Light Station at the east end of the Coinjock Canal, a job he kept until he retired in 1939. As a Keeper he was publicly addressed as "Captain," an honorary title accorded Keepers of Light Stations and Life-Saving Service Stations.

The years of 1910 to 1930 were a period of significant changes for the people of Kitty Hawk and their lifestyle, particularly with regards to transportation. Sailboats which had been for centuries the chief mode of transportation in the coastal areas and the work boat for fishing, hunting and other watermen activities were slowly being converted to power boats, or simply replaced by them. Automobiles, introduced into the community in the early 1920s, soon became commonplace for the inhabitants. While not every household owned an automobile, most families had access to a vehicle through a family member or neighbor and driving around just for fun became a favorite pastime on Sunday afternoons.

Scheduled ferry service between Kitty Hawk and Point Harbor on Currituck County mainland was initiated in 1926 and the schedules expanded as the demand increased. During this time a paved road from Shawboro, NC, south to Point Harbor was under construction so that soon one could drive to Elizabeth City instead of traveling there by boat; and there was talk of building a toll bridge from Currituck mainland to Kitty Hawk to replace the ferry.

With the announcement in 1927 of the President signing an act authorizing the construction of a monument to the Wright brothers on Kill Devil Hill, the public became more assured of the bridging of Currituck Sound and the paving of a road from that bridge along the beach to the Roanoke Sound Bridge, the gateway to Roanoke Island and the county seat at Manteo, NC.

While the announcement about the future monument to the Wright brothers atop Kill Devil Hill excited residents in the general area, the announcement also revived an earlier proposal to honor the Wright brothers in Kitty Hawk. Once again Captain William J. Tate came forward with his proposal for a Wright monument in the village. This time conditions were more favorable for his proposal. He no longer owned the property where he once lived and where the Wrights stayed as he had sold the home and adjoining land to the Kitty Hawk Methodist Church for a parsonage. The occupant of the parsonage, Rev. William A. Betts, fully supported the idea for a monument to the Wrights on the property.

The citizens of Kitty Hawk held a mass meeting on the evening of September 23, 1927, in the auditorium of the new Kitty Hawk School to discuss the proposal for a local monument. Captain Bill Tate, though no longer a resident of the community, attended and spoke eloquently of the proposed monument, the first to honor the Wright brothers in their home country. He recommended that a committee be appointed to pursue the proposal and in turn a committee composed of Captain Bill Tate, Chairman; Elijah W. Baum, Secretary; and Zene F. Perry, Treasurer, was appointed. Citizens of the community wanted this project to be a pure Kitty Hawk undertaking and agreed to limit the donations for purchasing of the monument to only Kitty Hawkers; past and present and their descendants.

Donations, either received or pledged for the monument, assured the committee that they would have the funding necessary for its purchase within several months. One unsolicited donation of $50 from a non-Kitty Hawk resident of California was returned with the thanks of the community.

The committee agreed on a 6 ½ foot gray Vermont marble obelisk to be purchased from the Elizabeth City Marble and Granite Works, D. T. Singleton, manager. On the face of the obelisk near the top would be a carving of the Wrights' 1900 glider being flown as a kite as shown in a 1900 Wright photograph in Tate's possession. Orville Wright reviewed and gave his approval for the glider design and text for the monument before the work was done.

Sculptor F. A. Berry of the Singleton firm did the glider carving and engraving of the inscription which read:

ON THIS SPOT
SEPT 17, 1900
WILBUR WRIGHT
BEGAN THE ASSEMBLY OF

THE
WRIGHT BROTHERS
FIRST EXPERIMENTAL
GLIDER
WHICH LED TO MAN'S
CONQUEST OF THE AIR
ERECTED BY
CITIZENS OF
KITTY HAWK, N.C. 1928

The monument cost $210. Contributors included: $5.00 each William J. Tate, Mrs. Addie M. Tate, Mrs. Pauline T. Woodard, Elijah William Tate, Mrs. Irene Tate Severn, Lewis J. Tate, Elijah W. Baum, Mrs. Hettie M. Baum, Orville L. Baum, Edna B. Baum, Elbert A. Baum, Willis G. Baum, Edward N. Baum, Ellsworth J. Baum, Alton E. Baum, James Burgess, Banister J. Hines, Mrs. Elizabeth P. Hines, Adolphus L. Hines, Truxton E. Midgett, Joseph E. Partridge, Benjamin F. Perry, Zenith F. Perry, Shepherd Perry, Thomas N. Sanderlin, Thomas N. Sanderlin, Jr., Pennel A. Tillett, Elton C. Twiford

$2.00 each Gaston F. Baum, Christopher C. Baum, McKinley Johnson, Dennis A. Twiford, Lafcadio Oliver Twiford

$1.00 each Jesse Etheridge Baum, Joseph Edward Baum, Mrs. Emeline Baum, Mrs. Matilda E. Baum, Miss Nora Baum, Miss Nellie Baum, Grandy Beasley, William A. Betts, Mrs. Lula Betts, William Betts, Gladys Betts, Henry Betts, Charles A. Caldwell, Theron S. Corbell, Miss Florence Clark, Herbert L. Gard, Graham Hollowell, Miss Lucile Jennings, Mrs. Mary Love Perry, Roland R. Perry, William T. Perry, Lawrence E. Perry

Theocanus "Canas" Tillett, William Lewis Tillett, Lloyd B. Owens

$ .50 each Ernest B. Beasley, Miss Minnie Parker

$ .40 each Ray Austin

$ .35 each Julian Lewark

$ .25 each Miss Maud Baum, Leland Beacham, Velora Baum, Mrs. Ella Parker, Washington Perry, Mrs. Zora Tillett, Avery 'BeLove" Tillett

$.10 each Shelton Midgett

$31.40 donation

The Ladies Aid Society of the Boaz Methodist Episcopal Church South, Kitty Hawk, NC, donated $31.40 out of the profits for food service on the occasion of the unveiling of the marker.

While the Wright monument committee worked on the details for the dedication and making arrangements for attendees, the monument company secured the Vermont marble obelisk and had it engraved and sculptured. The obelisk was delivered and placed on a slightly raised mount of earth in the front yard of the Kitty Hawk Methodist Parsonage by the first week in March 1928.

The program committee announced in late March 1928 that the unveiling and dedication of the monument would be May 11th. That particular date was selected since it was the reports of national newspaper for May 11, 1908, rather than December 17, 1903, that informed the public of the Wright brother's successful heavier-than-air powered driven flights. On that

The monument with its inscription once installed in Kitty Hawk.

date the Wrights had flown upwards of two miles, stayed aloft more than two minutes and flew straight lines as well as maneuvered through turns. Those May 1908 flights were just the prelude of things to come.

A week after the program committee had announced the dedication ceremonies for May 11th they corrected themselves and announced that the program would be on May 2nd. The change was necessary because high school graduation exercises were scheduled for the eleventh. For a community who was proud of its new high school and would be having only its second graduation class in history, those exercises would trump any other event regardless of historical significance.

Establishing a date for the unveiling and dedication was only one of many details to be addressed in planning for the program. Because of publicity for a federal sponsored monument on Kill Devil Hill and the prospect of construction of a bridge across Currituck Sound with connecting paved highways, Kitty Hawkers were anticipating a large turnout for their monument dedication and considerably more people than the existing ferry between Point Harbor and Kitty Hawk could accommodate. The program committee made arrangement with Alvin Griggs of Point Harbor for vehicle parking in one of his barnyards. The Committee also assembled a fleet of five private boats from Kitty Hawk to transport the visitors from Currituck to the village. Kitty Hawk citizens would provide ground transportation to the ceremonies.

Rev. Betts volunteered to have the grounds around the parsonage and the monument cleared of brush, briars and brambles for the celebration. About two weeks before the scheduled program, Rev. Betts assigned his two sons, Bill and Henry Betts, the task of clearing the parsonage lot. They performed their work well and piled up the clippings for burning. The clippings and brush was set afire, but unfortunately cinders caught the parsonage on fire, and the building was completely consumed. Rev. Betts and his family lost everything; clothing, furniture, personal items, and for Rev. Betts, his personal library from which he prepared a lifetime of sermons and religious teaching and his personal family genealogical records. There was no way Rev. Betts or the community could have saved the building or its contents. There was not a fire brigade or fire equipment in the community and the nearest water was a swamp ditch about 300 feet behind the structure. Transporting water by buckets, one at a time, for 300 feet, was an impractical exercise.

With the date of the ceremonies fast approaching, the community came together and removed all the fire debris from the parsonage property. Just the footprint of the former building was visible on May 2nd.

The speaker's platform before the program commencement of the unveiling. The Lucky Thirteen boys club from Kitty Hawk School, along with the ladies Ideal Literacy Club, served as honor guards for the ceremony. Reverend William A. Betts stands on the podium.

The planning committee had hoped for and expected a large turnout of people for the celebration. Also they wanted good representation from both the political and aviation communities. Orville Wright and Representative Lindsay C. Warren, the local representative in Congress and co-sponsor of legislation authorized the establishment of Kill Devil Hills Monument National Memorial,were invited but could not attend. William P.

McCracken, Assistant Secretary of Commerce for Aeronautics, and Assistant Secretary of the Navy for Aeronautics Edward P. Warner, were both invited to the celebration and accepted, provided the weather would permit them to fly in from Washington, D. C. The weather did not cooperate and they had to cancel their participation.

In spite of the absence of national figures, a reported crowd of 500 guests from surrounding Dare and Currituck County communities and Elizabeth City attended the May 2nd dedication. As a special event, the U. S. Army had scheduled its TC-5251 dirigible to land on the flats near the Kitty Hawk Coast Guard Station at 10:00 a.m. Additional Coast Guard personnel were assigned to assist the Kitty Hawk crew in securing lines from the dirigible for docking. The previous day, May 1st, the dirigible had been in the air over Kitty Hawk and had circled the site of the monument, probably as a practice for the following day, but high winds on May 2nd interceded and the dirigible flight was canceled.

The May 2nd program of unveiling the Kitty Hawk monument to the Wright brothers went very well. In the days before the unveiling the committee had a raised speaker's platform constructed and decorated with red, white and blue crepe paper and flags. Additionally, the exterior of the platform was covered with flowing dogwood boughs which added natural color and a special local flavor to the festivities. Additional significance and formality was given the program when female members of the Ideal Literary Society from the high school in their organizational dresses stood in front of the monument during the services and the male members of the Lucky Thirteen Society, also from the high school, likewise formally dressed in their special dress, stood in front of the speakers platform during the program.

The Ideal Literacy Society, serving as standard bearers at the monument unveiling

Rev. William A. Betts, pastor of the Boaz Methodist Episcopal Church South in Kitty Hawk, served as master of ceremonies for the ceremonies. The

Reverend Betts with the still wrapped obelisk in the background

program commenced with the unveiling of the memorial marker by Elmer R. Woodard, Jr., Captain Bill Tate's grandson, who removed the draped American flag from the marker. Students from the Kitty Hawk school, who had walked over a mile to the dedication site, lead the singing of The Airman's Hymn. The school piano had been brought to the dedication in the bed of a Model T Ford truck to accompany the singing. Nora Baum, the first grade teacher at Kitty Hawk school, undoubtedly played the piano for the congregation as she did at school functions.

Rev. Louis D. Hayman, a native Kitty Hawker and Methodist pastor in Troy, N. C., was scheduled to give the Invocation, but could not attend. Rev. Betts filled in for him and following the invocation gave a hardy welcome to those in attendance.

The main speaker for the day was Captain William James "Bill" Tate, who with his wife had been the first host of the Wright brothers when they came to Kitty Hawk in 1900. Captain Bill Tate became an enthusiastic supporter of the Wrights and their experiments and maintained a lifelong friendship with them. In this talk he related the experiences of Wilbur Wright's first trip to Kitty Hawk aboard Israel Perry's schooner, *CURLICUE*. He also spoke about other experiences and remembrances he had of the Wright brothers and their experiments. It was a narrative he would repeat many times to other groups throughout his life. In his closing remarks, as reported in the May 3rd, 1928, edition of *The Daily Advance*, Captain Tate stated, "No finer men ever graced our community with their presence than the brothers, Wilbur and Orville Wright. They were honorable in word, deed and thought, willing to win only on merit."

Visitors to the celebration admire the monument before moving to the picnic lunch

The formal program ended with the school students leading the assembly of attendees in the singing of The Old North State. The crowd then moved over to a picnic lunch prepared by the Ladies Aid Society of the Boaz Methodist Episcopal Church

South of Kitty Hawk. Profits from the picnic were applied to the cost of the monument marker.

For a short time, the monument stood in the empty field before the new parsonage could be built

With the dedication of the Wright brothers Memorial Marker at the site of the parsonage completed, the community, and especially the Methodist Church trustees, turned their attention to building a replacement for the destroyed parsonage. Unfortunately, the church did not have a building reserve fund and would have to depend on a donation subscription effort to fund the project. Within the first couple of weeks they had received several hundred dollars in donations to start the rebuilding fund. At the picnic following the dedication of the Wright Brothers Memorial Marker, R. Bruce Etheridge, a community leader in Dare County and on Roanoke Island personally appealed to visiting attendees to contribute to the rebuilding fund and raised approximately $100 through his appeal. The records of whatever other efforts were made have not survived, probably lost in the fire that destroyed the main church building in 1976. It is probably fair to say that the local people were very supportive and generous to the parsonage building fund. No doubt they encouraged donations from their friends and especially their business associates in Elizabeth City and surrounding communities. Although there are no local records to verify any contributions, it is possible that the Duke Endowment contributed to the construction cost. The endowment had been established three years earlier and assistance to rural churches was one of its stated goals. According to their rules, the endowment would only fund half of any building request.

By late July 1928, the church had sufficient funds to start the construction of the new parsonage. There are no records of who worked on the project, but Elijah W. Baum was designated the head carpenter. He undoubtedly was assisted by other volunteers from the church and community. He probably worked without pay, which was his custom when serving the church and most probably the other volunteeres also served without pay. Construction went well and the parsonage was finished in September. In fact, Reverend William A. Betts and his son, Henry Martyn Betts, painted the parsonage before Rev. Betts and family moved to his newly-assigned pastorate at Ocracoke, NC, in September 1928. The new parsonage served the church well through the years, until a new brick veneer parsonage on property next to the church replaced it in 1964.

The 1929 parsonage, newly built, with the original marker out front

With the placement and dedication of a granite marker on the site where Wilbur Wright began assembling his first glider at Kitty Hawk, the citizens of Kitty Hawk assumed that they had permanently memorialized the Wright brothers in their community, and in many ways they had. What they had not anticipated was that within a few years the memorial stone would begin to show signs of disintegrating. In a 1948 photograph, faint signs of cracking appeared on the surface of the marker although they may have been in evidence before that date without anyone noticing them. The first noticeable loss from the monument was a 14 inch long triangular shaped piece of granite from the southwest upper corner of the shaft. The detached granite piece was not saved and other smaller pieces also were lost from the marble monument.

What caused the cracking? No one knows for sure, but several theories have been advanced. Many people are convinced, because that is the story most often told, that the cracks were caused by someone throwing a bucket of water on the monument when the parsonage was burning. That is a quick and simple explanation – but it defies logic of understanding the village of 1928.

No one has left us a firsthand account of how, or even if, the fire was fought. In 1928, Kitty Hawk did not have any firefighting equipment, any fire brigade or municipal water system, or communication system to summon people to help in the emergency. The only water at the parsonage was a pitcher pump on the back porch of the house, while the closest surface water supply was Penny Toler Ditch about 100 yards west of the building. Penny Toler Ditch was more a swamp than a ditch, but there would have been water there.

When there was sufficient manpower to support an effort, a bucket brigade would normally be organized to fight a fire. There is no evidence, however, either written or oral, that a bucket brigade was formed for this fire; in fact there is a strong likelihood that there was insufficient manpower available for such a brigade. That position is based on the knowledge that in 1928 there were probably not more than 10 able bodied men living within a mile of the parsonage, if everyone was home at the time. Also, in 1928, the Kitty Hawk Coast Guard Station, located about a mile from the parsonage, was operating in a caretaker status with only two men serving as caretakers. The Betts family was most probably left to salvage what few personal items they could

268

when the fire first started and before the building became fully engulfed, then helplessly watch the fire burn.

It is unlikely and impractical to think that someone would go to Penny Toler Creek, collect a bucket of water, return and pass by the burning house to pour water on the granite marker located approximately 20 or 30 feet away from the building on the east side of the structure. A photograph of the building site taken after the burned debris, except for the foundation footing, had been removed shows the monument free of cracks on its left side. Certainly it is possible that there were cracks in the granite stone resulting from the fire, but the limited available physical evidence and lack of detail about the fire does not support that concept.

It is entirely possible and more logical that freezing and expansion of moisture trapped within the marker, which could enter the monument through natural hairline fissures, caused the damage to the marker. That idea is supported by the fact that from the time the cracks were first observed until the marker was moved inside the Kitty Hawk Town Hall, the cracks became wider, longer and more pronounced over time.

By the 1980s there was sufficient concern in the community that the monument would end up as a heap of rocks if something was not done to stabilize the damage. Late in 1983 the Albemarle Regional Planning and Development Commission notified municipalities and county governments in the region of a "Grants of Historic Attractions" program. Mayor Carlton P. Smith responded by requesting funding for the Kitty Hawk Memorial Marker on Moore Shore Road. The request did not qualify for a grant but the request set in motion the Town's commitment to address the deteriorating marker problem. Other funding sources were subsequently sought, including contacting the Honorable Charles D. Evans the local representative in the North Carolina House of Representatives, for special funding from the General Assembly, which did not materialize. In the meantime, the Town of Kitty Hawk applied for a Right-of-Way Encroachment Agreement with the North Carolina Department of Transportation to work on the marker which was partially in the road right-of-way. The marker in the right-of-way was grandfathered, but by

Departmental rules should the site be altered and/or the marker removed it could not be replaced on the same site.

In 1986, Administrator Larry G. Misenheimer of the Historic Sites Section, Division of Archives and History in the North Carolina Department of Cultural Resources visited Kitty Hawk and examined the Memorial Marker. On his return to Raleigh he discussed the condition of the marker with his division's preservationist. They concluded the marker stone was of poor quality; in fact they referred to it as "rotten marble". Additionally they suggested that even if the town could secure the services of a qualified craftsperson to repoint the stone and fill the cracks with a marble-dust/cement paste the long term life of the monument could not be assured. They recommended that the deteriorated marker be replaced with a reproduction.

The Kitty Hawk Civic Association under the leadership of Ward McCreedy took the lead in securing the replacement monument. A committee composed of Chairman Royal Breashears, Marilyn and Leo Antonucci, Betty Kelley, Anna May McCreedy, Christina Mank, Larry Mank, Robert and Jill Adams Morris, Jay Murphy, Etta Parrott, Paul Pruitt, and Webb and Sylvia Williams, was formed to raise funds for the replacement. The committee did their job well and raised $4,901 dollars from 395 contributors; a far cry from the $210 needed for the original monument. Clifton & Clifton Monument Company of Elizabeth City, NC, was contracted to provide the new monument reproduction. When they placed the new monument, the old one was stored in the town's maintenance yard until it could permanently displayed in a safe environment.

Dedication of the new monument was held on September 17, 1987, on the property where the original monument was located. The site of the new monument was altered slightly by being located a few feet west of the Moore Shore Road right-of-way and approximately 30 feet north of the original site so as to remove it from being directly in front of the Brown's home. The Browns, Steve and Barbara, deeded to the Town of Kitty Hawk a small parcel of land on which the new monument was erected so that there would be no property dispute in the future.

Geneva Harris Perry, a Kitty Hawk native and granddaughter of Elijah Baum, who was the first Kitty Hawker to meet Wilbur Wight when he came to the village in 1900, served as the Master of Ceremonies and welcomed those in attendance. She acknowledged and recognized the contributors to the replacement monument who were there and the descendants of the original contributors to the first monument in 1928.

First Flight Society President John Harris was the principal speaker at the dedication. He related stories about living conditions and life's challenges for the brothers while they were in camp near Kitty Hawk village. For two men who were used to all the conveniences of one of the most modern cities in the United States, living in a canvas tent sandblasted by the ever moving dunes in the area or occupied by hoards of mosquitoes would have been too much cultural shock for most people. But, the brothers persevered and achieved their goal of powered flight in spite of the adversities, and they contributed their success in part to their time at Kitty Hawk.

The dedication closed with President Ward McCreedy of the Kitty Hawk Citizens Association presenting a scroll with names of those who helped fund the reproduction marker. Mayor Elizabeth Smith accepted the scroll on behalf of the Town of Kitty Hawk and the Town's responsibility for caring for the new memorial marker.

The original marker was accorded special honor during the dedication in April 1998 of the new Town Hall by being permanently displayed in an alcove at the entrance to the new Town Hall. Its presence will remind all citizens and visitors of the special place Kitty Hawk had in the history of aviation.

AFTERWORD

My dad was passionate about historical places, photography, sharing local history, genealogy, and his beloved birthplace in "Mary Ann's Swamp" (see map) in Kitty Hawk Village. With a father in the National Park Service my family never passed a park on our travels that we didn't visit. He was interested in from whence people came. Many a time, he and I would be at a doctor's appointment and he'd strike up a conversation with a stranger and say, "Now, where are you from?" If it was remotely close to Kitty Hawk, the next question was always, "Now, who's your daddy?" This happened once in Elizabeth City on one such visit and the man answered, "Well. I'm from Kitty Hawk but joined the Coast Guard and have been here ever since." The next statement from my dad was, "Now your mom was a Rogers and my grandmother was so and so, and that makes us cousins." This happened often. It was incredible how my dad could just pull that information out, but he did quite a bit of genealogy research and had over 56,000 names in his Ancestery.com website. The first thing he did every morning was to check the obituaries to be sure first that he was not listed and then to see who may have been a local resident. He gave numerous speeches and interviews, all without using any notes or references. I asked him about this and he'd say, " I didn't know what I was going to say until I'd say it." "Shooting from the hip" worked well for him.

This book is compiled of conversations and information that William Harris gathered beginning in 1961 when he was completing his college education at Guilford College in Greensboro, NC. It was his Senior Thesis that began then, but continued throughout rest of his life until his passing in 2017. I didn't realize that he was continuing his research for his book about Kitty Hawk Village. I do recall as a young child hearing these loud voice recordings coming from our dining room until the late hours and my dad listening and taking notes. These recordings were residents from his younger days recalling stories and history from years ago. (These recordings can now be accessed at the Outer Banks History Center). I thought of them as old, loud people talking and keeping me awake at night. My mom, Fran Harris, was a big part of the effort it took to create this book. She was supportive of her husband's interests and as we worked to compile pictures for this book, I've found her handwriting on the backs of many pictures and documents.

As I was gathering information to complete this book in my dad's memory I ran across articles written about him by various correspondents like Kip Tabb. My father recalled his childhood, riding bikes to a country store and listening to the "old folks" tell stories and "tall tales" to anyone willing to listen. This obviously sparked his interest because he recorded those folks in his later years to assist with his research. Back in the "old days" he said that families would gather, tell stories and show pictures and then relate them to one another.

Fran Harris, Bill Harris, and Judith Harris Fearing

This passion of creating a book about Kitty Hawk Village took the course of 60 years. My father eventually retired from the National Park Service to his homeplace and became the Mayor of Kitty Hawk. He said on his 80th birthday in 2017 that his proudest professional accomplishment was overseeing the building of the Kitty Hawk Fire Department. He was so proud to be the mayor and made it a point to reach out to Kitty Hawk residents and make decisions for what was in the "best interest of Kitty Hawk." My mom often said he loved "Kitty Hawk more than the Lord" but that was just an old saying she'd heard from her elders. I hope this book is of interest to those who love Kitty Hawk and the Outer Banks area as much as he did and for all the natives of the area that call this piece of paradise home.

-Judith Harris Fearing, Sept 2024

SPECIAL THANKS

Special thanks to my mom, Fran Harris who for many years supported my dad and his efforts in documenting this life's work 1959-2017. Geneva H. Perry (Ward) who helped put the book together after Bill's passing. His dear friend, Tom Crouch for re-organizing the book to make it flow smoother. Joe Sledge, Editor/Publisher who brought the book to its fruition and made it happen with many, many hours of devotion to this book and assisting Judith Harris Fearing keep her promise to her dad to have his book finalized. Also, I'd like to thank the Outer Banks History Center/State Archives of North Carolina for their assistance with information and pictures. (Bill Harris' Papers can be referenced there by searching PC.5007) for additional information.

-Judith Harris Fearing

IMAGE CREDITS

Unless noted, all photos and images are used with permission or under public domain. No images may be reproduced without written permission by the owners. Author Bill Harris gathered many of these images directly from the residents of Kitty Hawk Village, with the expressed permission to use them in his book.

Other Image Credits

Kitty Hawk United Methodist Church, by Billy Payne, used with permission.

E.W. Baum General Store painting (cover) - Dawn Gray Moraga, used with permission

Afterword and About the Author - courtesy Judith Harris Fearing

Cover map by Bill Harris and Greg Ball

The background map on the cover is based on the 1900 Census of Kitty Hawk Village and can be viewed in its entirety at the Kitty Hawk Municipal building.

A Note From The Editor

Being able to merely touch this book, let alone help move it to print, has been a labor of love for me. I have great respect for anyone who can gather so much information and put it into order. Reading this book was a wonderful experience for me. I enjoyed seeing the names of people who shared a surname with adults I have known and kids with whom I grew up, as well as learning all the little bits and pieces of such a unique area, so close to my own home, though still far away as a little kid. I had attended Kitty Hawk Methodist Church as a child and young teen, and knew of how the village was at that time. So learning where it all had come from was very enlightening for me.

Editing this book, yes, it was a labor of love, but it was labor. I have endeavored to clean up the way it read, while leaving Bill's personal touch on the words. As such, I merely did some neatening of a few sentences, corrected some spelling, and added clarity. You would barely notice my hand in this book. At the same time, there still might be some errors, some spelling, that either I didn't catch or maybe I just left to keep the originality of the book. Forgive them and move ahead with the book with pleasure. It is as much a slice of life from Kitty Hawk Village as the stories that make up the book are.

-Joe Sledge, April 2024

ABOUT THE AUTHOR

William Aubrey "Bill" Harris was born March 2 1937 to Edna Baum and Aubrey Alonzo Harris in his grandparents' home in an area of Kitty Hawk Village known as "Mary Ann's Swamp" (see map in book). He joined his sister, Geneva Lee, and years later a younger brother, Roy Clavis Harris was born. Bill attended 1st and 2nd grade at the Kitty Hawk Elementary School on Kitty Hawk Road,

Bill Harris with Geneva Perry Ward

where his teacher was his aunt, Nora Baum. The Coast Guard took Bill's father and his immediate family to Elizabeth City for the remainder of Bill's elementary and high school years. During his junior year in high school Bill and several other boys joined the Coast Guard Reserves and traveled to Norfolk on Wednesday evenings for classes. During the weekends Bill could be found in Kitty Hawk Village staying with his grandparents or at their camp at the end of Elijah Baum Road on Kitty Hawk Bay. Upon graduation from Elizabeth City High School in 1955, Bill enlisted in the US Coast Guard and stayed on active duty through 1958. He remained in the Coast Guard Reserves for 5 additional years. In 1958 Bill returned to Kitty Hawk to try his hand at building homes with his grandfather, Elijah Baum. He soon realized that was not where his heart was. He enrolled in Guilford College, married his high school sweetheart, Frances Williams and they lived together at Guilford College while he attended classes to pursue a degree in U.S.History. His senior year of college was 1961-62 when he began work on his senior thesis which was an oral history of Kitty Hawk Residents. Upon graduation from Guilford College Bill began his profession with the National Park Service, which took him to 9 different parks around the United States. At these parks, Bill acted as superintendent or in an advisory position.

1962   Bodie Island Lighthouse, Wright Brothers Monument, Nags Head and Kill Devil Hills, North Carolina
1965 Fort McHenry, Baltimore, Maryland
1967 Mount Rushmore, Rapid City, South Dakota
1970-1972 Custer Battlefield National Park, Hardin, Montana
*This park was later renamed to Battle at Little BigHorn (due to Bill's research and advice to the Department of the Interior)
1972-1975   Fort Sumter and Fort Moultrie, Charleston, South Carolina
1975-1982   Cape Hatteras National Seashore, Hatteras, North Carolina
1982 Cumberland Island, St. Mary's, Georgia
             Department of Interior office in Atlanta, Georgia
1986   Cape Lookout National Seashore, Morehead City, North Carolina
1997 Wright Brothers National Monument

Bill's last move in 1997 brought him full circle back to his beloved Kitty Hawk where he continued his research for this book and completed his 38 year career in the National Park Service. Upon his return he built a home on his property that had been in the family for approximately 200 years. The property was previously owned by his great grandparents George W. and Matilda E. Baum, then later his aunt Nora Baum. Bill had been a member of the First Flight Society for many years prior to returning to the area, but upon his return he served as President and Treasurer and worked on numerous committees within the society to promote the history of this organization.

Bill worked tirelessly on the 2003 Centennial Committee (Wright Brother's Monument), and held an active membership in the Albemarle Genealogical Society, was a board member of the Outer Banks Community Foundation, a lifetime member of the local Mason Lodge, a member of the Kitty Hawk United Methodist Church Centennial Committee and the Austin Cemetery Association. Bill could be found doing interviews for UNC-TV, or locals like Ken Mann when he had his local history channel (Carolina on my Mind). Bill's hobbies, when not researching for this book, included photography of nature and local landmarks. On a daily basis he checked the local funeral homes websites for obituaries. He was constantly adding residents to his Ancestry website which ultimately included 56,000 names by the time of his death in March of 2017. Bill assisted well-known authors such as David McCullough, Larry Tise, and Tom Crouch in their research of the Wright brothers' history. Bill was regarded as a fount of local history knowledge and happily shared that with anyone interested.

www.ingramcontent.com/pod-product-compliance
Lightning Source LLC
Chambersburg PA
CBHW071142130626
46553CB00004B/1487